A Death in San Pietro

ALSO BY TIM BRADY

Twelve Desperate Miles: The Epic World War II
Voyage of the SS Contessa

A DEATH IN SAN PIETRO

THE UNTOLD STORY OF
Ernie Pyle, John Huston,
AND THE
Fight for Purple Heart Valley

TIM BRADY

DA CAPO PRESS
A Member of the Perseus Books Group

Printed in the United States of America.

For information, address Da Capo Press, 44 Farnsworth Street, 3rd Floor,
Boston, MA 02210.

Set in 12 point Adobe Garamond Pro by Marcovaldo Productions for
the Perseus Books Group

Cataloging-in-Publication data for this book is available from the Library
of Congress.
First Da Capo Press edition 2013
ISBN: 978-0-306-82214-8 (hardcover)
ISBN: 978-0-306-82215-5 (e-book)

Published by Da Capo Press
A Member of the Perseus Books Group
www.dacapopress.com

Da Capo Press books are available at special discounts for bulk purchases
in the U.S. by corporations, institutions, and other organizations. For
more information, please contact the Special Markets Department at the
Perseus Books Group, 2300 Chestnut Street, Suite 200, Philadelphia, PA,
19103, or call (800) 810-4145, ext. 5000, or e-mail special.markets@
perseusbooks.com.

10 9 8 7 6 5 4 3 2 1

To Susan, Sam, and Hannah

CONTENTS

PROLOGUE   1

CHAPTER 1   "The Hoosier Vagabond"   7

CHAPTER 2   The Texas Division   17

CHAPTER 3   Tunisia   27

CHAPTER 4   Morocco   43

CHAPTER 5   Pyle in Sicily   51

CHAPTER 6   Salerno   59

CHAPTER 7   Altavilla   77

CHAPTER 8   The Sorrento Peninsula   89

CHAPTER 9   Capri   109

CHAPTER 10   Why We Fight   119

CHAPTER 11   Pyle and Huston   129

CHAPTER 12   *Winterstellugen*   135

CHAPTER 13   Replacements   145

CHAPTER 14   Thanksgiving   153

CHAPTER 15   Observers   161

CHAPTER 16   Eve of Battle   167

Contents

CHAPTER 17 Sammucro   175

CHAPTER 18 A Bad Day on the Mountain   187

CHAPTER 19 Purple Heart Valley   195

CHAPTER 20 Aftermath   203

CHAPTER 21 New Year   211

CHAPTER 22 The Death of Captain Waskow   217

CHAPTER 23 Finishing Up   223

CHAPTER 24 Rapido   237

CHAPTER 25 A Final Posting   243

Notes   253
Sources   265
Acknowledgments   269
Index   271

Maps

Salerno Landing   95
Battle of San Pietro 1   180
Battle of San Pietro 2   199

A Death in San Pietro

Prologue

ONE UNIT OF SOLDIERS heading down the mountain, the other heading up. It was no easy task in either direction. Mt. Sammucro was a bare heap of rocks looming above the village of San Pietro: almost 4,000 feet high and so steep and craggy that the Italian mules carrying supplies to the American forces at its summit could only make it to the tree line, a third of the way up, before giving way to the sharp boulders and scree.

The constant precipitation on the mountain that fall, a mix of rain, sleet, and snow, didn't make the travel any easier. The rocks were greasy; the pebbly footing slipped away beneath combat boots. Both units were looking for a chance to pause among the hard ledges and catch their breath. Smoke a cigarette if they had 'em.

No one made a record of what the soldiers talked about that night, but there was business to discuss. Company B, moving up the mountain, would want to know the state of the defense above on the summit. Company I, moving down Sammucro, would be interested in what was going on at headquarters below. When would be the next assault on San Pietro?

There was a moment to talk about small things, too. Maybe something about the ironic circumstances that had brought both companies, each organized in neighboring small, south central Texas towns, to this Italian mountain just in time for Christmas 1943. Perhaps there was a passing mention of how the holiday would be celebrated back home.

In Belton, Texas, where Company I had been put together as a National Guard unit in the late 1930s, the Sunday school classes of the First Baptist Church were practicing a Christmas pageant, while the Presbyterians had already held theirs the Friday before. The Beltonian movie theater was showing *Watch on the Rhine* with Bette Davis.

Sixty miles to the northeast, in Mexia, Texas, the home base for Company B, rehearsals were under way for the annual Christmas concert held at the City Auditorium. The Black Cat Band would be performing Irving Berlin's "White Christmas" to highlight their show. War bonds would be available for sale at the door.

Both local papers had plenty of war news, too—"Soldier Letters Needed This Week for Dec. 24 News" read one column, reminding mothers to get news of their boys' overseas duty down to the paper if they wanted the reports to be printed by Christmas. But there was little mention of what was happening here in Italy, right on this mountain.

Both Companies B and I belonged to the 143rd Regiment of the 36th Infantry Division, part of the U.S. Fifth Army. They had arrived here together in Italy four months earlier; combat rookies, fresh from the port city of Oran, suddenly shoved out of their landing craft and onto the beaches of Salerno with no time to look back.

With the first splash of water came the terrible guns of war: the sputter of small arms fire, the endless scream of shells, the thump-whistle of mortars, and the deafening thunder of explosion after explosion. Dust and smoke and quaking ground. What remained for the eye to comprehend when all was settled made no sense at all: misshapen dead men, gaping holes in the landscape, strong, steel vehicles now twisted and mangled in heaps, solid stone buildings turned to rubble.

Three weeks of this brand of hell followed the landing, then came a moment of relative quiet, when the men of the 36th were able to actually see the foreign land they had arrived at. Ancient ruins and vistas, as beautiful as any these boys from the hill country of south central Texas had ever seen, dotted the landscape. They had heard of Vesuvius and Pompeii, Naples and the Isle of Capri. Now here they were amidst striking blue seas and dappled sunlight that glimmered through lemon trees and olive groves. There was finally time between the action to look, to contemplate the land, to eyeball its people: dirty, hungry, brutalized by war, yet grateful, oddly enough, given the amount of ammunition the Allies were dropping on their homes and villages, for the presence of the Americans.

But the 36th returned quickly to war. After Salerno and Naples came the abysmal crossing at Volturno River. And then rain and more rain, until now when they faced this line of mountains. The imposing range ran all the way across the mid-section of Italy from the Adriatic to the Tyrrhenian Seas. High, rock-strewn piles, bare of vegetation on the tallest of them, including Sammucro. Just great hunks of boulders, sharp arêtes, crags, ridges, and cliffs; but plenty of places for the young men on both sides of the fighting to crouch from the bullets and mortars, lean deep as possible into the shade of those rocks, and try to breathe deep, slow the racing of their hearts.

The goal of the Americans lay just on the other side of Sammucro, designated "Hill 1205" on army maps. There the Liri Valley spread out between the line of hills and mountains, and pointed northwest toward Rome. Down its center was Highway Six, the ancient Via Latina, which every Italian military leader from Caesar to Garibaldi to Il Duce knew as the link between the boot of Italy and its heart. This was the Allied treasure, though even now some wondered why. What was so important about the Liri Valley, about Rome, about whatever would come next in Italy? Wasn't the real goal to get to Berlin, and would that ever happen over the Alps?

That thinking was not encouraged among the men going down and coming up the mountain. They needed to focus on the thing preventing a simple sweep up the valley. The German army had built a rock solid line of defense across the peaks and down into the valley: concrete pillboxes, rock-walled machine gun nests, a ring of well-placed artillery, and spotters stationed along the crests of the mountains. They held the high ground as the Allies approached, and it was the work and duty of men in Companies B and I to take those positions from the Germans.

Five days earlier, Company B and the rest of 1st Battalion had taken the peak of Mt. Sammucro, and for three days fought tooth-and-nail to hold on, facing one counter-attack after another, until Company I of the 2nd Battalion, had relieved them. After two days down below, with Company I holding the position above, Company B returned to battle.

Huddled together on the hillside now, the two companies shared smokes and small talk. Not so much warriors, but exhausted, small town boys carrying weapons and heavy packs. In both units, going up and coming down, muscles ached and feet hurt. Emotions were kept in check. They were too tired to think in terms of fate or destiny—what was going to happen in this battle, who was going up the mountain, who was going down, who was going to live and who was going to die? Fate, however, was considering them.

CAPTAIN HENRY WASKOW knew both outfits. Raised near Belton, he had signed up for Company I along with two of his brothers, and a good many other young men in town, back in the late 1930s. Waskow had moved over to Company B when he was promoted to captain, while still stationed in the States.

Smooth-faced and slight of stature, quiet and unassuming, there was nothing physical that set Henry Waskow apart from the rest, nothing in his countenance that made him particularly impressive.

He thought of himself as a little odd, someone a bit out of step with the norm. Yet there was something obviously purposeful about Waskow that commanded the attention of the men in both companies. He was a man weighted with a sense of responsibility.

In an army composed of citizen soldiers, Henry Waskow was an ideal member. He acknowledged and accepted the responsibility of leading his men up the mountain once again. He felt the trust of those men as well as the trust his country had placed in him to lead them well. He believed fervently in the U.S. Army's mission and had volunteered for this service because, with deep sincerity, he knew his country needed him. That was who he was: a man with few adornments.

For all of his noble responsibility, however, Waskow might have remained as anonymous as the other members of Companies B and I, if not for a man hanging out with the Italian mules down below; a man, who despite his uniform and Army-issue cap would never be mistaken for a GI; a man deeply ambivalent about whether or not American soldiers should even be climbing this mountain, or laying down their young lives to take it.

Ernie Pyle and Henry Waskow would never cross paths on Mt. Sammucro, would never speak a word to each other, would never share a drink or a cigarette; but fate was about to draw them together.

And as fate would have it, they were about to make one of the great stories of World War II.

"The Hoosier Vagabond"

"It is hard for you at home to realize what an immense, complicated, sprawling institution a theater of war actually is. As it appears to you in the newspapers, war is a clear-cut matter of landing so many men overseas, moving them from port to the battlefield, advancing them against the enemy with guns firing, and they win or lose.

"To look at war that way is like seeing a trailer of a movie, and saying you've seen the whole picture . . ."

—*Ernie Pyle, Here Is Your War, 1943*

OFF THE COAST OF SICILY, JULY 1943

Ernie Pyle was in an unusual setting. After spending the past seven months tasting the grit and sand of terra firma in North Africa, most often from the foxholes, tents, and improvised lean-to's of U.S. Army infantrymen, the war correspondent was now at sea—a part of a vast armada of some two thousand U.S. and British ships, sailing from African ports to Sicily, there to wage war on the Italian and German forces arrayed to defend the island.

Among the many ships, scores of landing crafts whisked the tens of thousands of invading Allied troops onto the beaches of Sicily. There were tugs and minesweepers, destroyers and cruisers, submarines and sub-chasers—a large city of ships, as Pyle pictured them—all cruising in a vast sweep of ocean toward battle.

Global forces were at work here: enormous sums of money and human capital had been poured into the operation. Time, energy, natural resources, and endless supplies of manufactured goods. And more of this sort of massive enterprise was coming. The invasion of Sicily was just the second great step in the Allied war in Europe, coming quick on the heels of battle in North Africa, in which these same combined forces—U.S. and Great Britain—had driven the forces of Erwin Rommel and the German army from Tunisia.

Like Operation Torch, the invasion of Oran and Morocco seven months earlier, this huge collection of armies and ships sailing toward an impoverished island of Italy was prelude to even bigger conflicts to come. For more than a year, a steady stream of American forces and supplies had been shipped to Great Britain for storage and accumulation, all in preparation for the greatest invasion of them all: the one not yet definitively scheduled, but coming sometime in 1944, and aimed more directly than this assault, at the heart of Nazi Germany.

It was typical of Ernie Pyle that amid all these global forces, he chose to boil down his description of what was happening here off the shores of Sicily to the predicament of one young captain of a sub-chaser, coming around to a fleet flagship, looking for a small bit of help in the midst of the high drama.

Dusk was fast turning to dark night on the placid Mediterranean. All lights in the convoy were blacked out as Sicily neared. On board the U.S.S. *Biscayne*, the flagship on which Pyle was berthed, he watched as the sub-chaser appeared out of the gloaming and came to a softly puttering halt about thirty yards away. From his perch on the deck of the *Biscayne*, Pyle could not see the sub-chaser's skipper in the dark, but could hear his megaphoned voice calling out the problem. There was a troop-carrying barge back further in the armada. Her motor had broken down. What should he—could he—do to help?

Later on, when writing about this moment, Pyle imagined who this voice in the dark belonged to: "I could picture a youngster of a skipper out there with his blown hair and life jacket and binoculars, rolling to the sea in the Mediterranean dusk. Some young man who shortly before had been perhaps unaware of any sea at all—the bookkeeper in your bank, maybe—and then there he was, a strange new man in command of a ship, suddenly a person with acute responsibilities, carrying out with great intentness his special, small part of the enormous aggregate that is our war on all the lands and seas of the globe.

"In his unnatural presence, there in the heaving darkness of the Mediterranean," Pyle continued, "I realized vividly how everyone in America had changed, how every life had suddenly stopped and as suddenly had begun on a different course. Everything in this world had stopped except war and we were all men of a new profession out in a strange night of caring for one another."[1]

From the *Biscayne* instructions were megaphoned back on how to help the transport barge with its bad engine. The young captain of the sub-chaser called out his "aye-aye" and with a dash of new-found certainty, added that any subsequent problems would be dealt with on his ship alone. "If there is any change," he called to the *Biscayne's* commander, "I will use my own judgment and report to you again at dawn. Good night, sir."

Then off sailed the young sub-chaser captain, with his similarly young crew, to aid the stricken transport.

Pyle saluted the young skipper and all the others in the armada: "Not a pinpoint of light showed from those hundreds of ships as they surged on through the night toward their destiny, carrying across this ageless and indifferent sea, tens of thousands of young men of new professions, fighting for . . . for . . . well, at least for each other."

BY THE TIME Ernie Pyle's stay in the Mediterranean theater had stretched to this point, it was hard to know if he was a new man, a changed man, or a man who had found his calling.

After months of covering the war from every possible angle— frontline to aerodrome; signal corps to backstage with Mitzi May- fair—Pyle had grown so at ease with what he called the "magnificent simplicity" of life on the frontlines that he was almost uncomfort- able in any other setting. That included a pleasant cabin in the U.S.S. *Biscayne*, or the beaches of Tunisia, where he had been resting for a few weeks in the wake of the North African campaign. Pyle simply wasn't at ease away from those whose stories he had come here to tell.

Middle-aged in 1943 and a thin wisp of a man, Ernie Pyle's hair had once been a lively red but was now melding into to an ill- defined mixture of gray, white, and yellowish orange which he wore combed back and usually covered with some military-issue cap. At a fighting weight around 110 pounds on a five-foot-seven- inch frame, Pyle was so frail, he looked like he'd been raised on K-rations and Chesterfield cigarettes. Maybe it was that unassum- ing stature that helped Ernie Pyle fit in anywhere. No matter whether he was slipping into a circle of GI's leaning on a tank, or chatting with Ike himself, Pyle seemed to garner the confidence of everyone he met.

His goal was simply to tell the stories of the people who were gathered here to wage war. Pyle was, as one journalist later wrote of him, "a slight, gnome-like man who hated the whole business. He knew nothing of strategy or of military affairs, and so he concentrated on human-interest stories. No detail about life for the GI in Europe was too insignificant to report—he once wrote about the colour of the soldiers' foot ointment—no complaint too minor to mention, no message too mundane to relay . . ."[2]

Pyle was not the sort of man to claim he was serving some sort of higher cause by staying out in the field with his GI buddies. In fact, higher causes in general were not of great interest to him. For the length of his first twenty-some years as a journalist, Ernie Pyle had been an unassuming reporter; a writer less concerned with tackling big issues than in finding stories where others saw the commonplace and mundane.

As it turned out, by covering the war in this same fashion he was telling mothers, fathers, and girlfriends back home precisely what a growing number of them wanted to hear. They got enough of troop movements and battle descriptions from the wire services and in the dailies; what they longed for, it turned out, was a sense of how the boys were doing. Enter Pyle, for whom few details of a soldier's life were too picayune or prosaic for him to ask and write about. He told what they ate and how they ate it; how they set up camp after terrifying and exhausting days of battle; he described how they shaved and how they bathed; how they talked to one another and what they said in quiet moments when the war seemed as far away as their homes back in the States.

Pyle was hardly a saint and hardly without flaws. Lee Miller, his editor back in the U.S., caught the full brunt of Pyle's insecurities in letters Pyle sent home. He worried about his writing talents, the state of his unraveling marriage, his myriad illnesses, real and imagined, and whether or not he had the ability to honestly capture the war. He drank too much and moaned and groaned mightily. But for all his uncertainties and personal problems, in the grand scheme of things, and to a growing number of readers back home, Pyle seemed to be doing the work of the angels.

BORN IN SMALL-TOWN Indiana at the turn-of-the-century, Pyle was the only child of a farm family. His father was taciturn but kind hearted. His mother was opinionated and the driving force in the family. Pyle did the standard farm chores of the era, and generally hated doing them. He went to school, elementary and secondary, in the town of Dana. A trip to Chicago when he was a boy with his father might have prompted his first interest in journalism. He got his hands on some of the city dailies and was impressed with the comic-strip heroes and liked seeing the names of the writers in bylines.[3]

Ernie Pyle was slightly built even as a boy, and not much of an athlete. But like a lot of Indiana kids of his era, he became enamored with auto racing after the first running of the Indianapolis 500 in 1911. The family got a Model T soon after Henry Ford began mass-producing them, and Ernie, at age sixteen, was wheeling around Dana with buddies. His first heroes were the drivers at the "brickyard"—nicknamed for the paved bricks that served as the first track. Even later in life Pyle would get to the 500 whenever he was able, and press his ear to the radio when he wasn't.

After graduating from high school in the spring of 1918, Pyle enlisted in the U.S. Naval Reserve. He was sent to the University of Illinois for training and was just on his way to the Great Lakes Naval Training Station in Chicago when the war ended. By the fall of 1919, he had enrolled at Indiana University in Bloomington, about 90 miles from his hometown.

As a shy, small town freshman, Pyle mumbled to a counselor that he might be interested in the practice of journalism. Unfortunately Indiana did not yet offer degrees in that subject. Pyle started out studying economics, but as a sophomore, not only took his first course in journalism, but signed up for the staff of the *Daily Student*, the school newspaper. Predictably nicknamed "Red" for his hair color, Pyle loved covering sporting events because of the travel involved, and would find whatever means possible to get to out-of-town contests, including one trip to Cambridge, Massachusetts, when Indiana took on Harvard in a 1921 football game.

In the spring of 1922, the baseball team was set to travel to Japan for a series of games, and Pyle determined he would go, too. To finance the trip, he found a job as a cabin boy on the ship that was taking the team across the Pacific. The cruise brought him his first view of the wide world.

When he returned to school in the fall, Pyle became editor-in-chief of the *Daily Student*, but skipped finishing his senior year at the university when he was offered a job at the *LaPorte* [Indiana] *Herald*. Among his first assignments was covering a local meeting of the Ku Klux Klan, then a major force in Indiana politics. A newcomer to the town and a stranger at the meeting, he was quickly pinpointed as an interloper by attendees and Klan members followed him home to his room at the LaPorte YMCA. There Pyle was threatened by the KKK and told not to write anything about what he'd just seen. Undaunted, the cub reporter filed his story.

Just three months later, a friend from the *Daily Student* recommended Pyle to an editor at the *Washington Daily News* and Ernie got his first big-time job at $30 a week in the nation's capital. He worked first as a reporter, and then as a copy editor, where he honed the sort of crisp writing style that would become his trademark. He made friends with Lee Miller, another young reporter at the paper, and also developed a few eccentricities. Because Pyle didn't have to travel very far from his own desk, and always complained about feeling cold, he started to wear clothing that was hardly typical for a big city newsroom. He liked to match lumberjack shirts with a long stocking cap for warmth.

In 1923, Pyle fell in love with a young woman from Minnesota named Geraldine "Jerry" Siebolds, who worked as clerk at the Civil Service Commission in D.C. They made a good match: like Ernie, she was a bit of a free spirit, rolled her own cigarettes, read and wrote poetry, and liked to travel. They married in 1925 and took an apartment together in Washington, where they kept just a few pieces of furniture. The floor, according to Miller, was coated like a saloon's in small bits of tobacco fallen from haphazard rolling.[4]

Soon after the wedding, Pyle grew tired of his copyediting job. He and Jerry took their savings—$1000 stowed in the boot of a Ford Model T—and hit the road for a cross-country tour to L.A. and back to the east coast. A pause in New York turned into something longer when Pyle took back-to-back newspaper jobs, first with the *Evening World* and then with the *Post*. When Lee Miller took over as managing editor at the *Washington Daily News,* Pyle and Jerry packed up their few belongings and headed down the power corridor, back to D.C., where Ernie, with a bump in salary, served as a telegraph editor, a crucial function at any newspaper in the day. The ability to turn abbreviated telegrams into sharp prose was a highly admired skill, and Pyle did the job well. Still, he wasn't quite satisfied.

It was 1928. The year after Charles Lindbergh had flown the Atlantic and public interest in airplane flight was at its zenith. Pyle got the bug himself and soon began a four-year stint as one of the nation's first columnists on all matters of aviation. Over that time, he met all the hero fliers of the day, from mail pilots to Amelia Earhart. By logging almost 100,000 air miles, Pyle was able to gain the trust and confidence of the flying community, and his and Jerry's apartment in Washington became a salon of sorts for wingmen and women passing through the city.

Pyle liked the work and continued with the column even after Lee Miller left the *Daily News* to take another job in the Scripps-Howard chain. A couple of years after Miller's departure, Pyle was promoted to the managing editor job, which prompted a group of pilots so fond of Pyle and his work to gift him with a watch, presented by Earhart in a ceremony at the Washington-Hoover airport.

Two years of serving as the managing editor of the *Washington Daily News* was plenty for Pyle. The daily grind of turning out a newspaper wore thin and by late 1934, he was ready for a break. He and Jerry drove on another cross-country tour of the country. This time, he came back to the east coast by way of a steamer, through the Panama Canal, the Gulf of Mexico, and up the eastern seaboard. He happened to arrive back at the *Daily News* just as one of the paper's syndicated columnists, Heywood Broun, was on vacation. Pyle got permission from the editors to fill in with a series of stories describing his tour with Jerry; and thus was born his column, the "Hoosier Vagabond."

For the next five years, Ernie Pyle, usually accompanied by Jerry, traveled far and wide, beyond the continental U.S. to Hawaii and Alaska, Canada, and Central and South America. He wore out two cars and five sets of tires as he sought out stories and profiles that others had missed: Pyle wrote about a leper colony in Hawaii; the Dust Bowl in western Kansas; a cook in a Nashville restaurant who had once been a slave of President Andrew Johnson. He wrote about, in the words of one admirer, "the shepherds, hat-check girls, tugboat captains, crab fishermen, silver miners, moonshiners, revenuers, soda jerks, agate hunters, abalone divers, sharpshooters, and Death Valley cave-dwellers whom Pyle chatted up [along the way]."[5]

Jerry took on a persona of her own in the columns. Pyle referred to her as "That Girl" and she became, in his characterization, a slightly world-weary, but nonetheless game companion, offering the occasional sardonic note and far-off gaze to the "Hoosier Vagabond's" travel.

In fact, their life was not all carefree, windows-down, cross-country cruising. As the trips multiplied, so, too, did the bleak roadside motels and the lonely nights spent sliding a liquor bottle back-and-forth on the night table between them. Jerry grew reclusive on these trips, staying in their hotel rooms, reading, drinking, working crossword puzzles as Pyle ventured out, collecting his stories. She was depressive and her alcohol use exacerbated the condition. In 1937, 1938, and 1940, she had alcohol-related breakdowns that landed her in sanitariums for prolonged stays. In this era, when Alcoholics Anonymous was just getting organized and the disease model of the affliction was non-existent, effective help was hard to find. Despite Pyle's deep and loving concerns for a woman who had been for years, not only his wife, but his boon companion, Pyle himself frequently abused alcohol, too. He thought that Jerry's problems could be contained if she "just cut back on the booze."[6]

After her last breakdown, the two decided it would be a settling influence on their lives and Jerry's recovery if they had a permanent place to call home. They decided to build a house in a favorite spot—Albuquerque, New Mexico—and contractors were hired to construct a small ranch-style home just outside the city.

Even before it was finished, however, Ernie Pyle began to feel the tug of the great story of the day: the war in Europe. France fell to Germany that summer and the Luftwaffe began its almost nightly bombing of London in September. In somber, urgent tones, Edward R. Murrow reported the story as a struggle of good versus evil, and Pyle felt compelled to be there.

He asked Scripps-Howard to send him to England. His idea was to cover the war in the same way he'd covered everything else in his journalistic career. He wrote to Miller, who was working again at Scripps-Howard, telling the editor that he wasn't interested in reporting "a message" about what was happening in London, but to write on "the same old basis the column has always been written on, of making people at home see what I see." [7]

Scripps-Howard gave him the go-ahead. He left "That Girl" to deal with the contractors in Albuquerque and her own demons. Pyle headed off to become, at age 40, a war correspondent. The London Blitz loomed in his future.

2

The Texas Division

ON THE 4TH OF JULY, 1943, the 143rd Infantry Regiment of the U.S. Army's 36th Division, known variously as the Texas Division, or the T-Patchers, for the distinctive T insignia sewn onto the upper arms of their uniforms, marched in a holiday parade in Rabat, the capital of Morocco. Led by the Sultan's Guard, native troops dressed in bright red Moroccan garb, the parade also included U.S. Navy aviation personnel from the nearby Port Lyautey airfield and the 1st Armored Division. The marchers were followed by a single column of sand-caked vehicles, moving at a snail's pace. According to the commander of the 36th, General Fred Livingood Walker, who was at the head of the parade, the long line of loud, grungy tanks and trucks following the colorful regimental guidons and the brilliant native uniforms of the Sultan Guard discouraged a large number of parade spectators. The crowd soon began to dwindle as the procession dragged on.

For Walker and his division, it was nonetheless a good day. The regiment he had picked to show off the crisp military style of the 36th—the 143rd, which included Henry Waskow's Company B— had made positive impressions on visiting officers, including a handful of French generals, and Generals Mark Clark and Ernest Dawley,

Walker's commanding generals in the U.S. Fifth Army. Not only did he receive a number of compliments from his fellow officers on the presentation of the 143rd, more important, over lunch afterward, Walker learned from Clark that the 36th was finally being tapped for duty. After several false starts and last minute cancellations, they were going to see action soon.

The 36th had been in North Africa for three months now and was ready for combat. Comprised for the most part of Texas National Guard units (thus the division's nickname), with a few Oklahoma companies sprinkled in, the 36th had been first called into active duty in November 1940. Stationed at Camp Bowie in Texas at the start of its service, the division had been moved around the country for the next two years, taking part in the vast war games in Louisiana in the late summer of 1941 before returning to Texas. Then it was on to Florida, where they took part in more war games; and up to Camp Edwards in Massachusetts in August 1942, where the division heard its first rumors of being shipped overseas.

General George Patton visited Walker and the 36th on Cape Cod in late August, soon after the division arrived in Massachusetts. His appearance was marked by mystery regarding upcoming Allied plans. Patton had come from England where he had been assigned by General Eisenhower to head the Western Taskforce of Operation Torch—the portion of the invasion of North Africa aimed at Morocco in November 1942. He was home now to gather troops for that task. But the operation was top secret and Patton could make no mention of its details.

When he arrived at Camp Edwards, Patton asked to meet privately with Walker, where he confided that he wanted the 36th for a soon-to-happen Allied action. Patton, however, could not tell Walker where, when, or how this attack was to occur, or when the division would know with certainty that it was being called to combat. Still, the general asked Walker for leave to address the 36th in order to rouse them for upcoming battle.[1]

Walker was a long-time U.S. Army officer and knew enough of George Patton to take his drama with a grain of salt. In fact, he had something of a history with "Georgie," as Patton was called by most of his family and Army friends.

Walker had been a member of the Ohio National Guard as an undergraduate at Ohio State University and was commissioned in the regular army soon after graduating with a degree in mine engineering in 1911. He served in the Philippines as a second lieutenant, and with General John "Black Jack" Pershing in Mexio, prior to World War I.

Walker went to France in 1917 and earned a Distinguished Service Cross for bravery during the second battle of the Marne. Between the wars, he served once again in the Philippines as well as in China. He also graduated from the War College in Washington, D.C., served as an instructor there and at Fort Benning, Georgia, and was commandant at Shattuck Academy in Minnesota for five years in the late '20s and early '30s.

By the start of World War II, he was a well-respected field general but not a rising star in the army. His countenance suggested a man who understood that status. His gaze was forthright with just a hint of irony in the line of his mouth. His eyes were dark and eyebrows darker—both urged no nonsense. Fifty-four years old when he was appointed commander of the 36th, Fred Walker looked his age.

His appointment to the Texas Division came in the midst of a hurricane warning in Louisiana, just prior to the war games that the T-Patchers took part in that September 1941. Aside from the inauspicious weather, it was an appointment that Walker didn't immediately relish. Despite his beginnings as a soldier in the Ohio National Guard, Walker had long since turned "regular" army. He knew that guard units were often considered sloppy and amateurish by "regulars." Conversely, guard unit members could be suspicious and unfriendly toward regular army folk, especially those who were taking command as he was, after the 36th had been training on active duty for almost a full year. There was also the fact that as a commander of a National Guard division way out in Texas, Walker was a far sight from the career-changing happenings emanating from George Marshall's office and the War Department in Washington.[2]

But as the 36th and the general got to know each other through the following year, respect grew and became mutual. The young Texans under his command tended to be unassuming and hard-working characters, with the occasional streaks of wildness and lack of discipline that came with their age and the fact that they were, by and large, country boys who hadn't seen much of the world. Walker, on the other hand, was plain-spoken and liked plain-spoken people.

He was not the sort of officer to be overly impressed with a flamboyant general such as George Patton. In fact, after those war games back in Louisiana, Walker was one of a number of participants who had groused about the way Patton and his armored division had played. Down in the bayou a year earlier, Walker and the 36th had been assigned an area to defend against Patton's tanks, except the Army at the time had no anti-tank weaponry to supply his troops. In lieu of these, Walker and company had simply made handwritten signs that read "Tank Destroyer" and placed them strategically around the landscape as a means to indicate to the game umpires that the area was defended.

Another inventive group from the 36th anti-tank battalion had an officer whose father owned a machine ship in Fort Worth. Prior to the Louisiana game, he went to an auto salvage yard and then back to his dad's shop, where he welded a few mock guns, using axle housing for the barrel.[3]

It didn't matter in either case. Patton and his division simply ignored the signs and the judges who were there to point them out. What's more, in the after-games critique, Patton had the temerity to boast of how he had destroyed Walker's defenses. "I was furious," Walker later confided to his diary about the exercises, "but I was not as angry as my men who had to take to the brush to keep from being run over. If any of them had had live ammunition, I am sure some would have felt like using it."

Of course, all of this was history by the time of Patton's visit to Cape Cod. And Patton was Walker's superior. Plus he offered the possibility, no matter how skeptically Walker might view his visit, of getting the 36th into action. Walker granted Patton's request to address his troops and subsequently listened as "Georgie" gave a rousing speech in his surprisingly high-pitched voice to an assembly of officers from the 36th from the back of a jeep at Camp Edwards. "I watched the faces of my officers during his 'oratory,'" Walker recorded. "They showed surprise, bewilderment, and disgust." According to Walker, the Texas boys "were not favorably impressed" with Patton's habitual use of profanity and vulgarity.

Perhaps the memory of being nearly run over in Louisiana also affected his reception with the officers of the 36th. Whether or not their lack of interest in Patton was felt by him and influenced his decision is unrecorded; but, in fact, the Texas Division was not chosen to be a part of the Western Task Force of the Allied invasion of North Africa, and instead remained in Cape Cod for the next several months. It proceeded to invade Martha's Vineyard, not Morocco, not once, but twice (October and December 1942) before it settled in for the winter on the Cape.

The 36th stayed long enough at Camp Edwards, near Falmouth, to become favorites of the locals. After the many months in training, a number of Texas Division troops grew tired of life without their spouses and so they brought them up to Massachusetts, where quite a few Texan women and a handful of children occupied seasonal housing after the tourists left Cape Cod at the end of summer. If nightclub bands in the area didn't have the "Eyes of Texas" in their repertoires before the arrival of the 36th, they soon learned it or risked trouble from the crowd. Meanwhile the Texans acquired a taste for New England lobster and blueberry pie, continued with their endless drills, and, along with every recruit in the U.S. Army, watched a new training film produced by Hollywood director Frank Capra that November called Prelude to War. No reviews of the documentary were recorded among the members of the 36th.

The amphibious landings practiced by the division, sailing from Falmouth to the sands of Martha's Vineyard under live fire conditions, was in keeping with a long tradition within the U.S. military. John Glover's Marblehead seaman had practiced the same sort of military maneuvers on Martha's Vineyards before rowing George Washington and his troops across the Delaware on Christmas Eve nearly 170 years before Walker and the 36th made the same practice voyages.

The division remained on the Cape through the tragic post-Thanksgiving fire at the Cocoanut Grove nightclub in Boston, which killed 492 revelers in the deadliest such conflagration in the nation's history. They endured ten degree-below-zero temperatures during the week of Christmas. On December 30, Walker got word that one of his three infantry regiments would be soon shipped overseas; but just two and a half weeks later that departure was cancelled.

Walker dealt with a variety of discipline problems associated with troops stuck in the middle of a long New England winter: absenteeism, desertion, stealing food from company kitchens. Soldiers from the camp entertained the locals in New Bedford at the Empire Theater stage with a variety revue dubbed "The Khaki Parade." There were musicians, comedians, magicians, and a soldier in drag doing a Carmen Miranda number to the delight of the audience. In February, Lieutenant Joel Westbrook, the 1st Battalion operations officer, married a local girl named Elaine Summers at The Chapel of the 143rd in Camp Edwards. Westbrook was a recent grad of the University of Texas Law School and the son of an ally of Texas Senator Coke Stevenson, Lawrence Westbrook, who'd run the W.P.A. program in Texas.

Still the 36th didn't get the call to duty. In early March, Walker made a stop in Washington to find out what was going on and learned that the problems were more bureaucratic than anything else. There were simply too many inexperienced officers in too many offices trying to manage a rapidly expanding army, most of which was training in camps remote from Washington, such as Edwards up on Cape Cod, to effectively coordinate troop movements with U.S. Navy shipping.

He was advised that things would soon be sorted out, and they were. By the third week of March, it appeared the division was being prepared to ship out. Railroad cars began arriving in Massachusetts to carry troops and supplies away from Edwards, and packing began in earnest. Walker visited the Army Port of Embarkation in Brooklyn to check on preliminary arrangements. Five ships, the Brazil, the Argentina, the Gibbons, the Barry, and the Hawaiian Shipper were to take the entire division to North Africa.

Walker sailed on the Brazil with about 5,000 of his men, bunked in tiers four high. The Argentina had similar accommodations. Most of the division's equipment fit on the five transports, with the exception of a tank destroyer battalion and its twenty-four anti-tank vehicles, which were shipped in a vessel especially designed for the assignment. For entertainment purposes, Walker placed a regimental band on four of the five transports, with an orchestra on the fifth.

On April 1, the troop trains began pulling into the pier in Brooklyn at 6:30 in the morning, and the last unit, a battalion of the 143rd, climbed aboard its transport at 10 p.m. that night. The next morning the division sailed for North Africa.

It took two weeks for the 36th to land in Oran, Algeria, on the northern coast of Africa. On board the Brazil, General Walker caught up with some reading: the first volume of Douglas Southall Freeman's *Lee's Lieutenants* was his choice for the cruise.[4]

Elsewhere on the Brazil, a mimeographed division newspaper called the T-Patch, born soon after leaving New York harbor, provided lighter reading for the troops. Along with war news gleaned from the ship's radio, the paper provided Major League Baseball scores and the results of shipboard boxing matches and basketball games. The T-Patch also contained a bevy of drawings of scantily-clad women, sketched in full pin-up style with dreamy cut-lines suggesting that these buxom women might actually await them in North Africa: there was "Gertie from Bizerte," for instance, and "Cassie from Maknassy with the classy chassis." One woman drawn in diaphanous veil and stretched out on pillows, was described as "a cute kid from Sidi Bou Zid."

The Brazil disembarked at Oran on the evening of April 13, and the T-Patchers soon took a train to Magenta, 80 miles south, where the division made themselves at home in a countryside that reminded some of California.

Just after Easter, Walker left his division to fly from Oran to Rabat and then on to Casablanca, the area at the heart of the action of Patton's Western taskforce during the Operation Torch invasion of Morocco the previous November. At Rabat, Walker attended a meeting at Patton's headquarters that brought together much of the

North African command, including Patton himself. Here and at subsequent meetings through the rest of April to mid-May, Walker learned that the tug-of-war over where the 36th would be assigned remained ongoing. The division was a wishbone being yanked on one hand by Patton, who would command the U.S. Seventh Army in the next Allied operation after North Africa; and by Clark, who hoped to command the operation himself.

By the middle of May, and back at Magenta, Walker learned that the T-Patchers would not be accompanying Patton to Sicily, the next Allied target. Instead, with the exception of a battalion from the 141st, which ironically would be training some of Patton's forces for amphibious assault, the 36th was heading for a camp in the Marmora Forest of cork trees, between Port Lyautey and Rabat in northeastern Morocco.

Walker enjoyed his stay in Morocco, learning the ways and means of Moroccan society, both native and French colonial. He found the countryside stunning and was curious about Arab agriculture and military customs. He also had to deal with accidents and discipline problems. Three members of the 1st Division, from the group being trained by his 141st, were drowned in exercises off the Moroccan coast; members of 143rd were charged by local farmers, both Arab and French, with stealing watermelons ("Texas soldiers just can't resist watermelons," Walker noted in his diary); a forest fire eighteen miles from his headquarters needed to be put out, and the 143rd, sent to extinguish the flames, found a crashed B-25 there, the source of the flames, containing three charred American bodies.

But then came the 4th of July parade in Rabat, followed by the news from Mark Clark that the 36th would be joining him that fall for the next Allied action against the Axis. That post-parade confidence between the generals was quickly followed by the news that the Allies, including Patton and his Seventh Army, had invaded Sicily on July 10.

Two weeks later Walker and the 36th learned that they were headed back north to Arzew on the Mediterranean, where once again they would be practicing amphibious landings in preparation for whatever assault would follow.

It was practice that Walker knew his division did not need, but after all these months he thought he could say with some certainty that his division would soon be fighting.

3

Tunisia

BEING A WORLD WAR II war correspondent was still a relatively novel position in spring 1943—just twenty-six had landed with the troops during Operation Torch in November. By the time Pyle wound up on the U.S.S. *Biscayne* seven months later, he could count at least seventy-five American and British reporters in the Mediterranean theater.[1]

Correspondents were aided—and censored—by an Army department known to the journalists as INC, for Information and Censorship. Correspondents would cover what was happening in the field during the course of a typical day, and take turns getting jeep rides back to headquarters in Algiers from INC officers, in order to file prior to a 9 p.m. deadline. In the early weeks of the campaign, rules prohibited transmissions to just 200 words a day. By spring, that number had jumped to 450 words.[2]

Just what a war correspondent was supposed to do—and *be*—in this war was an evolving problem when Pyle arrived in North Africa in late November 1942. The dependence on the military for transportation, information, and access to personnel left World War II correspondents with little room for reporting any contradictions in the war, or stories that might cast military efforts in anything but a diligent and brave light. Then again, early in the war, there was little sense of urgency among the journalists to report anything but the positive. Almost to a man, they felt as if they were enemies of the Axis powers, too.

Eventually, there would be those who hung out at headquarters and covered the war from the point of view of its planners; and those who braved the frontlines and told what progress was being made from the ground up. There were romantic types, too, whose experiences, were fed by politics, and in some cases, by past associations with the cause and romance of the Spanish Civil War. These reporters might carry guns and rush toward the action, half hoping they would become a part of it (later in the war, Ernest Hemingway would actually claim to have raced ahead of Allied troops and "taken" a French town).[3]

Pyle, of course, had never been a "hard news" reporter and he wasn't going to change stripes in North Africa. Because he was writing a column, Pyle had no pressures to be absolutely up to date in his reporting. He could write about incidents well after they happened, so he wasn't a part of the wire service and daily news contingent who were constantly shuttling back-and-forth between frontlines and headquarters to send news back to the States.

After landing at Oran and spending his first few weeks in proximity to Allied headquarters, he began to venture out to various units spread across the North African war zone, essentially pursuing stories in the same fashion that he and Jerry had done when he was authoring his "Hoosier Vagabond" columns. His first stories were about the convoy that brought him to Algeria, about the landscape and the Arab people, about a unit of Rangers with whom he hooked up, about a signal corps unit.

Pyle did one exposé on Allied use of French fascists for assistance in the war effort, but it was atypical of his reporting and he quickly returned to his usual "beat." He wrote about a medical unit and camp life—the daily needs of the average GI, which were, according to Pyle: "(1) good mail service; (2) movies, radios, and phonographs; (3) cigarettes and candy."[4]

Pyle traveled light: just the clothes on his back, his typewriter, and a pouch of Bull Durham tobacco. He did what he had been doing for years now: sidled up to people who looked like they had something to say, and made himself easy to talk to.

Always careful to get the right spelling, full name, rank, and home address of his interviewees, he depicted camp life: the boxing tournaments, games of touch football, even badminton contests.

Pyle painted a picture of the North African countryside: he described the roads as macadamized and surprisingly good, said the landscape was similar to the American southwest, and told how the farming was done by beautiful Arabian horses.

The Arab people did a lot of waving at passing troops and their children offered "V for Victory" signs, but the populace was generally hard to get to know.

He did a story on Hollywood entertainers Martha Ray, Kay Francis, Mitzi Mayfair, and Carole Landis, traveling through North Africa's Allied airbases on one of the war's earliest entertainment tours. "Four good soldiers," Pyle called them.[5]

A column from an aerodrome in the desert was the first spine-tingling war story that he told. In quiet detail it outlined the tale of a wounded plane coming in hours late from a bombing mission over Bizerte. Pyle related how the clock ticked away on the chances of its return as a beautiful desert sunset painted the sky in stunning oranges and pinks and blues. Men at the base ate supper in silence, thinking of the crew. Everyone was aware of how much gasoline it carried and how much air time that would usually afford a bomber. Everyone knew that it had long since exceeded that standard equivalency, and as a consequence the ten lives on board—ten men, who a few hours earlier had been doing the ordinary things that young fliers did in preparation for a mission: the nervous chatter back and forth; the checking of gauges and mechanisms; the zipping of jackets and search for gloves—those smiling, laughing, youthful lives were now in jeopardy or lost.

"And then an electric thing happened," Pyle wrote. "Far off in the dusk a red flare shot into the sky. It made an arc against the dark background of the mountains and fell to the earth. It couldn't be anything else. It had to be. The ten dead men were coming home."[6]

His work started to get noticed. Miller wrote to Pyle that more newspapers were picking up his column: Keep up the good work. Do what you're doing.

For Pyle that meant living close to the soldiers he reported on. He got to know their habits and lifestyles, sat through their talks, small and deep. He heard their confessions, understood their fears and their dreams. Pyle was with them at quiet moments and moments of exploration—a trip to the headquarters of the French Foreign Legion at Sidi-bel-Abbès in the Algerian desert, for instance, was an otherworldly experience for Pyle and the five Army officers. These were, after all, young men—a dentist from Dallas, a brick salesman from Chicago, a lawyer in Milwaukee—who had never ventured far from home. Now they found themselves at the North African home of the fabled Legionnaires, where instead of a sand blown old fort, they wound up admiring, among other amenities, a magnificent new swimming pool, which rivaled "anything in Hollywood."[7]

He was hardly touring the countryside, however. Pyle spent weeks and weeks on the shifting frontlines in Tunisia. He came to like the infantry guys more than all others, primarily because theirs was the hardest and most thankless job in the war. He stuck with them as they moved at a snail's pace in endless nighttime convoys toward the frontlines. And he stayed with them through battle, including the German push at Sidi Bou Said in mid-February 1943, and the pell-mell exit from the Kasserine Pass a few days later.

Despite his experiences near the frontlines, Pyle was the first to admit that he was not particularly brave. In fact, he wrote of it in a column about a bomber crew that he'd first met in England. One day soon after a proscription that prevented journalists from flying on bombing missions had been lifted, Pyle was asked by this crew if he was interested in tagging along on a run over Bizerte.

He had dreaded the moment when he would have to answer this question. On the one hand, Pyle knew that there was not one practical function that he could serve and he would simply be dead weight on the flight.

On the other hand, he wondered if it wasn't cowardly to tell the stories about these brave men and not partake in the daily dangers that they were facing. After all, other journalists had flown. Could he truly understand their circumstances without himself going into the air?

When his answer finally came, it was a no, "I'm too old to be a hero," he told the crew. Their reaction was an immediate surprise. They not only understood; they were supportive. [8]

"Anybody who goes when he doesn't have to is a plain damned fool," one of the bombers said.

The soldiers' pragmatism was evident a few days earlier, when Pyle had been looking at photos printed in an American magazine. Pyle and the bomber crew pored over these war reports, full of dramatic and vivid images from around the globe. Pyle realized that one of the pictures was a photo of the long concrete pier in Oran, at which his ship had docked when he first arrived in Africa. This was the same quay that he had stepped onto a few months earlier with absolutely no sense of romance. It was just a bustling, loading zone. Now in this magazine, the Oran pier looked as exotic as an oasis rising on the edge of the desert.

To the men in the group, Pyle made his confession: though he was in the middle of a world war, it didn't seem at all dramatic to him.

One of the flyers in the group, a bomber squadron leader, admired and respected by all the others, agreed with Pyle. "It isn't to me either," said Major Quint Quick. "I know it should be, but it isn't. It's just hard work, and all I want is to finish it and get back home."[9]

This was the sort of sensibility that Pyle admired. This is what he recorded and sent back to his readers in the States. This is what they responded to in numbers that were making him the most widely read correspondent in North Africa. He didn't sugar coat the war for the folks. He painted it as rough, hard work, carried out mainly by young men who would rather be anywhere else. Nor did he focus on its horrors: the terrible wounds and gruesome deaths went undescribed as they did with every other journalist covering the war in its early days.

His readers responded to these stories in a remarkable fashion. When he left for North Africa in November 1942, Pyle's column for Scripps-Howard appeared in 42 newspapers. In just one month's time that number jumped to 65; by the end of March, the total was 82, and one month after that, 122 newspapers were carrying his stories with a total circulation near 9 million. By the time Pyle ended up, back at headquarters in Algiers that spring, 3 book publishers were vying to collect his columns into a book.[10] It was a pretty meteoric rise for a journalist who had been relatively obscure less than a year before and had never covered a war.

LONDON WAS, in a sense, a practice run for his subsequent work in North Africa that would take place nearly two years later. Pyle arrived there in early December 1940, after leaving Jerry behind to oversee the construction of their home in Albuquerque. Scripps-Howard had blessed his mission and off he flew to England. Once there, he explored the city for a few days, but in truth, he couldn't find much to write about. The great Battle of Britain that fall had temporarily abated and he worried to editor Lee Miller that his columns were having no emotional impact.[11]

Then on December 29, one of the great raids of the war erupted over the darkened skies of London. Pyle rushed to a balcony in the Hotel Savoy, where he was staying, and watched in awe as wave after wave of German bombers dropped their load on the city lighting 2,000 separate fires, including a massive blaze at the Cathedral of St. Paul.

Pyle's reaction was recorded in one of his most memorable columns: "Someday when peace has returned to this odd world I want to come to London again and stand on a certain balcony on a moonlit night and look down upon the peaceful silver curve of the Thames with its dark bridges," he wrote.

"And standing there, I want to tell somebody who has never seen it how London looked on a certain night in the holiday season of the year 1940.

"For on that night this old, old city—even though I must bite my tongue in shame for saying it—was the most beautiful sight I have ever seen.

"It was a night when London was ringed and stabbed with fire . . ."[12]

In vivid detail and great sympathy for the city, he described the awesome destruction visiting the streets below, all the time staying true to the promise he'd always made to his readers: to report, first of all, how he felt about what he was seeing. That meant admitting that as awful as this sight might be, there was a beauty in it, "a dreadful masterpiece," he called it. A "monstrous loveliness...London stabbed with great fires, shaken by explosions, its dark regions along the Thames sparkling with the pinpoints of white-hot bombs, all of it roofed over with a ceiling of pink that held bursting shells, balloons, flares and the grind of vicious engines. And in yourself the excitement and anticipation and wonder in your soul that this could be happening at all. These things all went together to make the most hateful, most beautiful single scene I have ever known."

The prose was beautiful and haunting; the column's contradictions made it feel true and meaningful to his readers. This was war in the modern age and it jumped off the page, as did subsequent stories that January, describing the British response to the Blitz: the quiet pluck and grit of the people; a city far more resilient than Adolph Hitler could imagine or appreciate.

Time magazine picked up his story on the London raid and reprinted it with a note describing Pyle as "an inconspicuous little man . . . not celebrated as a straight news reporter [until he wrote this column]." The head of Scripps-Howard sent Pyle a wire saying his columns were the "talk of New York"; and Pyle would soon be contacted by a publisher about the possibility of collecting his stories into a small book.[13]

But there were two more months in England, and subsequent columns lost some of the snap and emotion of the first few. Early in March, he learned that his mother had suffered a stroke and died in Indiana. Upon hearing the news, he returned to his room at the Savoy and conjured images of her life "attending neighborhood square dances, playing the violin, aiding sick animals, driving the family automobile in the local Fourth of July parade, and crying as he left to report for service with the naval reserves in World War I."[14]

The death was debilitating to his work and psyche. Pyle's brush with journalistic stardom wound quickly down, and by the end of March, he returned the States, trying to settle in with Jerry in their new home in Albuquerque. By summer, she suffered another relapse and refused to go to a sanitarium. Pyle was once again ensconced in a joint misery that continued into the fall.

Depression set in, and Pyle took a leave of absence from the column. He traveled to Indiana to visit his father and entered into a couple of unsatisfying affairs. They were unsatisfying for reasons beyond his guilt. Pyle suffered from sexual impotence, an ongoing condition that had begun in his relationship with Jerry several years earlier and had been unaided by his own heavy drinking and depressive nature.

To jar himself out of his melancholy and escape Jerry, Pyle made plans to take a long trip to Asia to report on conditions there. A flight to Honolulu, the first leg on his journey, scheduled for early December was postponed. The Japanese had struck Pearl Harbor on December 7.

Feeling restless and caged, Pyle fled to the West Coast to report on the helter-skelter activity and intense fear that the attack prompted up and down the coast, but according to Pyle biographer James Tobin, he spent most of his time, "struggling to write lackluster columns, drinking heavily and feeling a 'tight, swollen up feeling in my face and head . . . and a general all around debilitation and disinterest in everything.'"[15] By the spring of 1942, Pyle was deep in the trough of a serious depression.

He and Jerry entered a confused and mutually destructive dance of co-dependency. They could not live with one another; they could not live without one another. He suggested divorce; she suggested they try to conceive a child; he pointed out that neither of them was in a condition to bring children into the world; she continued to drink. In April, now at Jerry's request, they decided to divorce. "As an experiment," Pyle wrote to Miller, "on the gamble that that it might shock her into a realization that she had to face life like other people."[16]

Both of them seemed to finally understand that she needed to work at getting herself well, and that his presence was not helping matters. The marriage was officially dissolved in mid April, yet Pyle continued to stay in the house with her in Albuquerque. He also remained restless and itching to do something to get away. Pyle made an attempt to enlist in the service but at 110 pounds and 42 years old, he was not exactly fighting material.

Scripps-Howard stepped in and encouraged its columnist to return to what he did best, suggesting that he make a six-month tour of Army bases in Ireland and England, to report on the impending action in Europe. Still doubtful about his interest in writing, Pyle nonetheless decided to go after Jerry agreed to another trip to the sanitarium, and seemed to be getting somewhat better.

In late summer, Pyle shipped to Great Britain, where he spent the next five months gradually restoring his spirit as he donned the uniform of the war correspondent and got acquainted with the young men who were preparing to go to war with Hitler's Germany.

In September 1942, Pyle heard through the grapevine that the first action in the European Theater would be taking place in North Africa soon. He made plans to follow the invasion. Now on the brink of a new stage in his career and life, Pyle had little idea of the whirlwind that was about to engulf him. Not only was he about to learn a lot more about the "monstrous loveliness" of war, but he would also know something about fame. In less than a year, his name would be as familiar to the people of the United States as Ernest Hemingway or George Patton. It wasn't just the soldiers to whom he sidled up as he was shipping to North Africa who would know "this inconspicuous little man": the name Ernie Pyle would mean something to every G.I. in the theater.

For now, things felt right; they felt somewhat controlled. Jerry continued on the mend back in Albuquerque and Pyle could daydream about one day, perhaps, rejoining her in their bungalow and leading a quiet and peaceful existence. In the meantime, he was once again energized about writing, about doing what he did best, which was making the people back home see what he saw.

So hopeful was Pyle that one of the first things that he did after arriving in North Africa was to consult with an army lawyer about the possibility of once again marrying Jerry. Could he send a legal proxy to Jerry back in New Mexico? he asked the lawyer. It would be a written offer and legally binding agreement to remarry her, when and if she were willing. He was told, yes, he could do that and Pyle signed a document to that effect, drawn up by the lawyer, and sent it home to Jerry.

In the Spring of 1943, just before the climactic battles in the war for North Africa, Pyle learned from Jerry that she had signed the proxy. In the strange and convoluted world that was his domestic life, he and Jerry were once again, man and wife.

PYLE JOINED the 1st Infantry Division as the war headed north from central Tunisia toward Bizerte on the Mediterranean. As they neared the sea, the fighting grew more intense and difficult. The distances between the armies narrowed as Rommel and the Germans started to run out of room on the continent, and the Allies kept pushing.

The landscape was hilly and treeless. "It was walking and climbing and crawling country," Pyle wrote. "The mountains weren't big, but they were constant."

At each set of rolling hills, American soldiers would approach and let the artillery have first crack at the Germans, who would be ensconced on the reverse side of the slopes, digging in and under to escape the shelling. When the big guns on the Allied side had done their softening of the German lines, the troops of the 1st Division would sweep out wide of the army before them, in an attempt to take the Germans from the flank.

The repetition of the work, the consistency with which the young infantry men would rise each time they were ordered, and head toward each hill along the way to make their deadly progress into the German guns—to Pyle, these were feats of amazing young men. Night after night, day after day, death after death, working on half-starved stomachs, with little or no sleep, they marched, with no warmth or comforts, no dreams but to make it over the next hill safely

"I wish you could have seen just one of the unforgettable sights I saw," he wrote of that trek north toward Bizerte. "I was sitting among clumps of sword grass on a steep and rocky hillside that we had just taken, looking out over a vast and rolling country to the rear. A narrow path wound like a ribbon over a hill miles away, down a long slope, across a creek, up a slope and over another hill. All along the length of that ribbon there was a thin line of men. For four days and nights they had fought hard, eaten little, washed none, and slept hardly at all. Their nights had been violent with attack, fright, butchery, their days sleepless and miserable with the crash of artillery."[17]

Yet they kept on walking toward the hill, dispersed for safety reasons at about fifty feet per soldier. They came toward Pyle all day long, moving slowly, deliberately, dead tired and weighted down with ammunition, weapons, and what field gear they could manage.

By the first week of May, the British had pinched the Germans toward Tunis, while the American 2nd Corps, including the 1st Infantry Division, had forced the Axis troops against the sea at Bizerte. With the U.S. and British Navies at the their backs, preventing resupply and evacuation, German and Italian forces were trapped. Ultimately, somewhere in the neighborhood of 250,000 prisoners were taken by the Allies.

The U.S. army had taken some hard knocks, particularly at Kasserine, but they had learned and could now consider themselves veteran troops. North Africa had been a good testing ground for the green Americans. It was not vital ground to the Germans, not fought tooth-and-nail as other territory would soon be. And of course the veteran British troops had been there for years, parrying with Rommel, and taking the brunt of fighting on the eastern front. "Tunisia was a good warm-up field for our armies," Pyle wrote. "We would take an increasingly big part in the battles ahead."

Pyle offered a cautionary note to his readers in the States. He wanted his readers to know that a change had come to the now veteran troops that he'd followed through Tunisia. He recalled the thinking of the soldiers he'd met over the past several months, their consistent curiosity about two questions in particular: when do you think the war will be over and when do you think we'll get to go home?

Everyone still wanted to go home as soon as possible, homesickness remained deep and aching in the hearts of the troops; but they now knew it was pointless to ask when the war would be over. Pyle saw something deeper in their attitude: "It isn't any theatrical proclamation that the enemy must be destroyed in the name of freedom; it's just a vague but growing individual acceptance of the bitter fact that we must win the war or else, and that it can't be won by running excursion boats back and forth across the Atlantic carrying homesick vacationers."[18]

They felt a weary obligation to finish a necessary job. "Home gradually grows less vivid," Pyle wrote, "the separation from it less agonizing." Their eyes were less set on getting home to see the Statue of Liberty than to march into Paris or "down the streets of Berlin."[19]

A price was being paid for this change in the people at the front-lines, Pyle warned his readers back home. Their sons would not be coming back quite the same people they'd been before. "They are rougher than you knew them. Killing is a rough business. Their basic language has changed from mere profanity to obscenity."

He wrote of their longing for women, "their need for female companionship and the gentling effect of femininity." He warned that, "Our men have less regard for property than you raised them to have. Money value means nothing to them, either personally or in the aggregate." Pyle wrote that one of the most striking things he witnessed about the war was how wasteful it was. The necessities of war made soldiers "easily abandon equipment they can't take with them"; the urgency of war "prohibits normal caution in the handling of vehicles and supplies."[20] There wasn't time in war to be economical and there wasn't time for red tape. If a unit needed some piece of equipment and it was there for the taking, soldiers felt free to "requisition" what could help them survive. "The stress of war puts old virtues in a changed light," he wrote.

They were visitors in foreign lands, and war at times made them impatient and resentful of the strangers they were meeting in these strange lands. They were not yet internationalists, but Pyle foresaw a time when they would "brag about how they learned a little Arabic, and how swell the girls were in England, and how pretty the hills of Germany were."

Pyle recorded his thoughts a few weeks after the finish of the campaign as he rested on the shores of the Mediterranean, with the surf "caress[ing] the beach not a hundred yards away." The sky was cloudless; the water a deep blue.[21] He was finishing up a collection of stories that would soon be published back in the U.S. as *Here Is Your War*. The book would quickly rise up the bestseller charts, further adding to the fame that had come to him as he jeeped around North Africa in search of stories.

A hard-fought campaign just ended, and another one on its way. In a little more than seven-months time, Pyle had morphed, like those he was writing about, from a newcomer to a veteran. He was tired and feeling his age, but he was, by means of his book advance, getting wealthier than he'd ever been before. A part of him wanted to stay on this beach for a long time to come, but a part of him couldn't "deny that war is vastly exhilarating."[22]

It was that part of him that placed Pyle on the deck of the U.S.S. *Biscayne* the night before Allied troops set foot on the shores of Sicily. It was that part of him that would keep him close to the war effort all the way to the bitter end.

4

Morocco

THE 36TH DIVISION consisted of three infantry regiments (141st, 142nd, 143rd); the 111 Engineering Battalion; the 111th Medical Battalion; four artillery battalions and a division band. The distinctive shoulder patch worn by 36th members, the T-Patch, was actually a blue arrowhead pointed down the arm, with a green T in the middle. The arrowhead honored the Oklahoma units in the division and was meant to symbolize the state—originally the Indian Territory—from which they had come. The T, of course, stood for Texas.

The 36th was organized in October 1917 at Camp Bowie to help fight the World War I, and included both Texas and Oklahoma units from the start. Shipped to France in July 1918, the four infantry regiments in the 36th (there was a 144th in World War I and would be another one before this war was through) fought with distinction, particularly at the second battle of the Meuse -Argonne in October 1918, just before the end of the war. The division was put on reserve after the Armistice and shipped home in July 1919. Between the wars the regiments of the 36th participated in some disaster relief and a handful of training exercises. It was recalled to active duty in November 1940.

A number of companies had proud roots that stretched back to the founding of Texas. The 141st carried regimental colors honoring "The Republic of Texas," "The Alamo," and "San Jacinto." It had the longest lineage of the three infantry regiments in the 36th and was thus designated, the Texas 1st.

Many of the companies in the division were formed primarily from the populations of individual Texas towns, who proudly organized units for service in the guard. Company A of the 143rd, the regiment that was chosen to march in the 4th of July parade in Rabat, had been founded in Rusk, Texas and had a lineage that stretched back to a cavalry unit in the Civil War; Company B hailed primarily from the small town of Mexia, just east of Waco, and was formed in 1928; Company C was also formed between the wars in 1926, and was comprised mostly of Beaumont men.

At the start of the war, the soldiers in the 143rd were almost all from the east central part of Texas between Dallas and San Antonio, where the I-35 corridor runs today. Here the rolling hills of West Texas met the greener landscapes to the east. The troops came from cotton farms and cattle ranches and towns that supported the commerce of agriculture. In those hard times of the 1930s, many had signed up for duty out of economic necessity, in some cases exchanging bunks in CCC camps for bunks in the National Guard.

There were no African American soldiers in the division and more than a few hints, in documentary evidence, that they would not have been particularly welcome by most if they had been included—not just by the Texans, either. The native Ohioan, Walker, records with a decided lack of sympathy, the story of incidents at Camp Edwards where members of the 36th had used the word "nigger" toward African American staff at the camp. In response, he writes in his diary "of the tendency of some Negro soldiers to make a great deal out of a little and to cry out like children when they feel offended."[1]

Within each company, however, there was a mix of backgrounds and ethnicities, including a strong element of Tex-Mex culture and heritage. Hundreds of members of the Texas Division had Hispanic surnames and were descendants of Mexican families.

The units with roots in small-town Texas were formed by various socio-economic elements in those communities, from town leaders and sons of Main Street commerce, to laborers in local textile mills. They liked high school football and prayed, for the most part, to a Baptist God. Quite a few had been swatted hard by the Great Depression.

Company I came from Belton, Texas, near Killeen, just north of Austin. Belton was an agricultural community of a few thousand souls in the early '40s, set in the hill country of south central Texas. It served as a sort of dividing line in the area: to the east were small farms, mainly cotton; to the west was ranch country. However, the arrival in 1942 of Fort Hood, a new tank unit training facility (which would continue to grow throughout the war), was fast changing the economics of the region as well as booming the population.[2]

Company I was organized by a town councilman named Harry Carden. He became the unit's captain until it was called into active duty, at which time he gave way to an officer in the regular army.

Also a part of Company I was Jack White, son of a photographer in town, who had worked in his father's studio, played trumpet in a the Belton High School, and graduated in 1939, before which he'd signed up to be a part of Company I.

Twin brothers from nearby Temple, Ray and Roy Goad, signed up for duty in the company soon after high school graduation in 1940. They were tough, 155-pound all-district guards for the football Wildcats in the fall of '39.

Another group of brothers, the Waskows—August, John Otto, and Henry T.—signed up for Company I back in 1937. The men were part of a large tenant farm family of eight children—parents of

German descent—who worked land south of Temple and north of Belton in Bell County.

Henry, the youngest of the boys, and pondering either a teaching career (as his college friends assumed) or a career in the ministry (as his family thought), signed up last. He had attended a country school near the farm until it ran out of grades at the 9th. Henry matriculated to Belton High, where he graduated with top academic honors. He was quiet and serious; a country boy from impoverished circumstances, who according to one classmate, arrived at school as a freshman in a brand-new blue shirt and blue overalls and wore the same every day for his four years, until they were faded to the softest of baby blues by the time he graduated.[3]

Henry had the distinction of being class president, a member of the student council, and served, with Jack White's sister, among others, on the student newspaper. Afterward, he earned a scholarship to Temple Junior College, where he was awarded a teaching certificate in 1937 and won second place in a statewide oratory contest. Instead of taking a teaching job, however, he decided to go on to a four-year institution, Trinity College up in Waxahachie, just south of Dallas. At the same time, to earn a little extra money, Henry joined his brothers in Company I and spent weekends training and drilling with the boys of Belton as he worked toward his degree at Trinity. He'd hitchhike between Waxahachie and Belton on weekends to make his guard duties.[4]

Henry's ambitions and talents were evident in the Guard as well. He was promoted to corporal even before Company I was activated and ordered to report to Camp Bowie. He rose to lieutenant in camp and then was chosen for officer's training, which sent him to Fort Benning, Georgia. He was now outranking older brother August. (John Otto had to drop out of the unit when he injured a shoulder). August, now at the age of 30, was six years older than Henry and had the full muscled-body and thickness of a mature man. Henry, on the other hand, looked young and slight. A portrait of him taken at the time suggests his cheeks even had a cherubic hint of color. Nonetheless, it was Henry who was promoted to Captain when the Division moved to Camp Edwards in Massachusetts. It was also in Massachusetts that Henry Waskow was transferred to the command of Company B within the 143rd, leaving his brother and the Belton boys for another Texas-based unit.

Company B was formed in Mexia, just northeast of Belton, back in 1928. Like Company I it had an assortment of young friends from town, people such as Willie Slaughter and Jack Berry. Berry was another Texas high school footballer—a halfback for Mexia High prior to enlisting in the Guard. Slaughter was a lineman on that same team. He had dreams of saving enough money to start a cattle ranch after the war. Slaughter was one of fourteen descendants of Will Skelton of Cedar, Texas—thirteen grandsons, and one great-grandson—serving in the armed forces across the globe.

Jack Gibson had served for several years in the Civilian Conservation Corps before finding a job at the Mexia textile mill prior to the war. He was nearly thirty years old and the eldest son of a farm widow who had five other children when the Guard called him up.

A number of Wadle family members, cousins and brothers, were part of the unit, including Arthur A. Wadle, son of Annie of Mexia. Flynn Durbin, son of a railroad worker in Mexia, had a brother in the Navy and one serving as an Army medic in England. Richard Burrage, son of a railroad maintenance man and a native of Waco, Texas, was a recent graduate of Congressman Lyndon B. Johnson's alma mater in San Marcos, Southwest Texas State Teachers' College.

Riley Tidwell's mother had died when he was young, leaving her son, in his own words "essentially orphaned." Riley was taken in by a farm family in Fairfield, Texas, just east of Mexia. He grew up working for both his foster family and a ranch near the town of

Centerville, where he rode fence lines and got paid twenty-five cents a day plus room and board. He decided to sign up for National Guard service in Company B in 1939, after being turned down by the CCC. He needed the money and was hoping for the $30 a month offered by "the tree army," but had to settle for the $21 given new recruits by the Guard.

Tidwell was just sixteen years old when he enlisted, but stood six feet five inches tall, a fact that helped him when he went to sign up for the Guard. "How old are you?" He was asked. "Seventeen," he lied. "Got any kids?" Taken aback for a moment, Riley paused and said he had none. After the recruiter gave him a long look up and down, Tidwell was told he was a soldier.

He trained for a while in Mexia, but went to Camp Bowie after Company B was activated. Riley Tidwell went through maneuvers in Louisiana with the 36th, took his first train ride when the division was moved from Texas to Florida, got into a truck accident during more maneuvers in North Carolina, and then was shipped with his unit up to Camp Edwards, where he became the company runner under its new commander, soon-to-be captain, Henry Waskow.

They had met initially at Camp Bowie, where Waskow had served for a time as corporal of the camp guards. Tidwell had been one of his charges. They got along well, had some nice chats on duty, which probably helped Tidwell get the post of company runner. It was a job that required almost constant contact with the CO. The runner was the link between the captain and his various platoons, as well as battalion command. He also operated the radio for Waskow when called upon.

Tidwell had lean and lanky good looks and prominent ears accentuated by the military cut of his hair. He towered over his captain, who stood about five feet nine inches tall and according to Tidwell, came up to the runner's armpit.[5] Though Waskow was five or six years older than Tidwell, his smooth-skinned features and sandy blond hair actually gave him the look of a younger man. But despite this and his height advantage, Tidwell quickly began to look up to his commander and started to think of him like he would an older brother.

When the 36th finally moved out of Camp Edwards on April 1, and boarded ship for their journey overseas, Tidwell, as company runner, had to learn the ins-and-outs of the transport ship upon which they were sailing, so that he could pick up and deliver messages to Waskow while on board. No one found out they were going to North Africa until they were well out to sea. That night, the ship's mess served turkey—a meal that was not a favorite fare of Riley Tidwell anyway—and he and everyone else in the company got violently ill from salmonella.

Much like their stay on Cape Cod, more amphibious training continued when they arrived in Rabat, Morocco, where the division was only about a dozen miles from the Atlantic. There was time for sightseeing and collecting souvenirs. Jack White sent home a cigarette lighter, a compass, some French francs and Italian lira. He sent French cigarettes and a guide to the customs of North Africa to his parents in one package; in another, he mailed a pair of hand-sewn camel-hide shoes for his sister and a knife for his dad.[6] Henry Waskow sent watercolor postcards home to his younger sister, Mary Lee, with whom he'd always been particularly close.

While in Morocco, Company B spent time doing guard duty on the beaches near Port Lyautey. One day, they found barrels of North African brew washed ashore, presumably from a shipwreck. According to Riley Tidwell, Captain Waskow gained many points with his men by allowing them to open the kegs and fill their canteens with the local quaff. They weren't sure if they were drinking wine or beer but it didn't really matter.[7]

Both Jack White and Henry's brother, August, were assigned the duty of accompanying Italian and German P.O.W.'s from the North

African campaign back to the U.S. After their stateside voyage they were quickly back at Rabat.

War news dominated the front page of the Belton and Mexia papers in early August 1943. The battle for Sicily was of prominent concern, but so, too, were actions in the Pacific and the Soviet Union. Inner pages of the paper kept people informed about the price of cotton and a week's long revival meeting. Soldiers and sailors kept their families abreast of their circumstances and those families sent news to the local papers. Both Mexia and Belton editions had weekly features that described the doings.

August Waskow wrote what he knew would be the last letter from him that his mother would receive for awhile, letting her know that he'd earned a good conduct medal in North Africa, and that the Red Cross was doing a wonderful job helping troops there. Jack White echoed that salute to the Red Cross in a letter to his parents. He said the aid organization had shown a movie the night before that "gave me more laughs than I've had in a long time." White also seemed to confirm Walker's comments about watermelons and Texas soldiers. "I help eat from about one to six or seven [watermelons] every day. That's just about all we have to spend our money on around here. They are pretty high-priced unless you can out argue the Arabs and they are pretty good at arguing."

Of course none of the letters published in the local paper mentioned what was coming next for the soldiers of the 36th. There was a military proscription against those sort of loose lips. Beyond that, the T-Patchers themselves weren't absolutely certain where they were bound.

An awfully good guess, however, was Italy itself.

Pyle in Sicily

D-DAY FOR PYLE and the 3rd Division, which he was accompanying to the shores of Sicily, came on July 10 and was a relatively quiet affair. Lucian Truscott, the commanding general of the division, had been placed on the far western sector of the invading force near the city of Licata. He and his men were greeted by light resistance. The Italians, if they'd been there at all, had largely vanished, either down the coast or into the body of the island. While the 1st Division, about fifteen miles to the east of 3rd Division, was facing a stiff opposition, and the 45th, even further to the right of the 1st, faced rough seas and abysmal beach conditions, Truscott's troops fairly walked into Sicily and started unloading.

Pyle came in about six hours after the first wave. He found soldiers digging foxholes in hard ground, actually grousing about the fact the Italians had evaporated. *We didn't even get a chance to fire a shot!*

There was always in Pyle a bit of the Indiana farm boy, back at the Brickyard, marveling at quality engineering. On the beaches he found that quality in how quickly and efficiently engineers set about turning the beach into a great dock for the unloading of the thousands of tons of ammunition, weapons, vehicle, and supplies needed to be brought ashore in the next few hours and days.

A mild contempt for the Italian defenders pervaded the setting. "We'd come prepared to fight our way through a solid wall of mines, machine guns, artillery, barbed wire, and liquid fire, and we even expected to hit some fiendish new devices. Yet there was almost nothing to it. It was like stepping into the ring to meet Joe Louis and finding Caspar Milquetoast there. The Italians didn't even leave many booby traps for us."[1]

Even the countryside was vaguely disappointing. Having brought a romanticized notion of Mediterranean isles to Sicily, both Pyle and the troops were disappointed to find a drab brown landscape, largely treeless and dull. The one splash of color, however, proved immensely popular: fields of ripe tomatoes were soon picked bare by the infantry.

GENERAL GEORGE Patton's Seventh Army, including the 3rd, 45th, and 1st divisions, quickly burst out of the beachhead and steamed one hundred miles north toward Palermo. Ernie Pyle hustled after them, though he was starting to feel the many months he'd spent in the field. In fact, he was so deeply and obviously fatigued that one press colleague actually wrote to Lee Miller suggesting that Pyle be pulled home for a rest.[2]

Just a couple of days later, Pyle checked himself into a medical station run by the 45th Division, where he was first diagnosed with dysentery, then malaria. But the doctors decided later it was something they labeled "battlefield fever."

When Pyle confessed to his readers that for all his life, he actually liked being in hospitals, he was being only partially facetious. This was a way to slow down, to be cared for, to have someone else force you to take care. "On the third day I was scared to death for fear I was well enough to leave," Pyle wrote in his column. "But the doctor looked thoughtful and said he wanted me to stay another day. I would have kissed him if he had been a nurse instead of a man with a mustache and stethoscope."

Of course, Pyle continued to report while there. He wrote about his doctor, about medical care in the field, about the wounded soldiers who arrived and shared the station with him. An admirer and keen observer of well-run army logistical operations, Pyle described the triage that took place in the succession of battlefield medical stations. "The idea all along the way is to do as little surgical work as possible, but at each stop merely to keep a man in good enough condition to stand the trip back to the hospital, where there are full facilities for any kind of work."[3]

Pyle wrote about gruesome wounds and a trench outside the station that was filled with the bloody bits of clothing snipped from patients in the hospital. He wrote home about getting woozy looking at some of the injuries; but for the folks back home, he usually took a reassuring step back, telling, for instance, how one doctor, who'd practiced in New York prior to the war, "had never seen a body so badly smashed up in Sicily as he had in traffic accidents back in New York."[4]

It was obviously not that he was unaware of the horrors of war—in fact, that, in part was what was draining him and had sent him to the hospital in the first place—but like almost every Allied correspondent in the theater, he continued to hold a dual responsibility. Not only was he there to report on the war, but he was also there—professional responsibility or not—to support its goals and purpose. He was just too close to the men and women on the frontlines. He shared their interests, and at least early in the war that meant shielding the folks back home from the worst of what was happening—including the pair of incidents that happened when George Patton visited medical stations similar to the one Pyle was in.

The first occurred on August 3, 1943. A young private attached to the 1st Division had just been diagnosed with exhaustion, when General Patton, on a tour of the facility with a group of medical officers, happened by. After visiting with several wounded soldiers and commending them on their bravery, Patton saw the private slouched on a stool. He asked what was the matter, and the young soldier told his commander that he was nervous, that "he just couldn't take it anymore."

Patton immediately grew irate and slapped the private with his gloves, grabbed the soldier by his collar, and pulled him to the tent entrance. He then deposited the man outside, calling him a gutless bastard, and ordering him back to the front.

Just a week later, Patton repeated the exercise at another medical station. This time, he actually knocked the helmet off the soldier, pulled out one of his ivory-handled pistols, and threatened to shoot him.

Pyle was no friend of George Patton. In fact, according to press colleague A.P. correspondent Don Whitehead, he hated Patton for just this sort of reason: "Patton's bluster, show, and complete disregard for the dignity of the individual was the direct antithesis of Ernie's gentle character."[5] And yet like every reporter in Sicily, he refrained from reporting on the slaps.

Instead a group of correspondents went to General Eisenhower with details of the incidents. He asked that they repress the story. They in turn asked Eisenhower to fire Patton, which he did not do. Instead, Patton was made to apologize to both soldiers and to each of the divisions of his army. More fallout would come when the story ultimately broke in the press, but that was not until late in November, by which time Patton was already in limbo as far as the Allied command was concerned.

BACK ON his feet and out of the hospital, Pyle spent his last weeks in Sicily primarily in the company of engineers attached to the 3rd Division, as it was making its drive to Messina, at the very tip of northern Sicily. The infantry had hit a bottleneck along the coastal highway. The road followed tight against a coastal cliff until it came to a massive rock, which jutted out into the ocean. A tunnel had long ago been blasted through the obstacle, which would have been an obvious place for the German forces to seal in their retreat to Messina. Instead, they blasted the road shelf on the other side of the tunnel, making a crater that ran 150 feet deep, all the way to the sea down below.

Thousands of vehicles were backed up on the highway as the engineers went to work. "Bulldozers came to clear off the stone-blocked highway at the crater edge. Trucks, with long trailers bearing railroad irons and huge timbers, came and unloaded. Steel cable was brought up, and kegs of spikes, and all kinds of crowbars and sledges," Pyle reported.[6]

Through the night they worked, calling in 3rd Infantry help and a pair of Sicilian fishing boats to help nail planking down at sea level. The U.S. Navy came forward with supplies and landing craft. Dynamite charges were blasted to clear rock out of the hole. Truscott himself came forward to watch progress, smoking cigarettes as he waited.

By dawn, about a third of the crater had been leveled out enough to carry traffic.

Though it sagged and swayed, by 11 a.m. the new road was ready to be tested, and it was Truscott and his jeep driver who bravely made the inaugural voyage, with a two hundred foot drop to the sea a distinctly possible outcome. "The engineers had insisted they send a test jeep across first," Pyle wrote. "But when [Truscott] saw it was ready, the general just got in and went. It wasn't done dramatically but it was a dramatic thing. It showed that the Old Man had complete faith in his engineers. I heard soldiers speak of it appreciatively for an hour."[7]

WHEN MESSINA was taken and Sicily conquered, Pyle had had enough of war. He was exhausted and he felt like his work was growing exhausted, too. He backtracked his way off the island and theater: to Palermo, for a brief stay, then on to Algiers for a flight home.

He had been away from the States for well over a year and was eager to get home to his remarried-by-proxy wife and settle down for a time in Albuquerque. True R & R.

Of course much had changed in his absence: he had a sense of it in the theater; he knew that his writing had brought him some measure of fame, and his new book on the North African campaign, *Here Is Your War*, was on the precipice of bringing him even more. He also knew that the GIs with whom he'd been hanging out for this last year were not simply getting to know and recognize him, but to think of him, with deep fondness, as their letter-writer, the guy who with the simplest, clearest style could say what they might say about the war to their folks back home if they had his ability.

Pyle felt the responsibility but it was not a burden that he asked for or wanted. Still he felt obliged to explain to his readers why he was coming back. He knew that the Italian invasion was in the works, but just couldn't do it.

"I made that decision because I realized, in the middle of Sicily, that I had been too close to the war for too long." He was exhausted, he said fearful of "writing unconscious distortions and unwarranted pessimisms" about the war.

"When we fought through Sicily," he wrote, "it was to many of us like seeing the same movie for the fourth time. Battles differ from one another only in their physical environment – the emotions of fear and exhaustion and exaltation and hatred are about the same in all of them. Through repetition, I had worn clear down to the nub my ability to weight and describe. You can't do a painting when your oils have turned to water."

There would be more war to come for Ernie Pyle, but for now "you who read and I who write would both benefit in the long run if I came home to refreshen my sagging brain and drooping frame."[8]

He would go home to see Jerry in New Mexico and take care of some writing business.

6

Salerno

ON THE MORNING of September 8, 1943, General Fred Walker looked out of his porthole on the U.S.S. *Chase* and saw more than a hundred ships carrying troops from the British X Corps passing the U.S. convoy of which he, the 36th Division, and the *Chase* were a part. Both groups, British and American, were sailing on a placid sea from North Africa around Sicily, on their way to the Italian coast. There, the Brits would head to the north end of Salerno Bay, and point toward the city of Salerno and the beach that extended below it; the 36th would head at the ancient Greek settlement of Paestum on the south side of the Bay. If all went well, both forces would soon wind up northbound on the road to Naples, about fifty kilometers from Salerno.

After all the months of preparation and anticipation, Walker felt good to be, at last, a part of operations in Europe. There was finally a certainty about what would be happening the next morning. He and the 36th were committed to an invasion of Italy by the Allied command. All preparations were over; the months of training were about to be put to use.

On board the *Chase*, General Walker discussed with her commander, Admiral Hall, whether or not to put down a naval bombardment in advance of the 36th's landing the next morning. The British X Corps, landing to the north, had planned to unleash heavy fire against shore defenses, but in the last recon photos Walker saw that day, he could detect no organized defense of the beaches where his command was about to land. So he decided to forgo the bombardment: "I could see no point to killing a lot of peaceful Italians and destroying their homes," Walker confided to his diary. That didn't mean he wanted the 36th to go in uncovered by U.S. Navy fire; spotters were moving in on the third or fourth wave of landings, and Walker fully expected them to direct Navy fire once they arrived.[1]

Walker made one last adjustment in the landings that night: the craft that he and his party were to debark in the next morning was supposed to be lowered from the deck all the way into the water, as were the troop crafts. The rope ladder that Walker and others in his party would have to climb down was about four stories high. Many of his senior commanders were of an age near to his fifty-six years. Most were not in the sort of shape required to make that sort of rapel. He asked for and received different accommodations. A vessel that could be loaded on deck and lowered to the water was found and drafted into the general's service.

THE DECISIONS that brought Walker and the 36th to this moment had come after weeks, even months of debate, and were arrived at with little certitude. Until August, in fact, there had been no consensus among the Allies about where Mark Clark's Fifth Army should land, or if it should be on the Italian peninsula at all.

The strategic importance of taking Italy had long been debated among British and American war planners. While it seemed to make geographical sense to follow the successful campaigns in North Africa and Sicily with an invasion of Europe that began on the boot of Italy, strategically the situation was more complex.

By taking North Africa and Sicily, the Allies had essentially assumed power in the Mediterranean. That had been the first goal of their joint efforts, beginning with Operation Torch. But always, the main focus of Allied war efforts had been pointed toward the direct invasion of Europe, from the U.K., through France.

The meeting of FDR and Churchill in Casablanca in January 1943, had cemented the invasion of Sicily as the succeeding step to victory in North Africa. But any further activity in the Mediterranean would drain resources from the buildup of forces in Great Britain. Simply to pull up stakes in the Mediterranean and focus on the cross-channel invasion was problematic as well. It would lessen pressures against Hitler's Germany, and allow the Reich to focus stretched resources on their Eastern front—a prospect that did not please Stalin and the Soviet Union.

Always aware that it was fighting wars in two oceans against two world powers, the U.S. wanted to build up resources for the coming direct invasion of Europe. Great Britain, on the other hand, argued for maintaining a constant pressure on Germany. An attack on Italy would force the Germans to spread themselves thin and thus hamper their ability to conduct a two-front war.

The tick of the clock ultimately prompted the decision. As it became apparent through the spring of 1943 that the cross-channel invasion of Europe would not be a possibility until 1944 (shortages in shipping made prospects too risky to rush the assault), the British argument for some continued action in the Mediterranean became dominant. The question remained, where should that action be?

Again, the Allies split: the British favored an attack in the Adriatic and Aegean areas east of Italy. Their assumption was that an Allied assault in the eastern Mediterranean would aid guerilla efforts already in existence there, and might lure Turkey into the war on the Allied side. Counter-arguments quickly arose, however, pointing out that to focus attention on the Balkans would require a base in the boot of Italy, and would ultimately move Allied forces further away from the U.K. buildup, adding to expenses and tactical difficulties.[2]

The U.S. leaned, at least initially, toward an island-hopping campaign in the Tyrrhenian Sea to the west of Italy. The idea was to follow the victory in Sicily with a jump to Sardinia and then Corsica, in preparation for an invasion of Europe through the south of France. It was obvious, however, that Sardinia and Corsica had no strategic value to Germany and would not be vigorously defended. Which meant one of the prime reasons for the assaults—an effort to drain resources from Germany's war efforts elsewhere—would not be achieved. Plus the idea of a major invasion of Europe through the south of France was not practical for a number of reasons, beginning, once again with a lack of shipping resources available to Mediterranean operations.

In May, as fighting was coming to an end in North Africa, Allied leaders met in Washington to set a schedule for the July invasion of Sicily with a further goal of knocking Italy out of the war, and finalizing next steps. They still could not agree, however, on precisely what those were, so at the end of the month, George Marshall flew to Algiers for further discussions with Winston Churchill, British Chief of Staff Alan Brooke, General Eisenhower, and British and American officers of the Anglo-American Allied Force Headquarters. There, Eisenhower and his American staff continued to argue for the island-hopping option, and British commanders kept pushing for an assault on their original destination: the boot of Italy.

Eisenhower's considerations were dictated to a large extent by what was happening in the field. He was watching Sicily with an eye toward Italian resolve to continue fighting, and German strength in the region. He fully expected a hard battle in Sicily; one that might drag into October. The longer the fight, the less apt was Eisenhower to commit serious forces to the Italian campaign as that would draw troops and supplies away from the cross-channel invasion in '44. A tough fight, thought Eisenhower, would mitigate for the island-hopping movement—Sardinia followed by Corsica—and away from the mainland of Italy.

The unexpected ease with which Allied forces landed in Sicily on July 10, and the lack of determination of Italian forces fighting thereafter, quickly changed his thinking. Just five days after the invasion, Eisenhower's chief of intelligence, Major General George Strong, was arguing for a quick decisive move toward the mainland of Italy. Strong's information suggested that Italy could be knocked out of the war with a bold move toward the port of Naples. There were good beaches for landing troops nearby and the port of Naples itself was large and modern, and could serve the Allies well during the coming months of the war. Intelligence further suggested that Germany was not particularly interested in a fierce defense of southern Italy. [3]

Strong found an ally in General George Marshall, who quickly brought the idea to the Combined Chiefs. There it received support contingent on Eisenhower's view of matters in Sicily. The British generally liked the idea (more than the Sardinian invasion), but continued to lobby for a combined assault: at Naples with largely an American force; and at the foot of Italy with largely British troops.

The assumption that Italy was near the end of its fight was further enhanced when King Victor Emmanuel forced Mussolini from power late in July. An assault on the mainland would surely force Germany's lone major partner in the war out of action. Now the question of what size force would be needed for the job became of paramount consideration. Eisenhower decided that sending British forces across the narrow strait between Messina in Sicily and the toe of Italy remained a good idea, and one that would alleviate the need to send a vast force of Americans into Italy at Salerno. Always thinking of maintaining his forces for next year's cross-channel invasion of France, the invasion of Italy was to be undertaken with no flab in its budget.

When it was pointed out that Naples lay just beyond the range of Allied fighters flying from airbases in Sicily, Strong's initial location for invasion was revised slightly southward. Now the attack of Italy would be focused at Salerno, about fifty kilometers below Naples, on the other side of the rugged Sorrento Peninsula that held some of the most magnificent coastal views in all of Italy. Here a rough and rocky landscape plummeted dramatically from interior mountains down toward quaint fishing villages and tourist towns on the shores of the Tyrrhenian Sea. The famed city of Pompeii, buried in the ash of nearby erupting Mount Vesuvius in 79 A.D., was just down the coastline from Naples, between that city and the Sorrento Peninsula. The famed tourist haven, Capri, rested off the tip of the Sorrento, which separated the Gulf of Naples and the Gulf of Salerno. The towns of Amalfi, Sorrento, and Positano were among the best known of a dozen villages in the area; and just to the southwest of Salerno, sat the ruins of a Greek settlement, Paestum; here the Doric columns of a trio of fifth century B.C. temples graced this twentieth century landscape in ancient and otherworldly splendor.

This was the landmark for Walker's 36th Division; this was where they were aimed as their ships cruised just off the shores at Salerno Bay.

THE EVENING before D-Day, at 6:30 p.m., an announcement was heard from high command at Radio Rome. The Italian government had surrendered. Beaten to a pulp in Sicily, and with no heart for a further fight, no love for its Axis ally, Germany, and a growing hatred of its former leader, Mussolini, the Italians no longer wished to wage war against the Allies. General Eisenhower soon followed with his own radio message, confirming the news. On ships' loudspeakers throughout the convoy, the announcement caused cheers and backslapping. Many of the infantry on deck thought this meant that their landing would be a cakewalk. There was even some consternation among more than a few members of the 36th about missing action that they had long awaited.

Don Whitehead, Ernie Pyle's Associated Press reporter friend, was with the convoy, and heard the news about the Italians with a group of Army officers. They immediately began speculating on whether or not the capitulation would force the German army to retreat from the south of Italy to take up defensive positions in the north. In the middle of the conversation, they saw flashes come from shore and then heard shells whining over their heads. It didn't look like a retreat after all. After laying down a smokescreen, both the U.S. Navy destroyers and the British fleet to the north opened fired on coastal batteries. No one would need to worry about missing out on the combat. The German army remained in Italy to greet them.

At 1:00 a.m. the first landing ships were ordered over the side and the infantry soon followed down the rope ladders. Each soldier was geared with a pack of toiletries, mess kit, full canteen, one boxed K ration, and two chocolate bars. They wore wool uniforms and left fatigues and a blanket with company supply sergeants. Each rifleman carried two extra bandoleers of ammunition.[4]

Though there would be no Italians defending their nation's shores, estimates of the number of German troops facing the invasion that morning suggested a growing strength. Numbers varied widely, but the best guess put the figure at about 20,000 soldiers, with another 100,000 German soldiers within a day or two of travel from Salerno (coming from both the boot of Italy and the area around Rome). By comparison, Mark Clark's Fifth Army had about 30,000 British troops, and 25,000 Americans—hardly an overwhelming force, but one that was considered sufficient for the operation (and one that would not take too many resources from the buildup in England).[5]

Walker's 36th Division was scheduled to land in four waves on beaches operationally named Red, Green, Yellow and Blue. Two reinforced regiments, the 141st and the 142nd, were leading the way to shore in the first two waves. The 143rd was coming in an hour later in the third wave, and as planned earlier, would stand in reserve, waiting to see where it was needed as the battle progressed.

Centered on Paestum and the long stretch of beach that ran down all the way from near Sele River, the attack posted the 141st and supporting anti-tank, engineering and artillery battalions on the far right at Blue and Yellow beaches; the 142nd was aimed at Green and Red beaches to the north, accompanied by assault rifle companies, special beach-clearing units and more engineer companies and artillery units.

In the dark morning on calm seas, the landing craft helmsman steered toward the color-coded beaches and a 5,000-yard seawall, which stood fifty-feet high in some places, built from large stones that dated back to the Etruscans. The Doric columns of Paestum's Greek temples were not evident from the sea, but a tower, built by the Saracens in the Middle Ages, stood out large and looming in the night sky.

ON THE NORTHERN edge of the British landing site, where the Sorrento Peninsula jutted into the sea, the high road from Salerno to Amalfi had been, according to *Baedeker's*, "hewn from the cliffs" in the 1850s and still clung precariously to the mountainsides. The slopes were a mix of barren limestone and terraces growing olive, lemon and other fruit trees. A series of sixteenth century watch towers, built to guard the coast against pirates, had been refurbished as homes in modern times. Amalfi, a town of about 6,000 before the war, had become a tourist destination in the twentieth century, especially for English visitors. Hotels inhabited the high ground above the town, fifteen miles from Salerno and accessible via bus on a high asphalt road.

While *Baedeker's* called the road from Salerno to Amalfi "almost unsurpassed for magnificent scenery," it was less kind in describing the road to Paestum to the south, where Walker's division was focused. Here, "the coast is flat and monotonous, in a barren and desolate situation."[6] The land that stretched back from the coast south of Salerno, and sweeping back to the foothills of a range of mountains to the east, was actually a plain that held a variety of farms, including grain and tobacco. The Greek temples were a spectacular contrast to the setting; in fact they were the most imposing remnants of Greek architecture remaining on the Italian mainland. In Paestum's long history, stretching from the centuries before Christ to World War II, the town had been conquered by Romans, Lucanians, and Saracens; it had been ransacked by Normans and destroyed by Frederick II; it had been forgotten and revived in the eighteenth century when its temples were rediscovered. Now, it was to be visited again by force. As Allied troops swept from the southern reaches of Sicily to the north in July, their high commanders had settled on this old and unique site as the location of their next joint attack against the Axis and gave the operation the name "Avalanche."

Even as the landing began, questions remained both about the choice of Salerno and the idea of invading the mainland of Italy, but momentum quickly built in favor of the assault. The flat beaches south of Salerno were more receptive to landing than those closer to Naples; coastal defenses in the gulf were not as strong as on the Naples side of the Sorrento Peninsula; fighter planes could not only reach Salerno from Sicily but an excellent airfield near the city and close to the coastline would provide for continued operations.

There had also been some questions raised about the commander of the Fifth Army. Mark Clark was perhaps not the best choice. He had Eisenhower's confidence and had proven to be an excellent staff officer, but had no experience as a field commander. However, the two most obvious picks in the region, Patton and Bradley, were otherwise occupied finishing things up in Sicily. Beside which Patton's reputation and availability were further muddled in the wake of the two slapping incidents in Sicily.

Clark's star had risen quickly since the beginning of the war and he had achieved fame early on for a daring visit to North Africa in the days just before the invasion. Clark took a submarine to the shores of Algeria in order to meet with Vichy leaders in the hopes of negotiating some sort of accord with the French in North Africa prior to the invasion. Though the excursion was more colorful than effective, it helped promote Clark's name as a bold and decisive general—a description that Clark did not shy from. He lobbied hard for the command of the Fifth Army and General Eisenhower, an old friend of Clark's and with whom Clark had worked as deputy supreme commander in London through the summer and fall, decided to appoint him to that post in December 1942.

But Clark was not universally admired within the world of U.S. Army command. He had trouble disguising a healthy ego and was considered, according to one historian (in a piece defending Clark's abilities as a general) "a blatant careerist and glory hog, [whose] legion of attackers claim [his] ambition exceeded all bounds. He cared more about public relations and cultivating a heroic image than he did about fighting wars."[7] Clark was vain enough to insist that photographers shoot only his left side, which he thought presented a better profile; "he was cocky to the point of arrogant"; and was referred to by some within the Army as Marcus Aurelius Clarkus.

Walker's assessment of his commander would be colored by subsequent events, but his diary hints that even before his troubles with Clark began, Walker was not particularly enamored of him. Walker was old school and Clark was a part of a slightly younger generation of Army regulars. Clark was undoubtedly more attuned to the public relations aspect of command than was Walker. He annoyed the commander of the 36th early on by allocating precious space in a tightly packed convoy to a large contingent of journalists. It couldn't have helped matters that Clark jumped a grade past Walker when he was given his third star in North Africa.

Nonetheless Clark was given overall command of the Salerno invasion, whose Fifth Army forces would include Major General Ernest Dawley's American VI Corps and the British X Corps. In addition to the British forces under General Richard McCreery, Clark would have Matthew Ridgway's 82nd Airborne in reserve, Ernest Harmon's 1st Armored, Lucian Truscott's 3rd Division, the group of army commandos under Colonel William Orlando Darby who had come to be known as Darby's Rangers, and three infantry divisions composed primarily of former National Guard units. These were the 34th, the 45th, and Walker's Texas Division, the 36th, which of the three was the only unit to have yet seen combat.

In addition, Vice-Admiral Kent Hewitt would command more than 600 U.S. Naval vessels, including five aircraft carriers, in support of the invasion.

To the south, Field Marshall Bernard Montgomery would lead the British Eighth Army across the strait of Messina to the toe of Italy; from Bizerte in North Africa, another British force would aim directly to the "instep" of the Italian boot at Taranto.

Up the coast of Italy toward Naples, the British divisions would assault the north end of Salerno Bay directed at the Montecorvino Airport and the city of Battipaglia. The left flank of this force was to then curl to the northeast toward Naples and the Vietri Pass.

Walker's 36th was pointed at Paestum at the south end of the Bay. Once it successfully landed and took the beach, its forces were to advance both north toward Altavilla, and south, where the 36th would secure the right flank of the Allied position against German advance from the toe of Italy.

Separating the Allied forces by nearly five miles, approximately in the middle of their two positions, was the Sele River and its delta, which drained down into the bay from the mountainous interior.

Walker's plan was to send his 141st and 142nd Regiments onto the beach on D-Day, holding the 143rd in reserve until he could see where it was most needed. The total strength of the 36th was just under 14,000 officers and enlisted men.[8]

DESPITE THE tower landmark near the Greek temples, looming above the beach, not all units hit their targets in the morning's darkness. The first battalion of the 141st, to the far right on the assault, missed Blue Beach by about 500 yards to the south. Still the first two waves of the 141st assault came in relatively unscathed and quickly moved inland to about a mile distance. Their arrival, however, soon prompted a fearsome German response, which pinned the 3rd and 4th waves just 400 yards onto the beach.

To the north, the 142nd hit Red and Green beaches but German artillery and machine gun fire sent a few of the landing craft back out to sea, cluttering the waters and slowing their scheduled debarking. Despite opposition, they continued to move inland, heading toward their D-Day destination, Monte Soprano, which loomed as the highest point in the distance beyond the beach and plain.

Elements of the 142nd advanced far enough from the beach to be, like 2nd Battalion Sergeant Manual Gonzales of Fort Davis, Texas, within striking distance of German artillery. Gonzales singlehandedly put one gun crew out of commission with well-placed hand grenades. Another hero from the 142nd, James Logan, ran directly into machine gun fire in order to take out a pair of gunners who'd set up by the ancient wall that ran along the beach. Still fire rained down on the shore.

In fact, the 3rd and 4th waves hit a wall of mortars and bullets. Glenn Clift, a medic from the 111th Battalion attached to the 36th, described the Germans as "throwing the book" at the late arrivals. He described, "Soldiers crouched low in assault boats, planes roaring overhead, shells and machine gun fire raining against the sides and off the ramps of the landing craft." There were Panzer divisions dug into the high hills beyond the beach pummeling the sand, and blasting those screaming .88 shells overhead.

For all the chaos and violence, Clift heralded the stout response of the T-Patchers: "It sounds fishy and on the tall tale side but one company of our boys hit the beach, tore off their helmets, rolled up their sleeves and charged into Jerry tanks with their rifles and knifes and hand grenades."[9]

One lieutenant was just called "Foxhole" because once in North Africa he'd illustrated for the company how to properly get into a foxhole by taking a flying leap from about fifteen feet. According to Clift, Foxhole ran down the beach in heavy gunfire toward a landing craft that had been hit by a shell and was burning about forty yards from the shore. Soldiers immersed in flames were jumping from the open ramp, while others remained trapped inside.

Foxhole cajoled a couple of others to brave withering machine gunfire on the beach and race out to help. The three swam to the craft and saw four soldiers inside: a badly burned major and three enlisted men. The fire in the boat remained hot and getting hotter—so hot that steam started to rise from the wet uniforms of Foxhole and his friend when they climbed onto the boat. They hauled the three wounded infantrymen to the edge of the ramp and went back for the officer, whom they discovered was dead. Just then another shell hit the stern of the craft sending shrapnel clattering around its sides. The major would have to be left behind.

Foxhole and the two others swam the wounded enlisted men to shore with gunfire splashing in the water all around them. They hauled them to the beach and just as they arrived the gas tank on the LCI exploded and the boat they'd just come from was no more.

As the morning progressed, Red Beach was proving more accessible than Green, but landing craft avoiding the shelling, caused a continuing traffic jam on Red. Out in the bay on a destroyer cruising up and down the beach, Don Whitehead reported on the action in both the British and American sectors. The British assault to the north of the Sele River, up near Salerno, was aided by naval fire, but their infantry was met squarely by a Panzer division and batteries of .88-millimeter guns. The blasts between the cruisers at sea and the German shore batteries were relentless.

To the south, the Red and Green beaches in the U.S. sector could have used the same—at least according to the troops on the ground—but command had decided not to shell the area from the sea. As the U.S. Navy continued to ferry troops, tanks, and equipment toward shore, destroyers were cruising back and forth in front of the beaches, trailing black smoke screens behind them to cover the landing craft, while German guns in the hills beyond Salerno pounded the landing areas.

At 5:30 that morning, General Walker with eighteen officers and ten enlisted men, headed toward Red Beach, some twelve miles from the U.S.S. *Chase*. As he neared land, Walker was irritated to see off to the south a number of landing craft, circling "aimlessly about . . . carrying artillery and tanks that should have been ashore helping infantry. . ."[10]

These were the boats being driven away by the fire and traffic on Green Beach, and waiting their turn at landing on Red. According to Walker, the German fire on the beach was insufficient to prevent getting that equipment on shore and he blamed the fortitude of the Navy helmsmen charged with getting the troops ashore. His negative impression was further confirmed when he and his companions were unceremoniously deposited in waist-deep water about seventy-five feet from the beach by an operator, who was, Walker wrote sarcastically, "in a great hurry."[11]

As Walker waded in, he saw wide, long stretches of sand that were ideal for amphibious assault. "There were no real obstacles, only a few patches of barbed wire here and there . . ." He and his command crossed Red Beach with no difficulty. Immediately they headed inland, walking a mile and a half without seeing any Italians along the way or in the village of Paestum, when they arrived there.

All the homes were tightly closed with curtains drawn and a ghostly absence of citizens. Two abandoned radios in a home were still receiving messages in German, which Walker considered a good sign because it suggested that his troops had surprised their German operators, forcing them to flee in haste.

As he and the others in his group passed the ruined Greek temples, Walker had a feeling that the 36th was desecrating sacred ground. Two of the temples were dedicated to Hera and stood side-by-side in the village; the third, honoring Athena, was some distance away on the highest point of the village. All were constructed in classic Greek style—rectangular, with massive Doric columns framing a structure almost three-quarters of a football field in length. In contrast, a field of bright red tomatoes just beyond, brought him quickly back from the contemplation of antiquity to the reality of his empty stomach; he considered the prospects of using the local fruits as a supplement to the troops' bitter chocolate bars.

Walker and company met no small arms fire along the way, but from the hills to the east artillery fire thundered down as they moved further inland, slightly wounding one of Walker's officers. To the southeast, they saw the sun flashing off of moving vehicles that they later learned were German tanks heading to Beaches Yellow and Red to assault the 141st, but there were no direct assaults on their own unit.

When they reached the railroad, which ran north and south beyond the beach, the command team headed north about two miles toward a group of tobacco factory buildings built on a farm that Walker had picked out as a good command post while he was still in Oran and looking over recon photos. The several buildings of the factory were constructed in a circular fashion creating a fort-like perimeter. Open fields surrounded the post, and its largest building was a warehouse that still held racks of drying tobacco leaves.

As they approached, the Italian owner and his family, dressed in their Sunday best and the first locals to appear to them, came out to greet Walker. He welcomed the Americans to his home and farm, and invited them to use both. Walker and his staff immediately began setting up shop and soon were receiving reports from unit commanders and issuing orders. Antitank defenses at the site were incomplete as weapons were still being unloaded from the beaches.

It wasn't long before they were desperately needed. From one of the towers near the tobacco warehouse, a spotter saw thirteen German tanks racing toward the 143rd, still in reserve down by the beaches. Part of the 151st Field Artillery Battalion had arrived and set up just in time to begin firing at the tanks. Combined with ground fire from the 143rd, the artillery was able to knock out four of the German tanks and thwart the assault.

By noon, the command post was up and running and, though the 141st on the southern reaches of American beaches was still pinned down and Green Beach was still under fire, Red Beach was wide open, and supplies were continuing to arrive on shore. Progress was satisfactory.

Unfortunately radio communication between Walker and the command out in the bay—Admiral Hewitt and Generals Clark and Dawley on the flagship—was sketchy. Clark and Dawley were taking reports from wounded soldiers returning from the fighting to the convoy, and these sounded more desperate than circumstances warranted. The two shipbound generals feared all beaches were being opposed by fierce tank attacks and artillery, and the beachhead itself was in peril. Not satisfied with the information he was receiving, Clark decided to send Dawley ashore to see if he could find out what was happening.

In fact, by the time Dawley arrived that afternoon, progress was as well as could be expected for D-Day. Though there was still some confusion around Red Beach, where the bulk of the unloading of supplies was happening—just too many craft bunched up in too small an area—unloading continued throughout the afternoon and evening. Walker, out at the tobacco farm was pleased to note that as nighttime came, combat units had pushed to their assigned positions up and down the landing area, forming a perimeter twelve miles long and about four miles deep.

His infantry was not quite so sanguine.

7

Altavilla

LIKE EVERYONE ELSE IN THE CONVOY sailing toward the beaches surrounding Salerno Bay on D-Day, the individual companies of the 143rd had a moment of elation on the evening of September 8 when word of the Italian capitulation spread around the ship. Shouts of triumph were heard all around, but quickly died down with the realization that the 36th was still going ashore to fight Germans. They were ordered to bed down on the decks, in order to have quick access to the boats next morning. Not many slept soundly.

Riley Tidwell, going in with Captain Henry Waskow and Company B in the third of four waves, had been excited, like so many others, at the surrender announcement. He thought "it might be an easy deal" with just the Germans defending the beaches. Tidwell was equally thrilled to find that his landing craft was piloted by former light-heavyweight boxing champ Lou Jenkins. Jenkins was a Texas boy who had held the boxing crown for little more than a year back in the late '30s, much to the delight of other Texas boys like Riley Tidwell. Jenkins had lost the title after getting injured in a drunken motorcycle accident in New Jersey, followed by festering problems with booze and an acrimonious divorce.

After climbing over the side of the transport and roping down to the landing craft, Tidwell, Waskow and the rest of Company B were motored onto Red Beach near Paestum by Jenkins, and dropped off with little trouble. They headed east of the village, further inland, and made quick progress until they reached the highway.[1]

COMPANY I of the 143rd, the Belton boys, including Henry Waskow's brother, August, was roused at 2:00 a.m. on the U.S.S. *Stanton* and served a breakfast of navy beans. Then it was over the side for their brief ride to Italy's shoreline. Jack White, the son of the local photographer in Belton, was in a landing craft that got lost on its way to shore. It ended up arriving in the fourth, rather than the third wave, and daylight had arrived by the time White and the others hit the beach.

Company I was also near Paestum and White's platoon made a run toward the town, across the sand and barbed wire entanglements. White was a communication sergeant, so his first duty was to find out where the various platoons in I company were located. Amid the chaos of battle, he remained focused on his work, and it felt strangely like he was in the midst of another one of those Cape Cod maneuvers, except for the surreal fact that there were dead and wounded all around him.[2]

By noon, the unit was organized, and ordered to move toward the hills and the village of Cappaccio, where it settled in for the night with Company L of the 143rd, digging foxholes and dining on K and D rations—the latter, simply those dark chocolate candy bars. The next morning they rose to word that German tanks were descending upon Cappaccio, so the company was ordered by its Captain, Bill Yates of Temple, Texas, to quickly set up outside of town to the east. The threat turned out to be seven armored cars, rather than tanks and three of them were quickly knocked out of action, while the four others surrendered. White was deeply impressed by the abilities of a company bazooka, which blew one of the cars into pieces with a single shot.

BY LATE in the day, Monte Soprano, the peak that rose high above the landing area, had been taken by the 142nd.

On D-Day plus 1, the supporting 3rd Battalion of the 143rd, which included Company I, with Yates, White, and August Waskow, relieved the 142nd. Elsewhere along the American line, portions of the 45th Division arrived early that morning and were sent north of the Sele River to shore up the U.S. left flank near the British, who had taken Salerno to the northeast but were otherwise having trouble rooting out German troops near the city of Battipaglia. More tank and tank destroyer battalions also came ashore along with anti-aircraft defenses to further boost defenses on the beach.

Accompanying this equipment were Generals Clark and Dawley, who came on shore to judge how the 36th was progressing. Clark annoyed Walker by giving Hawley command of the just-arrived 45th on the left flank. It was a change in leadership that had never been discussed in the planning of the operation. During those talks, Walker had been assigned sole command for all troops south of the Sele. He now sensed that Clark was still nervous about the state of the beachhead, as he had been the day before in the early hours of the invasion. It was hardly a vote of confidence for his command.[3]

Nonetheless, Walker was pleased with the current situation at his post, and continued to solidify the American presence there through the course of the day. German troops south of Monte Soprano had vacated their position when that hill was taken by the 142nd, which alleviated a great deal of pressure on the beachheads. Artillery and machine gun fire were now absent from the shore, allowing Walker, still at the tobacco farm, to focus his attention on the ground north of Monte Soprano toward the area where the Sele and Calore Rivers forked. He felt comfortable enough with his situation at the end of the day on the 10th to begin planning his strike at the hills to the east of the tobacco warehouse, around the village of Altavilla where the battle would quickly grow more fierce.

Altavilla, rested near the middle of a 424-meter high hill whose summit had a panoramic view of both Salerno Bay to the west and the Sele River to the north. Altavilla, which was also called Silentina to distinguish it from the four other villages in Italy called Altavilla, was another ancient town whose history stretched back to antiquity. The Roman General Pompey was said to have put down the last of the slave revolt led by Spartacus near Altavilla around 71 B.C. Though it was ravaged and abandoned in later times, the Normans came through the area in the eleventh century and built the foundations of the modern town. Franciscan monks constructed the dominant structure in the village, a convent, in the fifteenth century; the villagers themselves had renamed the community in the nineteenth century by combining the names of the Sele River and another stream in the area, the Alento. Its name would be remembered by the young Texans ordered to take it on the morning of Saturday, September 11, for reasons other than its history. But initially, to the 1st Battalion of the 142nd, it was simply a collection of old buildings with too many windows, too many doors, too many blind alleys and rooftops.

In their first visit that morning, they felt their way through Altavilla gingerly and without a fight, emerging on the other side of town about halfway up Hill 424.

There, Companies A, B, and C of the 142nd were separated and placed above Altavilla to protect the battalions left and right flanks, and its center. An uneasy calm followed. Hill 424, like so many other mountains and heights in south central Italy, as the Allies would soon discover, was full of ridges and ravines, which, in turn, were full of Germans.

The first patrols of Americans and Germans ran into each other as they were feeling their way around the hill at about 2 a.m. the next morning, and firefights broke out all around. The 1st Battalion of the 142nd was in a vulnerable position particularly on its left flank, which couldn't seem to find any elements of Dawley's newly assigned 45th Division to hook up with (it would turn out that they were quite some distance away). Both Company B and Company A of the 142nd faced heavy mortar and small arms fire from German patrols all through the morning.

With daylight, the German artillery opened up on their positions as well. The fire got hot and communications between both companies and headquarters at the foot of the hill were lost. By noon, Company C on the right flank was also in trouble, pinned down by a German counterattack. When command was finally able to reach its units, Companies A and B were ordered back down the hill, taking a rightward shift as the they moved, in order to shore up Company C.

Company B, on the far left, tried to head back to Altavilla on its way to Company C, but couldn't break free from the Germans. Meanwhile, the 1st Battalion commander, Lieutenant Colonel Gaines Barron, had moved forward to help direct Company A toward its new position. Except they were not where he thought they were and Barron walked right into German lines and was captured.

When word of Barron's capture reached, second-in-command, Major William Mobley, Mobley ordered the battalion command post to pull back to Altavilla. By evening on September 11, they were joined there by scattered elements of all three companies that had headed out that morning, everyone now badly bruised and hurting.

GERMAN FORCES continued to pound the remnants of the 142nd the next morning, which was when the 3rd Battalion of the 143rd was called in for support. Companies I, K, and L, under the command of Colonel William Martin, spent most of the day moving several miles north from Monte Soprano to a position that took them around Altavilla to the northwest foot of Hill 424. By the end of the day, they were in position to attack the summit.

Companies I and L were chosen to lead the assault, with Company K and Heavy Weapons Company M, in reserve. At 3 a.m. the two companies moved out, with Captain Bill Yates's Company I on the left flank, and Company L on the right. In a couple of hours of slow climbing, as well as moving east toward the village, they finally neared Altavilla (on the right) and the summit of Hill 424 (on the left).

Suddenly deadly German .88 shells, the "screaming meemies," started to rain down on top of them. For two hours, the enemy blasted both the town of Altavilla and the surrounding hillside, arcing fire back and forth between targets like a deadly lawn sprinkler.

Jack White, up on the hillside, caught a fragment of a shell around 11 a.m. He felt a searing pain in his lower leg, fell to the ground, and saw a shattered left ankle. Five other members of the company were hit in the same blast. There were no medics nearby, so White crawled down the side of Hill 424 into the town of Altavilla and finally found someone to help. By this time, however, the village was cutoff from the rest of the American force, so no ambulances were there to evacuate the wounded. He was given what comfort the medic could supply and taken to shelter in one of the ubiquitous ravines outside the town.[4]

Meanwhile, near Altavilla, Company L on the right flank decided it needed more protection from Germans positioned on a smaller, unnumbered hill just beyond Altavilla to the east. The company proceeded over the hill, but in the process were hit hard from a draw to its left, where a German machine gun was wreaking havoc over the field. Lieutenant John Morrissey was dispatched with three infantrymen, including Private 1st Class Charles Kelly of Pittsburgh to clear the area.

The four ran into a snakepit of Germans down in the ravine. Over seventy enemy soldiers swarmed around the gun and then around Morissey and his men as they worked their way down the landscape. Kelly, armed with a BAR (Browning Automatic Rifle), was able to knock the machine gun out along with its crew. He immediately redirected fire at an advancing German platoon, emptying a full magazine in its direction. His companions, meanwhile, covered him with fire from a second BAR and a .30 caliber machine gun that Morissey fired from the hip as Kelly reloaded. Again Kelly opened up and more Germans died. Finally, with a break from the German assault, the four members of Company L retreated back to their unit and arrived there unscathed.[5]

Over on the left flank, Company I was in the midst of a harrowing back-and-forth battle. Just as the battalion was preparing to push up to the summit of Hill 424—I on the left, L on the right, with K down in Altavilla in reserve—it was hit by an attack from the Germans. Beginning at five o'clock and continuing until darkness, at least five assaults were brought against I and L. The first of these came so close to overrunning the 143rd that the field commander ordered bayonets drawn. Captain Yates of Company I, who'd been down at Altavilla at the start of the assaults returned to find his command in dire straits. The Germans were less than a hundred yards away on the rocky, hilly ground, and their relentless attacks were not only filling the space with dead Germans, but his own command was fast being depleted.

The left flank of Company I was under particularly severe attack, and it was here that Sergeant August Waskow was positioned. Early in the evening the Germans rounded the unit's left and began attacking Waskow's post. Fire was now coming simultaneously from both front and rear. In the midst of this ground fire, a mortar suddenly burst right in front of him and all went dark for Waskow.

On and on went the fight around him, with the Germans continuing to charge down from the crest of 424, and Companies I and L continuing to battle back. The American position was overrun and retaken, overrun again, and retaken again. August Waskow lay helpless on the field and now Captain Yates was out of commission, too, with a wound to the arm.[6] As night came, the Germans fired flares to the front and back of the 3rd Battalion's sector, framing the American troops in a deadly halo. Phone lines between the battalion and the regimental command down below the hillsides were cut, too. In the dark, German forces moved to surround the entirety of the 3rd. Word finally got to the battalion from headquarters that it should evacuate its position, but it was too late. As dawn came, so came the knowledge that Companies I and L had Germans all around them.

Through the course of the day, the men of Companies I and L valiantly maintained their positions. Some members of the two units were also now down in Altavilla, where they were engaged in street fighting with the Germans. Among these was Private Kelly, adrenalin still pumping from his earlier heroics. He now found himself ensconced with a group of T-Patchers on the top floor of a three-story terracotta home surrounded by Germans. The unit had Kelly's BAR, a bazooka, a .37 mm anti-tank gun, hand grenades and mortars. They employed all of them in their defense, including the mortars, which Kelly armed and implemented by removing the pins and dropping them nose down from his upper story balcony, right on top of advancing Germans.[7]

As darkness inched up the side of the hill, Captain Bowden of Company L and Lieutenant Langdon, who'd replaced the wounded Cpt. Yates in command of Company I, tried to lead their men out of the trap. The results were mixed: Bowden was able to get 44 soldiers off the hill; Langdon got separated from his men and ended up wending his way down the hill by himself.

Others made the same sort of escape, singly or in small groups. In all 20 officers and 536 enlisted men got back to battalion command; but trapped on the hill were scores more from the 3rd Battalion of the 143rd, including the wounded Belton men, Jack White, August Waskow, Bill Yates, as well as, Lieutenant Ray Goad, one of the twin football playing guards from Temple, Texas, and Captain Alfred Laughlin, another Company I officer, who was now part of the battalion command. Laughlin, like Waskow, was critically wounded.

As their fellow T-Patchers escaped Hill 424 and Altavilla, those too injured to move were left behind for their captors, and were soon carted away to a German aid station. For those men, prisoner of war camps loomed.

THE PLIGHT of the 3rd Battalion was not the only critical matter on the Salerno beachhead the morning of September 14. Simultaneous to the dispatch of the 3rd to Altavilla, the 2nd Battalion of the 143rd, had been ordered to an equally vulnerable position on the far left flank of the American lines, between the Sele and Calore Rivers. The battalion was supposed to hook up with British troops to the north, connecting the two Allied lines, but in fact, the Brits weren't there and a five-mile gap existed between the two elements of the Fifth Army. German Panzers were quick to exploit the hole. The nearest American troops to the 2nd Battalion were the 3rd Battalion of the 143rd, who, as August Waskow and many others could attest, were otherwise occupied.

Late in the afternoon of September 13, the 2nd Battalion's left flank was caved in by German tanks. Though the Texans fought gallantly, they didn't have a chance and were soon surrounded by the enemy troops. Just nine officers and 325 enlisted men of the battalion's near 900-strong were able to make it out of the fork between the two rivers. The rest were now POWs.

Counting heads that night was a desperate matter. The 142nd's 2nd Battalion had been gravely depleted by fighting at Altavilla on September 12; the 143rd's 3rd Battalion now needed rescuing on Hill 424; and the regiment's 2nd Battalion had largely been killed, captured or wounded. To use a naval euphemism, it was now time for all hands on deck to protect the Salerno beachhead and keep the 36th from being pushed all the way back to the ocean.

General Walker ordered a quick reorganization of defenses: he split the division front into three sectors and gave command of each to a brigadier general. Assigned to each area was a mix of units, including cannon and antitank battalions; tank and engineer companies; as well as infantry battalions left over from the 141st and 142nd. Two parachute units from the 504th Infantry Regiment of the 82nd Airborne, were also dropped in that night to land on the sandy beaches of Salerno, bolster defenses, and help in counterattacks.

Early in the afternoon, the Germans attacked on the north (left) flank of the division near the Calore River and were halted. Near Altavilla, later that afternoon, about thirty Panzer tanks were likewise thwarted by a pair of field artillery battalions. The battle had not quite turned, but the U.S. Army was holding.

In the midst of the action, Walker was again annoyed by General Clark, who arrived at Walker's command post at 2 p.m. to chide Walker about the performance of his division, most particularly the 143rd's 2nd and 3rd battalions. Walker, who felt he was fed bad information about 2nd Battalion's position by command (specifically, Ernest Dawley), held his tongue about that matter. He also held it about the lack of initiative on Dawley and the 45th's part in trying to link up with the 36th from the left. In other words, not only did he not tell Walker about the gap, he failed to do anything himself to close it.

Walker, who never seemed to doubt that the Allied beachhead would stiffen despite these troubles, was further irritated that afternoon when he received a follow-up note from Clark with what Walker considered to be melodramatic language to the effect: "There must be no retreat" and "Not one foot of ground is to be given up."

In addition, Walker was forced to expend an infantry battalion and a tank destroyer unit to the villa serving as Clarks' Fifth Army Headquarters. In Walker's estimation the estate was unnecessarily close to the frontlines, thus prompting the headquarter's request for the defensive units. Clark's staff had chosen it, according to Walker, because it was the finest villa in the area, one befitting Clark's command.

Despite these squabbles, the 36th, with the assistance of the 45th Division on the left flank, and the airborne troops now fighting near Altavilla, was pushing back. The 45th had moved into the triangular area between the Sele and Calore Rivers where the 2nd Battalion of the 143rd had been trapped two days earlier. Near Altavilla and Hill 424, after some very tough fighting, the 504th paratroopers finally began to turn the tide of battle. Though Walker was frustrated a number of times by the lack of air support, the U.S. Navy supplied effective assistance to the assaults, essentially leveling the village of Altavilla in the process. And from the south, elements of British Field Marshal Bernard Montgomery's Eighth Army were making their way into the area from the boot of Italy. By Saturday morning, September 18, the Germans had withdrawn from the front.

With more allies coming onto shore by the hour, the British Eighth Army moving in, and facing continued air, artillery and naval superiority, the jig was up for the Germans. Some would later suggest that their hour for victory had passed when they failed to deliver a knockout blow to the Allies when they'd overrun the 2nd Battalion of the 143rd near the confluence of the Sele and Calore Rivers. General Walker would later regret sending in 2nd Battalion into an area as fraught with danger as that one, but would also add that the 36th was never in danger of losing the field.[8] It was all a moot point a few days later, when, according to a veteran of the 16th Panzer Division, "the decimated and fatigued forces [on the German side had] no further hope . . . of forcing the enemy into the sea."[9]

If they could not push the Fifth Army back into the sea at Salerno, it hardly meant the Germans were giving up the fight. In fact, they had other ideas on where and how to make the Allies pay a dear price for this invasion of Italy.

8

The Sorrento Peninsula

HENRY WASKOW HAD NO IDEA that about thirty kilometers away, on another Italian hillside, his brother was not only badly injured, but a prisoner of the Third Reich. As August lay critically wounded above Altavilla, Captain Henry Waskow and his Company B were in a sector about as far from Henry's old Belton Company I as any American unit in the battle. On September 13, they were ensconced on the Sorrento peninsula, far from the action near Hill 424, having arrived at this destination in circuitous fashion.

AFTER THE ex-boxing champ Lou Jenkins set him, Riley Tidwell, and the rest of the company ashore on Red Beach on D-Day, Waskow and Company B raced inland through mortar and artillery fire to the regimental reorganization line. Company B was the last of the three companies of the 1st Battalion to arrive at the assembly area, along the railroad tracks northeast of Paestum.

Among others waiting there was Lieutenant Richard Burrage, the graduate of San Marcos college back in Texas, and now the 1st Battalion's intelligence officer. He had left the U.S.S. *Chase* in the first wave, at 1 a.m., with other elements of the battalion's G-2 staff. He landed in about six feet of surf amid hostile mortar fire. The

.88's were also screaming overhead, which helped speed Burrage and his comrades inland.

Commander of the battalion was Lieutenant Colonel Fred Walker, Jr.—son of the general—who had joined the 36th at Camp Edwards the fall before. A graduate of West Point and General Staff School at Fort Leavenworth, Lieutenant Colonel Walker, Jr. was summoned to the division command post with the other battalion commanders about an hour after the 1st had settled into its position. When Walker, Jr. returned to the 1st, he ordered his battalion closer to his father near the tobacco farm in order to provide security for the general's post.

Like everyone else near the beaches, the 143rd's 1st Battalion remained subject to artillery and mortar fire through all of D-Day. On September 10, the battalion was moved to a position two and half miles northwest of Capaccio near Monte Soprano, where they continued to be held in reserve.

Early the next day, the battalion received new marching orders directly from General Mark Clark.[1] The 1st was to boat to the village of Maiori, near Amalfi on the Sorrento Peninsula to the northwest of their position near Salerno Bay. There they would provide reinforcement to the command of Colonel William O. Darby, leader of the 6615th Ranger Force, which was already gaining fame as Darby's Rangers.

Darby, along with elements of the British X Corps, had been given the assignment of securing the peninsula for the Allied advance to Naples. He and his troops had landed on the northernmost part of the Salerno beaches on D-Day and quickly started to work their way west, out onto the peninsula; but he and his three Ranger battalions were now stuck in Maiori, precariously perched on the coastline beneath the interior mountains above them. They needed more men for a push up to the heights, and 1st Battalion was available.

Lieutenant Burrage was able to get a ride with Brigadier General Wilbur's command team on a PT Boat that zipped over the bay toward the high cliffs of the peninsula. "Being from Waco," he later noted, "I had never had an opportunity to ship out on such an impressive boat." The view of the Sorrento landscape impressed him, too. Its beauty was stunning even with the prospect of looming battle.[2]

At Maoiri, Colonel Darby greeted the early arriving parties from the 36th, including Lieutenant Colonel Walker, General Wilbur, and Lieutenant Burrage. He then sat everyone down for a description of the circumstances at his base, at the foot of the peninsula hills. The road into the mountains above Maiori ran on a pretty straight line, south to north, across the peninsula through the Chiunzi Pass, currently held by the Germans. The pass was near the mainland, while the bulk of the peninsula ran toward the Isle of Capri out to the west. Darby proposed sending his forces to secure the territory toward the west end of the peninsula, while the 1st Battalion captured and held both sides of the Chiunzi Pass, right above Maiori.[3]

As the joint forces organized command posts, assembly areas, and a medical evacuation plan, the rest of the 1st Battalion was loading back at Red Beach in landing craft. They arrived at Maoiri by midnight and next morning—while Company I was moving into position to scale Hill 424—Lieutenant Colonel Walker assembled his company commanders. Company A, headed by Captain Joseph Peterman of Beaumont, Texas, was to take his unit up the ridge and head for the west side of the road leading to and through the Chiunzi Pass. Captain Henry Waskow and Company B were to take the east side of the road and secure it. Company C was to follow in reserve. Two machine gun platoons from a weapons company, Company D, firing .30 caliber, water-cooled guns, were sent out, one each with Companies A and B for support; and D's commander, 1st Lieutenant Roy Goad, the second of the twin brother, all-regional football guards from Temple, was ordered to send out observers to set up a mortar defense for the front of the column as well. Like Henry Waskow with his brother August, Roy Goad had no idea his twin brother Ray was at that moment trapped on Hill 424.

By 8 a.m. on September 12, the company commanders had briefed their soldiers and headed out of Maiori, up the road toward the mountaintops in a six-mile, calf-burning climb. Just two hours into the hike, they had their first casualty: a burst of small arms fire accompanied by mortar rounds hit the column, and First Lieutenant Orlando Greely was struck and killed. It was the first small arms fire 1st Battalion had faced and it was quickly snuffed out by platoons from Company C and A. Shaken but undeterred, the unit subsequently reached the crest of the mountains without further fire. It set up positions, made range cards, ran telephone lines through the afternoon and evening, and basically established itself on the east side of the road, just as it had set out to do.

Riley Tidwell was for the first time in a live combat field with his unit, and he soon established a routine with Waskow. As company runner, Tidwell was not assigned to a particular platoon and didn't have to go through the ranks—platoon sergeant to First Sergeant to captain—to stay in touch with Waskow. Instead he stayed close to the CO until told otherwise, at which time he would set out with his big, long strides back and forth between command and the various units, delivering orders and returning with whatever information needed to get back to the CO.[4]

There were four platoons in the company. Waskow would typically take the lead if the platoon he was accompanying was on the move. Tidwell would follow quickly on Waskow's heels, then came the First Sergeant, trailed by the rest of the troops. If Waskow wanted the remaining platoons to know anything, Tidwell would be sent back to tell them; if he wanted to send information to battalion headquarters, Tidwell would go on this mission, too; if he wanted to send a message to battalion via radio, Tidwell sometimes operated that as well.

It was Waskow's style to lead more by example than command.[5] Not a rah-rah guy, he was as unassuming in style as he was in appearance,[6] which might have been why Tidwell was afraid of losing him on the trail or in combat. To keep a visual connection to the captain, Riley tied a white rag to the back of Waskow's pack, the signal was in part to ensure that Tidwell was always in touch with his CO, and in part an assurance that he wouldn't suddenly find himself leading the platoon. If Waskow went over a cliff at night, Tidwell would take the plunge, too, he guessed.

Though they had already gotten close in the months of training, beginning with those quiet dark nights serving guard duty back at Camp Bowie, Waskow and Tidwell quickly became combat-close on the Sorrento Peninsula. They would swap stories of back home and what they'd like to do when they got there. Waskow was a coffee man and Tidwell was not, so the company runner would give the captain his ration of "Joe" and even brew it for him. He'd also make the CO toast by taking a slice of bread and holding it over the same can of Sterno that he used to make Waskow's coffee. Out climbing the rocks, the ravines, the terraces of the Sorrento Peninsula around the Chiunzi Pass, a good cup of coffee and a warm slice of toast was genuine comfort food. And when Waskow dreamed of better days to come, he dreamed of toasters. He told Tidwell he wanted to get one of those new modern ones with the pop-up trigger and electrical coils. That seemed like good living up in the Sorrento hills.[7]

FROM HIS BASE at the San Francisco Hotel in Maiori, Colonel Darby oversaw the operation of his Rangers and the 1st Battalion of the 143rd above. To keep in touch with his units in the field, he would occasionally hop in a jeep, which had a .50 caliber machine gun attached to a swivel above its seat, and take quick trips up to the

Chiunzi Pass. Burrage, who as battalion intelligence officer roamed from unit to unit gathering information, saw much of what was happening on the peninsula. He was there once when Darby was informed that one of his Rangers was wounded just beyond the Pass and in dire need of evacuation. The soldier couldn't get out because his unit was pinned by enemy fire. Darby grabbed a driver and hopped in the back of the jeep behind the .50 caliber gun as it raced up to the Chiunzi. He arrived at the scene, spraying bullets toward both sides of the road, grabbed his wounded Ranger, and continued to fire as his driver backed up to the Pass, where a stone blockhouse guarded the position. Still going backward, Darby had his driver head back down the hill toward Maiori to deliver the wounded man to the British medical unit.[8]

The fight on the peninsula had its oddities. There were two British navy cruisers in the bay providing loud and persistent support to the infantry on shore, aided by spotters on the hillsides, pinpointing German positions. Likewise, artillery kept pounding at the enemy and Lieutenant Roy Goad's mortar platoon was "firing missions around the clock," according to Burrage. Yet, in the midst of this near constant shelling, just down the road from Maiori in Amalfi, at least one seaside resort continued to serve its patrons "exotic meals on fine china [with] table settings of sterling silver." One Ranger unit, returning from several hard days in the field, came upon this restaurant and decided to take advantage of its menu. "They were so overcome with the style of living [encountered at the resort] that they sent one course back to the kitchen, explaining that it was not suitable," wrote Burrage. "The hotel chef came out and apologized profusely and made everything right . . ." They got a free night at the resort and sumptuous breakfast, as well, before heading back to Darby in Maiori.[9]

That stone house up at Chiunzi Pass was also an interesting location. It served both the Rangers and the 1st Battalion as a forward

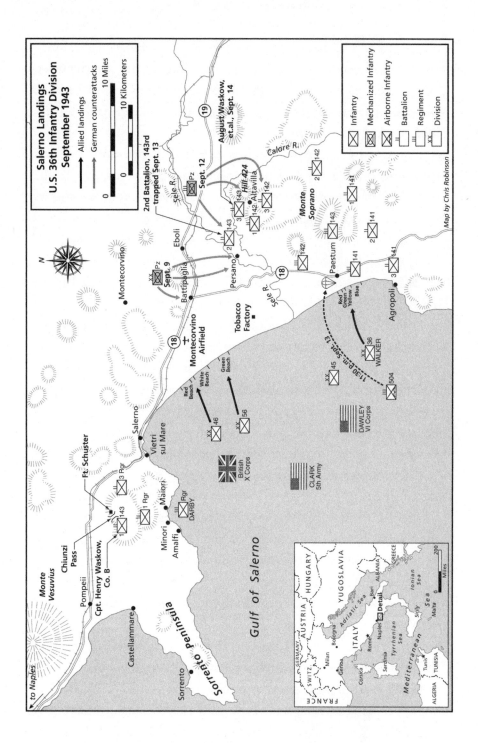

Salerno Landings
U.S. 36th Infantry Division
September 1943

Allied landings
German counterattacks

0   10 Miles
0   10 Kilometers

Infantry
Mechanized Infantry
Airborne Infantry
Battalion
Regiment
Division

Map by Chris Robinson

to Naples
Monte Vesuvius
Pompeii
Castellammare
Sorrento
Sorrento Peninsula
Chiunzi Pass
Cpt. Henry Waskow, Co. B
Ft. Schuster
1 143
1 Rgr
DARBY Rgr
Maiori
3 Rgr
Minori
Amalfi
Salerno
Vietri sul Mare
Montecorvino
18
Montecorvino Airfield
Battipaglia
XX Pz Sept. 9
Persano
Eboli
Sele R.
XX Pz Sept. 12
Sele R.
August Waskow, et.al., Sept. 14
19
2nd Battalion, 143rd trapped Sept. 13
2 143
3 143
1 142
3 143
2 142
Altavilla
Hill 424
3 142
Calore R.
Monte Soprano
1 142
2 142
1 143
Paestum
2 141
1 141
3 141
18
Green Beach
White Beach
Red Beach
XX 46
XX 56
British X Corps
CLARK 5th Army
45 XX
36 WALKER XX
11:30 p.m. Sept. 13
Red Green Yellow Blue
504 XX
DAWLEY VI Corps
Agropoli
Tobacco Factory

Gulf of Salerno

Detail
FRANCE
SWITZ.
GERMANY
AUSTRIA HUNGARY
YUGOSLAVIA
ITALY
Milan
Genoa
Bologna
Rome
Naples
Bari
GREECE
ALBANIA
Corsica
Sardinia
Tyrrhenian Sea
Adriatic Sea
Ionian Sea
Sicily
Malta
Mediterranean Sea
TUNISIA
ALGERIA
TUNIS
0   200
Miles

command post and an aid station headed by a Ranger medical officer, Emil Schuster. It quickly acquired the nickname, Fort Schuster, and become a focal point of the action around the Pass and on the peninsula. It was constantly being shelled by the Germans, but remained a depot of Allied activity.

From Mt. Pendolo, the highest height of the peninsula, it was easy to see the Bay of Naples and the entire city beyond it. To the northwest and nearer to the Sorrento was Mount Vesuvius and its surrounding valley, including the city of Pompeii. The Germans occupied the north side of the peninsula highlands and the lowlands in between. Their artillery kept up a steady shelling of the heights above, where British troops, as well as the Rangers and the 143rd's 1st Battalion parried with the German infantry.

A tactic nicknamed "shoot and scoot" developed on the American side. One day, a platoon of Rangers would occupy a hill on the peninsula and leave after a firefight with the Germans. The next day a platoon from Company A or B would move in and continue the encounter. [10] Alternating the units made it hard for the Germans to know if they were facing a patrol, a company, or a larger force.[11] The Germans, meanwhile, effectively confused their unit identifications and strengths by mixing troops from a variety of commands into assault teams.

On September 18, Waskow's Company B was sent on one of these raids down into the valley on the north side of the peninsula, near the village of Nocera. They took off at 9 p.m. accompanied by Lieutenant Roy Goad's mortar squad, always a welcome addition on these forays. His Company D laid down a carpet of shells, just ahead of Waskow and his soldiers.

At the valley floor, Waskow sent a platoon, led by Staff Sergeant Jack Berry, the old Mexia high football halfback, up a hillside to investigate a farmhouse set in the midst of a vineyard. When they were within a hundred yards of the house, the Germans suddenly let loose with scalding small arms fire. Berry asked his old teammate, Willie Slaughter, if he could get close enough to lob a couple of grenades at the German machine gun nest. The two of them, along with a third Mexia soldier, Arthur Wadle, proceeded to crawl on elbows and knees as close as they safely could. Slaughter, who was on the eve of his twenty-first birthday, sprang up waist high and accurately delivered a grenade.

Another German nest quickly opened fire. The trio repeated the exercise and knocked that one out, too. For good measure, Slaughter killed two snipers with his machine gun. All in all their heroics lasted a little more than half an hour before the platoon scrambled back to Waskow.[12] Company B killed a handful of the enemy and ultimately overran the position, but Waskow lost three men in the process. The action allowed the company to provide detailed diagrams of enemy positions around Nocera, which were soon to be of great value to Allied forces.

Company B headed back to battalion headquarters for a day in reserve. On September 20, they were back in the field, heading to the assistance of a battalion from the 325th Glider Infantry Regiment. The airborne unit was in danger of being overrun near Mount San Angelo, the highest point on the eastern side of the peninsula, and one that was bare of cover, except for numerous rock crevasses. Company B left headquarters at 3 p.m. and Waskow was able to report back, less than two hours later, that they'd made a remarkably quick climb up the hill and had arrived to aid the 325th.

In writing a note on the action to command, Waskow gave tribute to his men: "I think the men of Company B deserve a lot of credit for this successful counterattack. Previously, we had never scaled that mountain in less than three hours. This time we did it less than one and a half hours and not a single man fell out. I was more proud of my company that day than ever before or after." Once again, Company D had supplied mortar support and Waskow gave them credit, too. He wrote that, "fire support turned the tide," and the men of Company D despite being burdened with heavy mortar gear, "kept up with the riflemen."[13] By the time they'd reached the summit, the German's assault team had started back down the hill, thinking they were facing a much larger group. The next day, the shoot and scoot strategy was once again employed and Company B was replaced by the 504th Battalion from the 82nd Airborne.

That same day, General Mark Clark arrived to check on the progress of the battle at Maiori with Colonel Darby. He was accompanied by the young, 26-year-old journalist Richard Tregaskis, whose book *Guadalcanal Diary*, an in-the-trenches account of the Marine invasion of Guadalcanal in the south Pacific, was a bestseller and the source for a soon-to-be-released Hollywood film. General Walker would no doubt have noted how often Clark seemed to be accompanied by best-selling authors. At any rate, Clark congratulated Darby and Lieutenant Colonel Walker on their work, keeping the Germans from occupying the tops of the Sorrento hills. He also discussed next moves for the Rangers and 1st Battalion—an action that would have the Americans descend from the hills down to the Vesuvian plain and on into Naples. By the end of the day, Clark and Tregaskis were on their way back to the fighting on the east side of the peninsula.

Their visit was quickly followed by the arrival of another well-known journalist, photographer Robert Capa. Dark-haired, dark-browed, dark-eyed, with a wry smile that seem to suggest some ironic thought passing behind the grin, Capa had seen as much, or more, war as any of the soldiers he would soon be photographing on the peninsula. A Hungarian-born Jew whose given name was Andre Friedmann, Capa grew up in Budapest, the son of a tailor. From childhood, he had a daring and restless spirit, and as a teenager, started to get involved in leftist activism. He was more of a romancer than a political soul, however, and as a young man, he left the discord of Hungary for the excitement of Berlin. Though at first he studied politics, he soon became interested in journalism and found work at a large photographer's agency. Here he started to take images on his own using the famed Leica camera, which was revolutionizing photojournalism by means of its high-speed lens and focal plane shutters that brought exposures down to 1/1000 of a second.

Capa's first big break came when his agency gave him the opportunity to take shots of Leon Trotsky addressing a large audience in Copenhagen stadium. These turned out to be the last shots of Trotsky speaking before an audience, prior to the Russian's assassination, and they were published in *Der Spiegel*.

The rise of Adolph Hitler and the Nazis drove Capa from Berlin. After the burning of the Reichstag, he moved to Paris, where he had little success finding work. According to his friend, the American writer John Hersey, Capa's chief source of income during this time was achieved by carrying his Leica "to and from the pawnshop."[14]

His lover, Gerda Taro, helped steer him toward a more stable life when the two of them established a photography business in Paris. He took on the name and persona of Robert "Bob" Capa, an American photographer working out of Paris—he thought it would make his work more salable in U.S. markets—and began to sell his photos on a regular basis.[15]

Together he and Gerda went to Spain in 1936 to cover the civil war for the French photography magazine *Vu*. Here, on a bare Spanish hillside, Capa captured one of the most memorable wartime images in the history of photography. Traveling with a group of Spanish militia who were suddenly attacked on that hillside, Capa dove for cover but kept shooting images by holding his Leica above his head and pointing it back toward a nearby militiaman. He managed to capture the exact moment a bullet struck the Spanish Loyalist, and the resulting image was a stunning portrait. The man's body reels back; his eyes are shut; arms dropped behind him, as if to catch his fall. He is suspended on his way to the barren ground. One moment living, one moment dead, and Capa's image caught the intersection.[16]

The photo appeared in *Vu* in September 1936 and made Capa's reputation as a photographer "so daring he was there to capture the instant of a man's death." He and Gerda continued to cover the war in Spain, where they met and congregated with a host of famed writers and journalists who were also flocking to the war, including Ernest Hemingway, John Dos Passos, and Martha Gellhorn.

There was a romance to this conflict from the start: unlike World War I, which had soured so many in "The Lost Generation" on the brute powers of Europe, here was a fight with a cause they could believe in. "The Spanish Civil War," according to Hemingway, "was the happiest period of our lives. We were truly happy then, for when people died it seemed as though death was justified and important. For they died for something they believed in and that was going to happen."[17]

But it all ended badly for Capa. The Loyalists were defeated, and Gerda was killed gruesomely, run over by a tank.

Nonetheless, he kept looking for action. Capa went to China to cover the war in Manchuria between the Japanese and Chinese; he moved to the U.S. and did work for a number of American magazines. He visited Hemingway and Martha Gellhorn in Sun Valley, Idaho; and finally returned to Europe to cover the war, first in England and then North Africa, where he hooked up for a time with Ernie Pyle. Finally, he went to Sicily where he began to grow tired of the action, saying, "this war is like an aging actress: more and more dangerous and less and less photogenic."[18]

Still, he waited with other journalists to cover the invasion of Italy. A number of these were put up by the Army's P.R. office in the official press hotel, the Aletti in Algiers. A.J. Liebling, John Steinbeck, Ernie Pyle (who was on his way out of the theater at the time),

Jack Belden (*Time-Life*), and Capa were among eighteen journalists crowded into a single room in the hotel. Capa, looking for a scoop, was told by General Matthew Ridgway that he would let the photographer parachute into Rome with the 82nd airborne on the first day of the invasion. Capa was excited by the prospect and imagined himself photographing Mussolini at the deposed leader's home while others were taking photos of "dreary beaches and local mayors." Unfortunately for him, the idea of parachuting into Rome—promulgated by the notion that the Italian surrender would make the invasion a cakewalk—turned out to be wishful thinking.

Capa wound up instead coming ashore at Paestum on September 15 with Richard Tregaskis. They spent a couple of days together at Altavilla with the 504th of the 82nd Airborne, and then moved to Maiori.

Capa quickly found a center for his work that suited him just fine. He moved up to Fort Schuster at the Chiunzi Pass with his fellow *Life* correspondent, writer Will Lang, and made himself as comfortable as possible given the near constant shelling. "Whisky was offered to us as we sat and talked in the command post, and whisky was necessary," recalled Lang. "As each nearby explosion blew open the front door, Capa would put down his glass, raise his camera, and, still seated, photograph the dust and confusion through the doorway, remarking, 'This is the only way to cover a war.'"

Capa was also enamored of the half-track employed by one of the Ranger companies. It carried a 105 mm cannon, which it would lug up to the crest of the hill at Chiunzi Pass. The half-track crew would lob shells down on the valley below, before quickly backtracking to Fort Shuster and beyond, out of harm's way.

Capa did venture out with the troops, both the Rangers and Henry Waskow's Company B, a unit which he met and traveled with on patrol. Riley Tidwell had his picture taken by Capa as the company was nearing a house that held a sniper that Company B was trying to decommission. Tidwell took some shots at a window in the house with his carbine as Capa snapped away. Then a first sergeant from the company got to the door, kicked it open, and silenced the German with his tommy gun.

According to Tidwell, Capa told the platoon that they were craziest bunch of soldiers he'd ever seen. He was amazed that after they'd taken care of the sniper, they set up in the middle of a vineyard outside the house and started to reach up and pluck grapes from the vines, even as they continued to fire at the nearby Germans. It turned out that they were half a mile inside German lines at the time.[19]

BRITISH COMMANDO forces had been waging battle to the east of the American Rangers and the143rd since D-Day. They were at a location centered on the village of Vietri, which lay between Salerno to the east and Maiori to the west, right at the crook of the Bay of Salerno. Though the commandoes had been pretty badly battered for the first couple of days of the invasion, they had managed to secure the heights above Vietri, now at a place dubbed Commando Hill. The heights were taken with a heavy toll: when the battalions who'd waged the fight were finally relieved, their replacements saw a battlefield that would become a familiar sight in Italy: a rocky hillside covered with the dead bodies of both British and German soldiers. The Germans had used phosphorus shells in the fighting and the acrid smell of the chemical was all over the field, including the still smoldering bodies of dead British soldiers. Among those killed in the shelling was the Duke of Wellington, Sir Henry Wellesley.

It was about this time that Lieutenant Burrage, as battalion information office, received a copy of the first casualty report written by Clark to General Eisenhower. Since D-Day, the British X Corps had lost 531 killed, 1,915 wounded, and 1,561 missing. The American VI Corps had 225 killed, 835 wounded, and 589 missing. And the two forces were only now in a position to begin the push toward Naples.

ON SEPTEMBER 25, the British 23rd Armored Brigade began moving out of Vietri along the very narrow road to Maiori. The plan was for the British brigade to join forces with 1st Battalion and the Rangers, and head down the Chiunzi Pass road to the Vesuvius Plain. From there, the two units would link with the 82nd Airborne and move toward Naples along a central highway and coastal roads. A second British armored brigade would come at Naples after sweeping around the north side of Vesuvius.

It was no easy task to move the armored brigade between Vietri and Maiori. The highway between the two towns chiseled into the cliffs of the peninsula was hardly conducive for Sherman tanks and two-and-a-half ton trucks. The trek along the winding and narrow macadam road was achingly slow and laborious. According to Burrage, vehicles were stacked up all the way from Maiori to Vietri, at least seven or eight kilometers. It wasn't until the evening of September 27, that the joined forces began the descent down the hills from the Chiunzi Pass.

Company B entered the village of St. Egido the next morning, expecting to find Germans, but the enemy had pulled out in the night. Waskow was ordered to move on and occupy the nearby village of St. Lorenzo, which Company B did by noon. Here and in towns yet to come, Italian villagers greeted Americans as heroes, despite the fact that the air force and artillery had decimated scores of homes.

The next morning, the Texans had the otherworldly experience of passing through Pompeii, frozen in time since 79 A.D. Within the city wall and along the excavated streets, the GI's gaped at the ruins of homes caught in mid-day destruction. New archaeological work on the eastern end of the city, along what was called the Strada Abbondanza—the Street of Abundance—had been interrupted by the war.

Here the lives of wealthy Pompeiian business leaders had faced their own interruption in the ash of Vesuvius almost two thousand years earlier. Nearby, a sunken amphitheater, large enough to hold a crowd of 20,000, was likewise buried and now recently revealed.

On the northeast side of Pompeii, 1st Battalion was linked to a Royal Scot brigade and trucked on to the village of Torre del Greco, tight to the shore of the Gulf of Naples, and just to the southeast of the city. The Allies were given the assignment of taking a castle built on a promontory high above Toro del Greco, held currently by some three hundred German troops. Company B was chosen to take the lead in the assault and found itself facing a wooded terrain honeycombed with concrete walls eight to- ten feet high. The enemy had filled the area leading up to the castle with snipers and machine gun nests and Waskow's company was almost immediately stymied. After nearly seven hours of intense fighting, which devolved into "hand grenading" the machine gun posts, they were still two thousand yards from the castle, and thankful, at the end of the day, when they were pulled back to their original position.[20]

The fight at the castle turned out to be a rearguard action to slow the Allied advance into Naples. By October 1, the city was empty of Germans.

THAT SAME MORNING, General Walker, who hadn't received a word of the 1st Battalion's activities for days, set out for Naples from his division command near Altavilla. He drove with his aides northeast through Battapaglia, which had been racked by U.S. Navy shelling. The destruction appalled him. He couldn't see a single building left intact, and told his diary, "We could smell the dead bodies buried in the rubble."

Continuing on Highway 18, the main thoroughfare to Naples, Walker noted the wreckage of the railroad yards near Salerno and the "bewilderment" of the Italians standing around, looking at their ruined homes. "But even in the midst of destruction and grief, they were friendly toward us," he noted.[21]

They took a quick tour of Pompeii, which had been spared by both Germans and Allies. From nearby Vesuvius, Walker and his aides could see smoke drifting skyward from the crater. Like his stroll through the temples at Paestum, the general had a sense that he was treading on sacred ground as he walked along the streets of old Pompeii.

Walker griped about the pace in which the British X Corps had moved against the Germans. The fact that he came upon two sets of graves, British and German, between Salerno and Naples, indicated to him that the enemy had "retired voluntarily and were followed, not pushed, by the British."

Walker also cast an eye on the Sorrento mountains that his son, Lieutenant Colonel Walker, Jr., and the 143rd's 1st Battalion had been navigating for the past few weeks. He pronounced them rugged and speculated that "[the 143rd] must have had very rough going."

General Walker found his son and the 1st Battalion at the outskirts of Naples. They were there along with the 505th of the 82nd Airborne and the British 23rd Armored, waiting for orders on how to proceed into Naples.

Just as they were about to advance, a jeep from General Clark's command came speeding up to Colonel James Gavin, who was commanding the 505th. Clark himself wanted to lead the contingent into the city in triumphal fashion, said the messengers in the vehicle.[22] The 143rd's 1st Battalion and the 23rd Armored were told to continue on the coastal road into the city. Clark, in an armored half-track, would lead the 505th, riding mostly in trucks, into the Piazza Garibaldi, where a crowd of Neapolitans was expected to cheer his entrance.

As it turned out, however, the citizens of Naples mostly stayed indoors, which meant the triumphal entry was conducted through largely deserted streets. In fact there were some Italians waiting to greet the Americans in another plaza in the city (the Plaza del Plebiscito), but the hook-up between commanding general and adoring natives was never made, and Clark wound up turning around and heading back to the outskirts of Naples.

General Walker followed Clark into the city and was impressed with the complete destruction of the railroad yards and piers. "Both are a total wreck," he noted.[23] Again, he saw small groups of Italians, who, despite the devastation "were pleased to see the Americans in their city."

Heading back toward Altavilla late that afternoon, Walker and his aides came across clusters of young girls near Pompeii, waiting to throw bouquets at the passing troops. They also tossed walnuts into the divisional jeeps and gave Walker yellow flowers. In return, some of the aides broke up pieces of their dark chocolate bars and handed them out to the malnourished and sickly children.

Walker thought that it would be a kind of justice to drive Hitler and Mussolini through scenes like those he had witnessed that day, the misery and heartache brought to their own people, "and then behead both of them with a dull axe."

Walker noted one other sight on his way back to camp: he ran across several groups of discharged Italian soldiers heading to homes in southern Italy. Some were helping local farmers harvest their damaged crops in exchange for something to eat; some were begging for rides. To Walker, they were reminiscent of how he imagined Confederate soldiers, headed for home at the end of the Civil War.

HENRY WASKOW's Company B had its own interesting encounters with the local population. After its aborted entry into the heart of Naples, 1st Battalion was posted to a village on the north side of the city, and found one of its biggest difficulties was keeping order between the citizens of Morano and the German stragglers and Italian

Fascists who were left behind. Along with dealing with minefields laid by the evacuating Germans, Waskow and company had to break up several lynching parties, which were trying to stretch the necks of local followers of Il Duce.

In Morano, Waskow experienced a familiar phenomenon to American troops both in Sicily and Italy. As he headed Company B into the village, a well-dressed man approached "with a cigar in one hand and a walking cane in the other." His first words were, "Hey Bud, what's doing in the United States?" Like many others in the region, he'd lived for a number of years in America and was stranded in his homeland by the war. He insisted that Waskow accompany him to the garden behind his home, where he dug out his passport and a bottle of whisky. He'd been saving the Scotch for the first American officer who happened his way, and that officer happened to be Captain Henry Waskow.[24]

Of course not all was light-hearted greetings in the mop-up around Naples. On October 3 outside the village of Guigliano, Lieutenant Colonel Walker ordered the battalion, minus Company B, to attack a rearguard unit of Germans ensconced in a walnut grove. A late afternoon assault took Companies A and C within 300 yards of the village when sharp small arms fire halted the battalion. They were ordered to hold their position and resume the attack in the morning. Among the seriously wounded was Lieutenant Warren Klinger of Monahan, Texas and Company A, an old friend of Captain Waskow. Klinger had been at Camp Edwards with Waskow, had shipped with him to North Africa, and served with Waskow at the Chiunzi Pass. When he was being evacuated on a stretcher from the battlefield, Waskow came to his side and offered words of encouragement.[25]

On October 4, the two companies discovered that the Germans had pulled out of the town. They advanced against light resistance all the way through the village piazza. Once through Guigliano, however, they were hit by devastating artillery. A dozen officers and enlisted men were killed, and fourteen more were wounded. Gone in an instant were Captain Joseph Peterman, Company A commander, Major James Land, the battalion executive officer, Captain Ray Pederson, and seven enlisted men from Company A. It was the deadliest day for the 1st Battalion through the entire campaign. It was also the last day.[26]

The following morning, as Burrage was sitting down with Lieutenant Colonel Walker to begin drafting a report of what had happened the day before, Walker's father arrived with new orders for his son: Fred, Jr. was moving back to division headquarters where he would serve as the division's new operations officer. A few hours later, a convoy of trucks showed up from the 36th, there to haul 1st Battalion back to their comrades near Altavilla. After almost a month's absence the 1st Battalion would be linked again to the rest of the T-Patchers.

For Henry Waskow and Roy Goad, both with brothers last known to be wounded and in the hands of the enemy, the reunion would come with mixed emotions.

9

Capri

BACK IN THE MIDDLE of September, the mortar blast that knocked August Waskow off his pins and unconscious on Hill 424 also knocked him out of the war. In one instant, he was crouched tight to a rocky hillside in Italy, wishing he could dig his way to safe-keeping; in the next, he was a bloody mess, lying helpless and wounded as the battle continued to rage around him. More than thirty pieces of shrapnel from the mortar blast had pierced his body: both legs and arms, his chest, and face had been hit. One fragment had lodged behind his right eye, blinding it.[1] When he finally came to, he felt weightless, floating away from Hill 424 on a jostling, rocking flight, before he realized he was being carried away from the battlefield on a stretcher. In his groggy, semi-blinded state, it looked to Waskow that the men toting him from the field were wearing odd-looking caps. It took him awhile to realize that the helmets were indeed strange to him: he was being hauled away by Germans.[2]

Waskow wound up in a church-turned-field hospital in Altavilla, where he was reunited with others of Company I, including Captain Laughlin, Captain Yates, Ray Goad, and Jack White, all now wounded prisoners of the Germans.

White, who'd been hit in the ankle just hours into Company I's initial battle, was actually captured twice by the Germans. The first time, the enemy had taken him to one aid station in Altavilla, but they soon abandoned it when the Allies counter-attacked. Unfortunately for White, no Americans came for him. He wound up spending the afternoon of September 14 lying in an open field while the .88's screamed and burst over his head. That night, the Germans reappeared, and once again took the field. Early the next morning, they carried White and the other non-ambulatory wounded away with them to the church where he was reunited with others of his company.

Captain Kratka, the battalion surgeon had aided the badly wounded Laughlin on Hill 424, and stayed with him all the way to the German field hospital. Six other captured aid men from the battalion were there as well. With the help of a German doctor and medic, they tended to the wounds of about 40 American casualties, including August Waskow.

On September 15, the changing tide of battle forced the Germans to evacuate their wounded prisoners from Altavilla. Those Americans who could not walk were loaded in the back of trucks and driven off to an old stone building serving as a hospital about twenty miles from the battlefield. Those that could walk began to march in the same direction.

At the new medical station, the Germans fed the wounded prisoners with black bread, Limburger cheese, liverwurst, and soup. Captain Kratka and his aid men continued to care for the Americans, working side-by-side with a German doctor. Kratka did surgeries in an operating room at the hospital, including the amputation of one soldier's arm.

Three days passed in the stone hospital, after which the Germans received word that they were to evacuate the medical prisoners to a hospital even further behind their lines. That afternoon, the medical station admitted a host of wounded enemy troops. The German medics were too immersed in caring for their own wounded to pay much attention to the Americans, and eventually, when the order to evacuate became more pressing, the Germans decided to take only the American walking-wounded with them. That included Ray Goad and Bill Yates.

Among those left behind were White, Waskow, and Laughlin. Kratka was left to care for them and the others. He was spared, Kratka thought, because the German doctor with whom he'd worked had learned that the American doctor had two children back home and felt empathy for his situation. There were kindnesses in this war. And there was luck, too. In all about twenty-eight wounded remained behind. The Germans left them with more black bread, more liverwurst spread, jam, and cans of sardines.

Some locals offered assistance, bringing eggs and bread. Kratka attached a Red Cross flag to the top of the building to prevent strafing. Two days after the Germans left, the doctor sent an English-speaking Italian man in search of American help. The next morning, September 21, a jeep arrived from divisional headquarters, and soon after that, seven ambulances were pulling up to the building to take the wounded back to American field hospitals.[3, 4]

HENRY WASKOW remained uncertain about his brother's fate once he and Company B got back to the rest of the division after Naples.[5] He quickly learned of August's wounds, but in searching the area for his whereabouts, Henry discovered that there was confusion about whether or not his brother was still a prisoner of the Germans, or had even survived. Some Italians, trying to be helpful, added to his uncertainty; they took him to a freshly dug grave and told Henry that August had been killed and was buried there.[6]

After the shock of this initial misinformation, Captain Waskow finally learned that August had, in fact, survived and was currently on a hospital ship in the Gulf of Naples. Henry wrote home to his mother and sister Mary Lee to let them know of his and August's circumstances—in case they hadn't been informed of his brother's wounds by the Army. In fact, the family hadn't heard from either brother since just before Salerno. Word from Henry was obviously welcome, though news of August's wounds was frightening.

The Waskow family passed Henry's V-mail on to the Belton newspaper. He had made some interesting observations about the fighting in Italy, and he colored those comments with the sort of bravado that the local Texas papers loved to hear from their soldiers, especially early in the war. "We can lick the Germans anytime and anywhere," Waskow wrote. "They are tough, that's true, but our men are much, much tougher; and a lot more courageous."

Henry offered a brief description of the country and its people: "The Italians have greeted us everywhere with cheers. I have never been kissed so much in all my life . . . men, women, and kids."

Always conscientious about saluting the men in his command, he gave them a bow in this letter, too: "I wish I could tell you the stories of individual heroism among the men, but let's just say they are all heroes and 'the infantry with the dirt behind their ears, just keeps rolling along.'"

And thinking of Robert Capa and the time the photographer and Life writer Will Lang spent with Company B, Waskow let his folks know that he and the others in his outfit might be in the news. "Be sure to watch *Time* and *Life* magazines about this date [October 9]," he wrote with obvious excitement and pride.

Then Henry, who always seemed aware of his role in the grand scheme of things, got back to the big picture: the status of the war and the condition of Italy. "History will never forget what the Fascists have done to destroy this country," he wrote, "one would think he was living 100 or so years ago, for the civilization has just stopped."

Waskow closed the letter with a reassuring note about August. He was "okeh and safe" and getting some mail from home.[7]

As with the Belton paper, the *Mexia Weekly Herald* was also happy to publish letters from the front, especially those tinged with bravado. Willie Slaughter, one of the thirteen grandsons in the war, and eventual winner of two Silver Stars (one for his heroics in the Sorrento campaign) sent a note to his mother that she shared with the local paper: "Tell granddad I got my German," he wrote. "Shot him out of a tree with my tommy gun."

Slaughter said that he had been in action from the day he landed in Italy for a full month afterward. "The Germans have kept me pretty busy dodging bullets and artillery shells."

There had been some little time to admire the countryside. According to Slaughter, "Italy was pretty except for the war torn parts." And, oh by the way, he asked his mother, "Can you send a pair of leather gloves from home? And it sure would be nice to get some candy, too."[8]

Other Mexia soldiers writing home from Italy included Jack Berry, Hubert Ingram, Charles Morgan, and Billie Sunday. All reported themselves safe and sound, with Sunday adding, "The Italian people seem to be real proud to see us. They give us apples, grapes, and English walnuts. The parts of Italy that I have been through are pretty well torn up."[9]

Even in the midst of the brave postures exhibited in the letters, however, were the unavoidable tragedies of death and injury that were also being reported to the people back in Belton and Mexia. Word was coming home to Texas that the 36th was taking a lot of casualties in Italy. In Belton, the *Journal* reported the first two deaths from Company I, First Lieutenant Mallory Miller and Private Walter Roy Cole. Miller had worked in Belton as a constable and was a volunteer fireman. Cole was the son of a military man. Also reported in early October was the wounding of Corporal Jack White.

WITH A CAMPAIGN under his belt and more fighting expected soon, General Walker thought it would be a good time to offer some relaxation for his men. In mid-October, Captain Henry Waskow was rewarded with a trip to Capri for being the best company commander through the Naples campaign. No one recorded exactly how long he stayed on the island, or what exactly he did there, except for the fact that he picked up a folder postcard of its sights, with the intention of sending it later to his sister Mary Lee.

Then, as now, Capri was a beautiful tourist haven. In the days after the invasion, the Allies quickly turned it back to its former purpose and it bustled with soldiers and journalists. The isle of Capri is about 3.75 miles long and a mile and a half wide, and consists of two ridges of Apennine limestone with a high point of 1,920 feet. Before the war, there were about 7,700 inhabitants. The city of Capri was built in the saddle between the two ridges. A funicular dominated its heart. *Baedecker's* noted that the city offered fruit, oil and good red and white wines. "The walks in the island are all more or less steep," cautioned the guide.[10]

Blue Grotto on the north side of the island, a cavern hollowed by the waves, was the most celebrated of a number of these grottoes on the island. Then (and now) small boats entered a space less than three feet high, which opened up to an enormous interior cavern nearly fifty feet high and the size of a football field. Within the grotto, objects in the water assume a silvery appearance, and, for a few lire, local boys would dive in to create the silvery effect for the tourists. But it was cheaper just to stick your own arm into the water to create the illusion, according to *Baedeker's*. Near the middle of the grotto, a rift in the rock about sixty-five yards long was once thought to connect to the villa of the Roman Emperor Tiberius— another indication both of the antiquity of the area, and the antiquity of Capri as a getaway spot for vacationers.

John Steinbeck, only forty-one years old, but already author of *Grapes of Wrath, Of Mice and Men,* and *Tortilla Flats,* was in Capri that month as well, reporting on the war for the *New York Herald Tribune.* He came to Italy in the aftermath of Salerno and would soon head out with the U.S. Navy on a special operations mission along the coast north of Rome. In the interim, he visited Naples, Salerno, and Capri, and wrote pieces on the predilection of American soldiers for collecting souvenirs ("It is said, and with some truth, that while the Germans fight for world domination and the English for the defense of England, the Americans fight for souvenirs");[11] and on the soldiers' habits of stuffing their pockets with good-luck charms and amulets.

Henry Waskow, with his souvenir postcards in his pocket, might have been interested to know that Robert Capa also visited Capri after the Naples campaign.

Capa entered Naples on October 1 with Colonel Gavin and the 505th of the 82nd Airborne. Like everyone else on the Allied side moving into the city, he joined in the initial sense of accomplishment and elation, but soon the sight of dead bodies lying helter skelter on every street and in every piazza sobered him. The retreating Germans had taken out their anger and rage against the Neapolitans for Italy's surrender on the eve of the Allied invasion. No corner of the city was spared; hospitals were looted; public works were destroyed. Even schools were attacked. Huge parts of the city, which had already suffered through Allied bomb attacks, were largely turned into rubble by the Germans.

Capa snapped shots of the devastated waterfront, where boats and ships were piled in heaps, one on top of another, as if in the wake of a hurricane. He took photos of an Italian mob surrounding a trio of Fascists who had assisted the Germans in their defense of Naples. He took shots of a British tank crew washing up and shaving, getting gussied up for their triumphant entry into the city. He grabbed images of the pockmarked road through the suburbs into the city.

On October 7, one of the many booby-trap bombs left behind by the Germans exploded in the midst of a crowd gathered outside the Naples post office. Both Italians and members of the 82nd Airborne were in the streets. In all, more than 100 people were killed. Capa was only a few hundred yards away and took shots of the chaos and destruction.

When the fighting was all over in Naples and the bombs quit exploding, Capa sent his photos off to *Life* magazine and took a trip to Capri. There he took photos of an old Italian hero of the antifascist movement, sailed around the island, bedded a wealthy Italian countess in her beautiful seaside villa and did a little shopping in the village of Capri. In a few days times, he would be back in Naples, ready to cover the next advance of the Allies.

Meanwhile, on October 18, *Life* published not only his shots of Naples, but a second photo essay, devoted to the "Battle of Chiunzi Pass." There were images of the hills, several photos of the half-tracks that seemed to fascinate Capa; shots of the interior of Fort Schuster with American and British officers pointing spy glasses out a window, spotting German positions. Then came a series of photos of the T-Patchers: first, moving off through vineyard with Mt. Vesuvius steaming in the background; then a shot of a Texan, kneeling with his Garand rifle across his thigh, "coolly puffing a cigarette" in silhouette in a lemon grove, on his way to root out Germans at the base of Vesuvius; a continuation of the scene with Vesuvius even more prominent in the distance and a line of T-Patchers moving cautiously through an orchard. Finally, the last shot shows the same group from the 143rd's 1st Battalion outside an old vine-covered farmhouse, damaged by shells but still basically intact. The photo depicts GIs stand outside the front door of the home with guns leveled. Writer Will Lang's copy tells us that they've just shot the bolts off the door and have sprayed rounds within, but any Germans inside are dead or gone. He quotes an unnamed Texas private as muttering "It's a shame to hafta do things like this to people's homes."[12]

10

Why We Fight

As AMERICAN TROOPS WERE winding down the first step in their invasion of Italy, Hollywood directors Frank Capra and John Huston were in London, working on a documentary film that would ultimately receive decidedly mixed reviews. A joint production between British and American filmmakers, *Tunisian Victory* was supposed to detail the Allied victory in North Africa, but the movie turned out to be a hodge-podge of footage that suffered from a lack of quality shots of American participation as well as suffering from the ongoing disputes between the Allies about who ought to receive the bulk of the credit for the North African victory.

Prior to coming to London to take advantage of a much higher quality of film shot by British crews during the Tunisian campaign, Capra and Huston had been laboring jointly to re-create shots that were absent from American footage shot during the fighting itself. A single film crew had been employed by the U.S. Army Signal Corps to take moving pictures during the invasion of North Africa. All of that footage was subsequently sunk in port with the ship that was to carry it back to the States for editing.

President Roosevelt himself had expressed an interest in seeing film coverage of the North African invasion. According to Huston, the Signal Corps was so embarrassed that it had none, that when he and Capra were asked to re-create footage, they were advised to keep their re-creation on the low down, on the off chance that word of their activities would reach the president. Capra and Huston went to an Army training facility in the Mojave Desert in California where they shot footage of mock troop movements and artillery fire in conditions that approximated Tunisia. To get aerial shots, Huston went to Orlando, Florida, where he filmed some P-39 fighters planes in action.[1]

The re-created footage didn't work out so well. After trying, with little success, to fashion it into a quality film in New York, someone put forward the idea that the Americans ought to combine their efforts with the Brits, which is how Huston and Capra wound up in London putting together *Tunisian Victory.*

The two of them arrived in England in August, and shared a suite at the famed Claridge's Hotel. They spent the bulk of their time at the offices of the British Army Film Unit butting heads with their English counterparts over such issues as the title of the film, whether or not an all-American roster of actors should be used to provide commentary for the documentary, and the general tenor and direction of the film. They found time to have dinner with Bob Hope and his singer, Frances Langford, at the home of British actor, John Mills. And Huston spent some time squiring a red-headed opera singer named Lennie, but for the most part, they were kept busy trying to resolve the issues of the film.

Major Capra was Captain Huston's superior in the film work, and took the lead in the enterprise. Huston would later confess some embarrassment about what transpired. Capra apparently had refused to let the British see the film footage that he and Huston had recreated in the Mojave and Florida prior to the meetings. Had the Brits known the poor quality of the footage, Huston hinted, they would never have agreed to a joint production. In other words, what merit there was in *Tunisian Victory* came principally from British film work in the field; and yet Capra was able to not only elbow his way into a joint venture, he would actually come to dominate the subsequent debate over how it ought to be put together.[2]

BY THIS STAGE of the war, Frank Capra was an old hand in Army filmmaking procedures. In fact, he had been at it since shortly after Pearl Harbor, having enlisted the week after the attack (one of the first Hollywood directors to do so).

Not only was Capra quickly put to work, he was sent straight to the top of command. In February, 1942, the director of *It Happened One Night, Mr. Smith Goes to Washington, Mr. Deeds Goes to Town,* and *You Can't Take It With You* was called to the War Munitions Building in Washington, D.C., where he found himself standing before the door of Army Chief of Staff George Marshall. A man as ego-driven as any in Hollywood, Capra's knees were nevertheless rattled at the prospect of meeting the most powerful military man in the United States, in the midst of the nation's greatest war crisis in eighty years.

He had been given Marshall's reasons for wanting this chat a few days earlier, soon after his arrival in Washington. Capra's new boss at the Signal Corps told him that the general had handpicked the director for special duty within a newly created morale division of the Army's Signal Corps, Special Services unit. Marshall wanted someone with the highest-level of filmmaking skills to produce a series of informational training movies to show to every member of the U.S. Army before they shipped off to war. The idea was that it was not just important, but crucial, for all American servicemen to understand why they were in uniform, why they were being called upon to wage war on behalf of the nation.

The task was considered so essential that Marshall wanted the very best man available. He didn't quite trust the well-established

Signal Corps to do justice to the idea, despite its long history of directing Army communications of every stripe stretching all the way back to the Civil War. Long a Hollywood film buff who well-knew the quality of Capra's work, Marshall was a man already known in the Army for his ability to pick the best man for a given job. In fact, for years Marshall had kept a little black book in which he'd jot notes on the talents and abilities of the officers that he trained and served with over his long career in the Army. It was a list that had generally served him well, first when he was named Chief of Staff of the Army in 1939 and now, in the frenetically paced few weeks after Pear Harbor, when Marshall was organizing the Allied war effort with the President, the Joint Chiefs of Staff, and Winston Churchill and the military forces of Great Britain.

Capra had been given time after his enlistment to finish editing his latest film, a quirky comedy adapted from a popular Broadway play called *Arsenic and Old Lace*. Then he'd crossed the nation from one Union Station in Los Angeles, to another in Washington, D.C., wearing a crisp new uniform just purchased from the Hollywood Army-Navy store and tailored to fit his compact frame. He was spiffed with the leaves of an Army Major and the crossed-flag insignia of U.S. Army Signal Corps, all topped by a slightly oversized cap, which Capra had made the mistake of purchasing just prior to a military haircut.

Capra was always animated by a sense of challenge and this was a large one. One of his principal motives for enlisting in the army was a need for a new direction in his life. In a career that stretched back to just after World War I, Capra had conquered the world of motion pictures; now he needed new tests. "I'm an uphill man," he wrote. "When my motor races uphill, my interest rises, when it idles on the flat, I'm bored."[3]

Capra's successes, however, failed by a long shot to explain exactly why he was outside Marshall's door that February day. Marshall, after all, was a man whose labors, post December 7, were monumental. From the moment Marshall sat down to read the fourteen-point diplomatic ultimatum from the Japanese that had been placed on his desk after Pearl Harbor, he knew immediately that all had changed. His most immediate concerns at that moment turned toward protecting American shores and military interests from further Japanese attack, particularly in the Philippines. But quick on the heels of the necessary defensive measures at the start of the conflict, came the need to plan and implement a comprehensive strategy for world war.

So why, in the midst of these trying and dangerous times were precious moments belonging to George Marshall being expended on a discussion of training films with a Hollywood movie director?

When Capra entered the general's office, Marshall glanced up from his work, looking like a "sad-eyed Okie," according to the director.[4] George Marshall was not a man people relaxed around. Not simply because of his rank, or because he could be brusque; it was more that Marshall projected such a no-nonsense face to the world that those in his presence felt a need to get to the point as well.

Marshall began without preamble: Within a short time, he said, the U.S. Army had grown and would continue to grow from the two hundred thousand who were troops when Marshall became Chief of Staff in 1939, to numbers in the millions (around 8 ultimately). These young men would have many fine qualities but they would not be professional soldiers. In fact, the new recruits would outnumber veteran army professionals by a measure of about forty to one.

What most concerned Marshall, however, was how these young recruits would react when they were on the other side of the world. Marshall believed "A man's fighting quality, his stamina, his relentless purpose, comes most strongly from the association with his home." That association didn't exist in the current situation. The question that troubled him was whether American troops would fight with the necessary resolve and toughness when "they were thousands of miles from home-in the southwest Pacific, and Italy, in Africa, in places that they had hardly ever heard of."[5] When "there was none of that tremendous spirit that comes of defending your own home-your own wife and children . . ."

Marshall felt this need to inform in a deeply personal way. As General Pershing's aide-de-camp at the end of World War I, Marshall had been given a curious assignment in the waning days of the Army's stay in Europe. In the spring of 1919, several months after the Armistice, as American troops were being organized to be sent home, it came to the attention of Pershing's command that there was a high level of dissatisfaction among the troops. They wanted to get home, and not only were they having a hard time understanding the sort of bureaucratic delays slowing their departure, but they were further grousing about the causes that brought them to France in the first place. Marshall was given the assignment of explaining the war to the men who had just fought it. The backwardness of this after-the-war approach was striking to Marshall and stayed with him until the next world war.

Obviously, the problems of educating the troops in the causes of the war would not be confined solely to its beginnings. The films that he had in mind were not to answer the question of why we are fighting now. The Japanese attack on Pearl Harbor had helped explain that matter. More importantly, the question would need to be answered as the conflict dragged on for months and even years; when soldiers were not simply enduring the terrors of warfare, but also its monotony, its discomforts, its loneliness; when the soldiers in the American army fully understood that there was no going home until the bitter end.

The time would come, Marshall knew, when they had to have the answer to the question of "Why We Fight" engrained in their being. They had to know in their hearts what this was about. And these films had to be of the highest quality or else they simply wouldn't work. That's why Capra was here. Marshall did not want the sort of training film "presented after lunch" that would put his new recruits to sleep.[6] He wanted them inspired by the man who had put Mr. Deeds on the screen, the man who'd invented Mr. Smith and sent him to Washington.

Marshall finally arrived at the specific charge he was giving Capra: the young men in Allied uniforms were capable of being not only the equal, but superior to the soldiers of the totalitarian powers they were facing, he said, "if—and this is a large if, indeed—they are given answers as to why they are in uniform, and if the answers they get are worth fighting and dying for.

"And that, Capra, is our job—and your job. To win this war we must win the battle for men's minds," Marshall said. What he wanted specifically was for Capra "to make a series of documented, factual –information films—the first in our history—that will explain to our boys in the Army why we are fighting, and the principles for which we are fighting."[7]

GIVEN THIS daunting assignment, Frank Capra headed out to do just that. Capra had never made a documentary film before. As a successful commercial Hollywood filmmaker, he didn't have much respect for them either. He thought they were primarily the province of "kooks with long hair." Nonetheless, the director quickly set out to learn how they were made. He went to New York's Museum of Modern Art, where he was able to view a copy of Leni Riefenstahl's *Triumph of the Will*, the famed Nazi propaganda film. He was impressed by the way "it destroyed the will to resist" in a viewer.[8]

Also at MOMA, he watched several other German propaganda films of the pre-war era and was likewise impressed with their propagandizing. Slowly the idea began to take shape in his mind that the best way to convey the horrors of fascism was through the actual words and images that were being produced in the Axis nations. "Let their own films kill them," is how Capra put it to one of his assistants.[9]

Back in Washington, he tried to round up as much newsreel footage as he could, looking for film taken in Germany and Japan over the past few years that would help describe, as he put it, "what kind of bastards [our boys] are fighting—and why."[10]

Capra was ultimately given his own special film detachment, the 834th, within the Special Services Division of the Signal Corps. Between April and August 1942, the basic outline for the seven movies that ultimately comprised the *Why We Fight* documentary series was put together in Washington and Hollywood, where Capra and company moved in July, after the filmmaker became more comfortable with his standing on the project. Soon Capra's group was made up of a host of accomplished Hollywood filmmakers, including the young director John Huston.[11]

By October, the first of the series, *Prelude to Victory,* was complete and sent to Washington for a viewing. Once again, Capra and Marshall sat down together, this time to watch the fruits of their collaboration.

Marshall was deeply impressed. When the lights came up after the showing, he fairly gushed—something Marshall was not prone to doing. "How did you do it," he said to Capra, "that is the most wonderful thing."

Marshall was so happy with the outcome of the film that he made immediate plans to get it out to the troops, thousands of whom were already being prepped, like General Walker's Texas Division, for shipping to war zones overseas.

As SUCCESSFUL as Frank Capra's movie might have been, the fact of the matter was, like all the training measures furiously conducted by U.S. military leaders in the months prior to the advent of ground fighting in Europe, it was all preparation for what was to come; just another prelude to the moment, as Marshall envisioned, when American troops would be thousands of miles from home, cowering in some hellhole in a distant land, wondering just what they were doing there.

The deepest doubts about this war would not come in its first few months, when patriotic fervor and gung-ho spirit energized the troops landing on the shores of North Africa and Sicily. Now, almost a full year later, as the war had come to Italy, and the bodies began to stack up on the beaches of Salerno, and soon, on the road to Rome, the young soldiers slogging their way to an uncertain destination would need to know, in the depths of their being, just why they were fighting.

It was also not enough to show footage of German propaganda reels or fake tank battles staged in the California desert. By the spring of 1943, it was understood at the highest level of the administration—meaning in the offices of FDR, Henry Stimson, and George Marshall—that the enormous and ongoing sacrifices required of the American people in this war demanded a forthright depiction of what the fighting was like.

Roosevelt himself issued a memorandum to Signal Corps offices that "the public be shown the grimness and hardness of war through still and motion pictures."[12] It was language reiterated in a War Department radiogram of September 3, sent to the Signal Section of the U.S. Fifth Army, even as the troops were preparing to invade Salerno. It gave a direct sense of the FDR's feelings: "The President is dissatisfied with our photographic coverage. Motion and still photography of combat operations compare unfavorably with that of our Allies. Production of first-rate pictures of this type is essential to give the American people a visual accounting of the accomplishments of our soldiers overseas . . .

"Thus far, excessive filming of rear area activities instead of front line action has been noticed. In order to relate the dangers and grimness of war, the work of all arms and services in front lines during operations must be covered by both still and motion picture photography. Combat action must be filmed as it happens, so suitably equipped photographic personnel must accompany the front line troops. Fill-in and background shots can be made either after or before an operation . . ."[13]

Capra understood the need as well. Under the circumstances, a stitched together documentary like *Tunisian Victory* was not going to cut it. What was needed and wanted was a film shot in the midst of action with "especially energetic and capable direction in the field."[14]

The War Department assumed that the Fifth Army Signal Corps had the necessary camera teams in the Mediterranean Theater to make a quality documentary. But in going through its own list of personnel, the Fifth Army Signal Corps unit acknowledged that it had no director with motion picture experience "and insufficient competent motion picture cameramen."[15]

Fifth Army Signal Corps headquarters sent a radiogram back to the War Department advising them of the absence of a quality director. They also said a writer would be a good idea. A quick response from the War Department advised the unit that George Stevens, who had directed films in Hollywood for RKO and Universal, before joining the Signal Corps, was available along with a pair of writers.

Capra had other ideas, however. He contemplated the idea of going to Italy himself, but realized he had responsibilities here in London, and back in D.C. He did have a man that he thought could do justice to the task at hand and when contacted by the War Department about the idea of making a documentary about the campaign in Italy, he made his suggestion.

Instead of Stevens, director John Huston would be arriving shortly from England.

On the beach at Paestum. Day 1 at Salerno Bay.

A 143rd infantry combat team comes ashore at Salerno Bay.

An aerial view of
Paestum Beach
with the Saracen
Tower and Greek
temples inland.

The tobacco
factory.
Headquarters at
Salerno for the
36th Division.

Maiori, on
the Sorrento
Peninsula
(foreground),
and the road to
Fort Schuster.

Naples, looking south, with Mt. Vesuvius in the background.

American troops crossing the Volurno River.

Incessant rains and consequent mud bogged down the American advance north of Naples.

The German "Winter Lines" were laden with mines.

Mt. Sammucro, looking east from Mt. Lungo, across the Liri Valley.

Mt. Lungo, looking north, with Mt. Sammucro looming to the east and the Liri Valley above.

San Pietro in the immediate aftermath of the battle.

Members of 163rd Signal Corps enjoy their Christmas meal, Dec. 25, 1943.

Colonel Martin of the 143rd entering San Pietro on December 17, 1943.

A collection
area for
troops
brought
down
from Mt.
Sammucro.

The ruins of
San Pietro.

The body of a soldier
brought down off
the mountain on the
back of a mule.

A medical
detachment heading
into San Pietro in the
wake of the battle.

Ernie Pyle (right) with a
gun crew in Italy.

Gen. Dwight
Eisenhower,
with Lt. Gen.
Mark Clark
(near right),
Maj. Gen.
John Lucas
(far right),
and Maj.
Gen. Lucian
Truscott, in
Italy.

Eisenhower and
Mark Clark
confer in Italy.

Ernie Pyle
(hatless, with
cigarette) soon
before his death
in Okinawa.

11

Pyle and Huston

ERNIE PYLE KNEW HIS REPORTING struck a chord with vast numbers of readers across the country. But he was unprepared for the sort of attention that rained down on him from the moment he landed at LaGuardia airfield in early September, 1943. Even as he and his friend Lee Miller taxied in from the airport and settled in the Algonquin Hotel, Pyle started fielding requests for interviews, endorsement deals, lecture tours, and meetings with Army brass.[1]

In the words of a soon-to-be-published *Life* profile, Pyle had returned from Sicily "to find that he now occupies a place in American journalistic letters which no other correspondent of this war has achieved. His smooth, friendly prose had succeeded in bridging a gap between soldier and civilian where written words usually fail." His book about the North African campaign, *Here Is Your War*, had just come out from Holt publishing company and had been picked up, not only by the Book-of-the-Month Club, but the Council on Books for Wartime, which supplied books for soldiers serving overseas. That meant printing an extra 50,000 copies of *Here Is Your War*.

Chesterfield Cigarettes paid him $1,000 for use of his picture in an advertisement and Secretary of War Henry Stimson invited him to lunch in the capitol. Autograph hunters sought him out in hotel lobbies.[2]

Not only that, but Hollywood was calling, interested in doing a movie based on the reporting in his book—and these efforts were being encouraged by the U.S. Army's publicity machine, which had come to see Pyle's reporting and its real world description of an infantryman's life as a sort of necessary correlative to the war effort. Besides which, the Army felt that movies thus far coming from Hollywood in the war were overemphasizing the Navy's role in the action; it was time for a good film about the ground effort in the Mediterranean.[3]

Pyle went to Indiana for a quick visit with his father, and then headed back to Jerry and the bungalow in Albuquerque for some rest and relaxation. But the Hollywood production company had hired a young writer named Arthur Miller—the same thick, dark-rimmed glasses-wearing, intense New York intellectual, who would soon emerge as one of the country's premier playwrights—to write a script based on Ernie's work. And he was waiting for Pyle in Albuquerque. There was little rest from his labors—and little time for Jerry.

Pyle and Arthur Miller were mismatched from the outset. As Ernie settled into a planned four-week stay in New Mexico, the two began a back-and-forth exchange about the way the movie ought to be written. Miller was respectful of Pyle's work but thought the script should provide deeper meaning into what the war was all about. As for Ernie, it was precisely the avoidance of abstraction that was at the heart of his work; he was interested in the concrete, in the day-to-day, in reporting on the way his infantrymen lived their lives; not in how they thought about the causes for which they fought. As one Pyle biographer put it, "Miller yearned to say what the war ought to be; Ernie aimed to say what it was."[4]

Meanwhile, Pyle's life with Jerry quickly resumed old patterns. She had taken a job at a local air base in his absence and it seemed to help her deal with her emotional and psychological issues. This was the first time they had seen each other since their peculiar remarriage-by-proxy, but the visit was hardly a second honeymoon. The fact that he was determined to head back overseas shortly helped matters not at all; and as Ernie prepared to go to Italy at the end of October, Jerry started drinking again and quickly spun out of control. She asked to be returned to the hospital and Pyle agreed.

On October 28, he headed to Washington on the train where he found himself once again awash in celebrity. His book was getting rave reviews and had sold out a first run of 150,000 copies. *Life* called about the profile it was running. Despite his differences with Arthur Miller, there was more talk with producers about the movie, which would proceed as he was away in Europe.

Continuing old destructive habits of dealing with the pain of his relationship with Jerry, Pyle had a fling with an old friend while in Washington, meeting her for an afternoon tryst at the Hay-Adams Hotel. In the middle of this dalliance Pyle received an unexpected call. A big fan of his, the First Lady, was on the phone. Mrs. Eleanor Roosevelt invited him for afternoon tea at the White House.[5]

Pyle and the First Lay chatted about the burdens of writing columns (she wrote a daily piece called *My Day*), she praised him extravagantly, and asked if he might consider continuing his column in the South Pacific. It would be a great benefit to all.

That shift to the Pacific would come in time. For now, he was headed back to the Mediterranean, by way of Miami and Algiers.

LIKE FRANK CAPRA, John Huston was one of the first big-name Hollywood directors to raise his hand and volunteer for service in the U.S. Army Signal Corps. Huston signed up in January 1942 while in the midst of shooting a film called *Across the Pacific*, which Huston called a "follow-up" to his first film, *The Maltese Falcon*, because that 1941 hit had employed so many members of the cast, including Humphrey Bogart, Mary Astor and Sidney Greenstreet. Years later, Huston puckishly recalled leaving the filming mid-shoot, giving the poor director hired by Warner Brothers to replace him the task of getting Bogart out of a scene in which he was surrounded by Japanese soldiers. The script was unfinished and Huston's parting words of advice for the substitute director were, "Bogie will know how to get out."

Thirty-five-years-old when the war began, Huston cut a Bohemian figure in the Hollywood of the day. He had been given the assignment to direct *The Maltese Falcon* after an early career in which "deviation from the norm" had been his standard characteristic. Like a flesh and blood figure from a Hemingway novel, Huston had boxed, he'd written, he'd studied art, lived in Paris and had affairs with a lengthy list of women prior to establishing himself in the movies. A lanky, deep-voiced man, who oozed volatility on the set, Huston was given the nickname "The Great Unpressed" by his cast for his ability "to achieve a remarkable rumpled effect after about a minute and a half in any given set of clothes."[6]

Huston was born in 1906 the son of a Canadian engineer turned Vaudeville actor named Walter Huston. When he was a boy, his parents divorced and John wound up in Los Angeles with his mother, while his father worked mainly in off-Broadway theaters in New York.

Born restless and rebellious, Huston left high school in his midteens to try his hand at professional boxing. When that didn't promise a future, he went to New York and took a brief turn at his father's profession, acting. Here, too, he found his career stymied. Huston drifted to Mexico where he somehow wound up spending a couple of years in the national cavalry before heading back to Los Angeles He had begun writing while in Mexico and sold a couple of stories to H.L. Mencken's *American Mercury* magazine. Now back in Hollywood, Huston took a job as a script editor for Samuel Goldwyn and worked on the new "talkies" that were being produced.

Tragedy sent him adrift again—he struck and killed a woman while driving in Los Angeles and wound up afterwards in Paris where he studied art and immersed himself in café life for a time. He finally returned to the States, before settling down again in Hollywood, where he began to forge a screenwriting career. He got assignments for a couple of major scripts, *Sergeant York* and *High Sierra*, the latter of which became a hit for both Huston and its star, Humphrey Bogart.

Because of these successes, Jack Warner, head of Warner Bros. Studios, offered Huston his first directing job. As his source material, Huston chose a Dashiell Hammett novel that had been twice made into a film with little success. But by casting Humphrey Bogart as Detective Sam Spade and surrounding him with a memorable supporting crew, *The Maltese Falcon* became one of the most talked about films of 1941.

John Huston was a young man on the rise when he volunteered for service in World War II. Still wild and unpredictable, still something of a rake, and in the midst of directing his new movie, he didn't take notice of the letter from the U.S. Army telling him where and when to report. The haste with which he left the set was due to the Army Signal Corps insisting that he report to duty in Washington on the double.[7] In April 1942, he got his assignment. Huston was to fly to the Aleutian Islands in Alaska, there to make a documentary of the war effort in the far northwest.

He attacked the job with his typical brio. Huston quickly arranged to take his film crew on bombing missions out on the western edge of the Aleutians toward Japan. Time and again, he flew on bombing runs to the outer island, making friends with the crews along the way, including Jack Chennault, the son of Claire Chennault of Flying Tiger fame. Jack would later assist Huston in Orlando, by arranging the mock bombing missions filmed for *Tunisian Victory*.

Huston put his footage together in Hollywood, named the film *Report from the Aleutians,* and then carried it across country to the Signal Corps production studios in Astoria, New York, where more editing was done. An initial showing in Washington followed; and then there was a trip back to L.A. to add music to the documentary. Huston was just finishing up in California, when he got a call from Frank Capra. He was needed for a special assignment, a film on the desert triumph in Tunisia.

That led him with Capra to London; and during his stay in London, he met an English writer of suspense novels working with the British Film Unit. Huston and Eric Ambler quickly formed a collegial bond.

According to Ambler, it was Capra's idea to get Huston to Italy to work on a documentary. The pressures to get quality American filmmakers into the combat theater were growing daily. After an initial bump at Salerno, things seemed to be going well for the Fifth Army in Italy. Why not have Huston hook up with Mark Clark for the army's presumed triumphal march to Rome? The subsequent film, complete with images of cheering Italians and caring Allied soldiers, would be shown as psychological tool in occupied territories.[8]

In the spirit of the Allied film ventures represented (or not) by *Tunisian Victory,* Huston asked Ambler if he would like to travel to Italy on this new documentary project. Ambler agreed to serve as writer, and Capra became the Executive Producer of the project. Conferences in London with representatives of the American Office of War Information, the British Ministry of Information, and the Public Relations office of European Theater of Operations U.S. Army (ETOUSA) produced a title, "Welcome to Italy," but not much else in terms of content and outline.[9]

Huston and Ambler packed and readied for their trip as best they could. They had no real idea what might lie ahead in the mountains of Italy.

12

Winterstellugen

"Italy would break their backs, their bones, and nearly their spirits. But first it would break their hearts, and that heartbreak began north of the Volturno, where the terrain steepened, the weather worsened, and the enemy stiffened."[1]

—Rick Atkinson, Day of Battle

AT FIRST GLANCE, the Naples campaign looked to Allied command like a qualified success. The near disaster in mid-September at Salerno—the day when the Germans had exploited the gap between the Sele and Calore Rivers and nearly drove the American Fifth Army all the way back to the beach—was set aside. Mistakes had been made. There had been some indecisiveness and a lack of communication in the command, and Ernest Dawley ended up paying the price for those mistakes. Clark was encouraged by Eisenhower to cashier the general and he did.

But in spite of some messiness, the landings in Italy had taken place and Allied troops now had boots on the ground in Europe, seemingly poised to move quickly up the peninsula toward Rome. In fact, talk of taking the Eternal City by Christmas was heard not just among enthusiastic soldiers, but with Allied commanders as

well. Eisenhower cabled Marshall on October 4 to say that both he
and British Field Marshal Alexander felt that Rome might be actually taken by the end of October. Churchill and Roosevelt were
likewise encouraged. FDR sent a message to Stalin that "It looks as
if American and British armies should be in Rome in another few
weeks."[2]

It had taken the Allies just a month to take Naples and the cost,
while high had not been alarmingly so—12,500 British and American casualties: 2,000 killed in action, 7,000 wounded, and 3,500
missing.[3] Of course, Naples' harbor was virtually destroyed in the
process, negating its value as an Allied port. And the aims of the invasion remained soft. Of the two stated purposes —to take Italy out
of the war, and to keep German divisions occupied and away from
other fronts, East and West—the first had been attained even before
the first troops set down in Italy; and the second was not so much a
goal as a continuing task.

Despite these cautions, some Allied strategists began to double-
down on the original plans. This thinking went that taking Italy all
the way to the Alps would be advantageous to the entire European
theater. It would make an attack on southern France, timed to co-
incide with next year's cross-channel invasion, an easier chore if
troops were fully occupying the Italian peninsula. It would further
mean that German troops were fighting in Italy rather than France
or on the Eastern Front. There was a strong feeling, too, that German resistance would be less obstinate on the road to Rome. It just
didn't make a lot of sense, went this line of thinking, for the Germans to expend a lot of military capital in the defense of Italy. The
more they did so, the greater the advantage to the Allies elsewhere
in Europe.

In fact, within the German high command a fierce debate about
how much of Italy to defend *was* being waged. Erwin Rommel, who
commanded Italian troops in the north, argued forcefully for a Ger-

man retreat to just below the Po River. It simply wasn't worth it, in his estimation, to be waging a strong defensive war in a strategically unimportant land.

Albert Kesselring commanded the eight divisions in southern Italy, and argued just as forcefully that Rome ought to be defended. The narrowest part of the Italian peninsula could be found just north of Naples, he said. Eighty-five miles of rocky, mountainous terrain made for an ideal defensive line running across the waist of Italy. It was perfect territory in which to bog down the Allied advance and make British and American forces pay a heavy price for every inch of ground. In an argument that exactly mirrored optimistic Allied thinking, Kesselring suggested that if a large contingent of Allied forces were fighting in Italy, they would not be amassing in England for a more direct assault on Europe. In early October, he was able to convince Hitler of the efficacy of defending this line, despite Rommel's objections.[4]

Allied interrogation of German prisoners of war taken at the end of the Naples campaigns revealed that the Germans were setting up a series of *Winterstellungen,* or winter positions. Constructed by German reserves and forced Italian labor, along the narrow stretch of central Italy, the lines were being built from the Tyrrhenian Sea all the way across to the Adriatic, in order to stop Allied advances south of Rome for the winter.

The landscape was daunting enough anyway. North of the Volturno River, just above Naples, was about forty miles of rugged hills and mountains characterized by narrow roads, steep climbs and rocky streams running from the heights toward the coast. The mountains were part of the Appenine range, which ran down Italy's mid-section like a nobby spine, and ranged from heights near four thousand feet downward.

Beyond this cluster of mountains lay the Liri Valley, an expanse that ran north toward Rome and was key to the Allied advance and the German defense. The main German Winter Line, called the Gustav, followed the Garigliano River up from the Tyrrhenian coast, where it hooked up with the Rapido River, running down from the heights around an old monastery on top of Monte Cassino. This was the staunchest German defensive post, the one that Kesselring felt would be extremely difficult to breech and would be asked to hold the Allies through the whole of the coming season.

As an additional measure however, the Germans constructed another line just ahead of the Gustav. This was called the Bernhardt, or the first Winter Line, and it was constructed south of the Gustav, along the entrance to the Liri. The Bernhardt was meant to halt the Allies temporarily, but it would ultimately prove as formidable as the Gustav Line.

The Bernhardt Line was a series of interconnecting defensive positions centered around a cluster of mountains and villages on the north side of the Volturno River plain. Highway 6, the famed Via Latina, the ancient pathway to Rome, ran through this plain and squeezed between the mountains, before coming out again in the Liri Valley. The tallest of the peaks was Mt. Sammucro, an almost 4,000-foot high rocky massif that overlooked the Liri Valley to the east, and shaded the village of San Pietro, which was built into its side. Fronting Sammucro on the road from Naples, were the smaller mountains: Mignano, Lungo, Rotundo, Camino, La Difensa, Maggiore. All were formidable and more than able to present difficulties for an advancing army.

To the northeast of Sammucro, ran the spiny ridges of the Appenine mountain chain, which extended back into the Italian interior and across the narrow mid-section of the country. Here four-thousand-foot summits became commonplace, but villages and people were not. Just two narrow and hazardous roads probed the region from Highway 6, clinging to hillsides as they traversed the mountains. So restrictive was the access to the region that the German Winter Lines evaporated not far into the mountain range.

In the days following the capture of Naples, Mark Clark set up his Fifth Army Headquarters in the stunning Palace of Caserta, an eighteenth century, 1,200-room structure built by the Bourbon monarchs of Naples on vast grounds about twenty kilometers from Naples. It was just south of the Volturno, which would be the first obstacle the army would face on its continued path to Rome. The allied plan was for the brunt of the assault to begin here in October, with the Fifth leading an initial push toward Rome.

The next step was for the British Eighth Army, fighting all the way over on the east coast of Italy, to take up the cudgel around mid-November. The operation called for the Eighth to sweep up the Adriatic coast and then swing quickly across the peninsula to attack Rome from the northeast. Meanwhile, the rested Fifth Army would reengage the Germans at the end of November to continue the push from the south.[5]

Anyone holding a topographical map of Italy could sense a problem in this plan. The geography of the country made it obvious that the German defenders would hold the high ground and all the mountain passes. To enhance this natural advantage, German engineers had made every possible use of terrain to construct solid rock and concrete fortifications all along the Fifth Army front. They blew up bridges and culverts; they mined roads and mountain passes. They spent the weeks of October working on their lines, hiding machine gun and mortar nests in impregnable rocky sites, zeroed in on every possible path Allied forces might use.

Razor-sharp concertina wire was strung along points beyond thickly laid minefields; artillery was hidden behind hundreds of mountain crags and crests and spotted throughout the region on bivouac sites, highways, and every conceivable path. Concrete pillboxes shored up the lines in the Liri Valley and around Cassino.

Each of the mountains just north of the Volturno—Sammucro, Rotondo, Cannavinelle, Mignano, Lungo, Camino, La Difensa, Maggiore—bristled with German posts. Five enemy divisions, the XIV Panzer Corps, would man the defenses with reinforcements from the north, quickly available.

The Germans were going to contest every yard on the way to Rome.

THE POSITIONS of the German Panzer troops stood squarely in front of the Fifth Army at Caserta. It was here that the American divisions that had swept through Sicily—the 3rd, the 34th, the 45th— took the lead in the October fight in Italy. Lucian Truscott's 3rd Division stepped off on October 13 and soon splashed into the Volturno itself. To their left flank, nearer the Tyrrhenian Coast, British divisions from the X Corps headed out through the boggy and mine-filled grounds.

With virtually every bridge across the meandering river blown, Truscott found it was easier to get troops across the river than his tanks and other vehicles. The Volturno flowed in a winding northeast-to-southwest direction, at a slight angle to Truscott's northerly march. The river snaked back on itself so often that in order for troops to move forward in some semblance of a straight line, they had to cross and re-cross the river, as if they were working their way up a coiled spring. That meant that engineers were forced to bridge and re-bridge the river as well. Engineers worked feverishly to construct and keep open the flow of vehicle traffic over the Volturno even as German artillery landed around their labors. Despite all of the difficulties, by the afternoon of October 14, a good flow of equipment was streaming across the river.

It wasn't the river alone that provided engineering challenges for Lucian Truscott's advance. Cold, wet weather moved into the region and settled, soon making a quagmire of the low-lying areas leading up to the first line of hills north of the Volturno. Allied vehicles using the limited number of roads heading northeast towards Rome were either mired in mud, or susceptible to German sabotage. They had mined everything. Or as British High Commander Harold Alexander put it, "All roads lead to Rome, but all roads are mined."[6]

The Volturno and its tributaries kept overflowing their banks in the autumn rain, destroying just built Allied pontoon bridges and the corduroy roads that had been constructed to negotiate the mire. The Germans blocked village streets by blowing up stone buildings; they cratered roads; they hid mines on footpaths and farm trails, river fords and back alleys. The mines didn't just slow vehicle traffic: they took their toll on the infantry as well. Booby traps took life and limb. The muck and mire sapped spirit. Every step forward was slowed either by mud or the need for caution.

For all the headaches and difficulties, the push north of the Volturno toward the mountains, slowly continued. The Germans yielded ground, delaying but not halting the Allied advance, allowing it closer to those hills, where even as Truscott and his divisions came nearer, the Germans were fine-tuning their next impediments at the Bernhardt Line.

Since early October, the Germans had stripped the village of San Pietro of its manpower and draft animals to labor on defenses. Two hundred men between the ages of fifteen and forty-five were forced to haul supplies up the mountains and build entrenchments for the Germans. Knowing what was coming to the area, most of the remaining residents of the village evacuated themselves to a miserable life in a number of caves that dotted the hillsides surrounding the village. Food quickly began to run out. The town well, dug in the heart of San Pietro, was inaccessible. Periodically the Germans would sweep through the village and the caves, looking for San Pietrans fit enough to provide more slave labor in building more defenses in the area.[7]

Even before the Bernhardt Line, the Germans had constructed a chain of outposts meant to delay the Allies once they crossed the Volturno. These ran across the Mignano Gap and Highway 6, up into the mountains on either side of these lowlands. Given the delays caused by the German defenses, the overflowing Volturno, and the deplorable weather, Truscott's divisions moved as quickly as possible to a point where they were ready to probe the German positions.

What they could see in the distance as they approached the Bernhardt Line was Sammucro, the tall, bare mountain that loomed above San Pietro and everything else in the area. Below Sammucro down to the south in the direction of Naples, was Mt. Rotondo and Mt. Cannavinelle. Mt. Lungo was to the southwest, and between it and Mt. Rotondo, to the south, was the Mignano Ridge and Mignano Gap. Running through the gap and into the Liri Valley was Highway 6. Nearest to the Fifth Army position were Mt. Camino and Mt. La Difensa.

As Truscott and his 3rd Division prepared to face the defenses in front of them, they were already exhausted from their month-long effort. So, too, were the 34th and 45th divisions, positioned on the 3rd's right flank. The same was true of the two British divisions on Truscott's left.

Relief was in the works: the 36th Division was prepping for the moment—coming soon—when it would replace the 3rd Division at the center of the Allied assault. But at the same time, the pressure to continue moving forward was intense. Rome by Christmas might not have been a realistic timetable any longer, but after the victory in Tunisia, and the swift taking of Sicily, continued expectations of a well-paced advance were high. A whole month had passed and the Fifth Army was only a few miles further along the Italian peninsula than they were in Naples.

The realization that the Germans were digging in to defend Rome and central Italy against the Allied advance seemed almost

like an affront to public sentiment. The Germans simply weren't doing the expected. They were dragging the Allies into a fight at some
godawful site in the mountains of Italy. But any second thoughts
about the operation among Allied command were stifled: a commitment had been made to invade Italy, and now a commitment was
made to make something of that invasion.

Clark decided to probe German forces. The British divisions on
the left were asked to swing around Mt. Camino, the first of the
rocky, barren summits on the way to the Liri Valley. On November
5, the Brits set off and ran smack into the Bernhardt Line, with all
its "mines, machine guns, and mortar pits . . ." The fighting quickly
turned murderous with British soldiers "claw[ing] up a succession of
summits only to find that they were false crests overshadowed by
still higher ground."[8] The German positions were so well laid out
that it felt like they had been there for years. In spite of this, the
British forces somehow made it to the summit.

Panzer counterattacks came close to sweeping the British brigade
off Camino, but they hung on—without winter gear and desperately short of food and water—for a full week before Clark merci-
fully called for their withdrawal.

In the meantime, Truscott's troops had begun an assault on the
ridge that connected Mt. Camino and Mt. La Difensa. The ridge
was likewise well-defended by the Germans. The 3rd, after a tough,
ten-day fight, was ultimately as unsuccessful as the British.

Not to be thwarted, Clark asked Truscott to send his infantry
against both Mt. Lungo, which rose above the Mignano Gap, and
Mt. Rotondo, which stood to the east of Lungo on the other side of
the Gap. The 3rd Infantry was able to capture the summit of the
brush covered Rotondo, but could only grasp a toehold on Mt.
Lungo.

On the far right of the American line, the 34th and 45th Divisions made some headway into the mountains, but here, deeper in

the Italian interior, the Appenine terrain was even rougher than the sections surrounding San Pietro. So rough, in fact, that the Germans discounted their ability to make any meaningful headway against them. As one German commander put it, "Enemy gains constituted no grave threat and every step forward into the mountainous terrain merely increased his difficulties."[9]

His men exhausted, his division depleted by more than 8,500 casualties since its arrival in Sicily, the time was nigh for Lucian Truscott to pack it in and wait for the 36th to arrive and take over the struggle.

Rome still lay in the distance.

13

Replacements

ON OCTOBER 8, GENERAL FRED WALKER learned from Mark Clark in Naples that General John Lucas had been chosen to replace Ernest Dawley as Corps Commander, despite the fact that Clark had promised Walker that post "if anything happened to Dawley." Again, Walker swallowed his disappointment, telling his diary, "I am satisified where I am."[1]

He was otherwise occupied with the demands of his command. The 36th headed into reserve for a few weeks while the 3rd Division took over primary combat duties. The 36th's bivouac area was moved closer to the front—near the city of Nola, northeast of Naples and southeast of Caserta, where Clark had set up Fifth Army headquarters. Walker authorized visits from 36th Division troops to Capri, Pompeii and Naples. Many got to tour Vesuvius and Pompeii as well.

The weather turned damp, chill and rainy as the move to Nola was made. Toward the end of October, Walker visited Clark at Caserta and learned that he was considering an amphibious assault against the Germans in an attempt to outflank the line that the enemy was establishing north of the Volturno. A lack of amphibious assault craft and the difficult terrain at potential landing sites made the planning seem impractical to Walker, who hoped that Clark would not order such an effort.

Replacement troops were filling the ranks of the 143rd and the rest of the 36th Division after the operations in Salerno and the Sorrento Peninsula. They were sorely needed. Of its near 14,000-man strength at the start of the campaign, the 36th had lost almost 2,000 killed, wounded, or missing in action. The 143rd was hit hardest: 8 officers were killed in action, as were 124 enlisted men. Total wounded was above 300. Captured were 35 officers and 153 enlisted men, and missing in action, most of whom were presumed prisoners of the Germans, numbered 4 officers and 488 enlisted men. The bulk of these were lost from the 2nd Battalion in the fighting between the Sele and Calore Rivers during the second week of the battle.[2]

The Texas Division quickly grew less Texan, as its ranks were filled with newcomers from all corners of the country, including Ben Palmer, a farm kid from upstate New York. Palmer had spent his senior year in high school on an assembly line, building military transport planes at the Curtiss-Wright plant in Buffalo. Before the school year was done he turned eighteen, registered for the draft, and entered the U.S. Army in February 1943. After five months of basic training, he shipped out of Norfolk, Virginia for North Africa in late July.

After landing in Casablanca, Palmer and his fellow soldiers, now dubbed the 36th Replacement Battalion, spent a few days in Morocco before being shipped by train to Oran and then Bizerte. Palmer, blond-haired and full-cheeked, looked younger than his eighteen years and was still wide-eyed. He noted that the old Moroccan steam engines had been made in Elmyra, New York, just 120 miles from his home. They moved so slowly that it took days to make the journey from Casablanca to Oran, and troops were actually able to jump out of their cars on the journey and grab melons from the passing fields and jump back before the train passed away. Apparently, the allure of Moroccan melons remained irresistible within the 36th.

Soon after he'd arrived in Bizerte, Palmer and the others heard news that the 36th had been involved in the invasion of Italy at Salerno. It wasn't until October, however that the replacements shipped to Naples, and got their first sight of the devastation wrought by the Germans as they were evacuating. The city was a shambles and the streets were full of little boys begging for food.

It was here that Palmer got his assignment: he was to serve as a replacement in the 143rd Infantry Regiment, whose strength had been depleted by 65 percent. Specifically, he was to join Henry Waskow's Company B.

When he arrived at Nola, Palmer was informed by company veterans—those same men who had never experienced combat until a month earlier—that Waskow was a standup guy. Aside from a quick greeting, Palmer had no conversation with the captain. He was told to join up with the platoon headed by Sergeant Herbert Golden, a Mexia native. Palmer shared a tent with six other GI's and slept on a canvas cot elevated above the soggy Italian soil by a wooden platform. A large kitchen tent provided hot meals for the company, and showers were available behind a canvas screen. It was pretty sumptuous living by field camp standards.[3]

Especially by comparison to the Italian villagers, who had taken to hillside caves during the battle and consequent destruction of their homes. The natives hung around the camp begging for food and sustenance. Their lives, impoverished to begin with, had turned destitute with invasion. They'd bring buckets and hang out outside the kitchen tent, waiting for soldiers to scrape leftovers into their tins.

In the first week of November, the 143rd executed a practice river crossing of the Volturno—just surmounted by Truscott and company—in preparation for future operations that winter. The Rapido River lay just in front of the Gustav line near Cassino and would need to be crossed for the advance to Rome to continue. For now, it seemed to the infantrymen slogging over the Volturno that this was just another of the endless amphibious exercises they had undertaken, like those back at Cape Cod, Morocco, and Oran.

Maps soon arrived at 143rd headquarters indicating just where they were headed on the frontline. Along with the rest of the 36th, they would be taking the battle directly to the German Winter Line, even now being firmed up in the mountains beyond the Volturno.

ERNIE PYLE's fame followed him back to the front. On just his second day back in the Mediterranean theater, he found himself standing in Dwight Eisenhower's office in Algiers, autographing a copy of his book for the commander. The next day, he was on a flight to Naples and just hours after that, he was heading north toward the front to join an artillery unit nearing the German Winter Line.

Pyle was given a room at the palace in Caserta, along with others in the press corps. He took a moment to write a letter to Jerry, but Pyle was in a dark mood and afterward worried about passing his afflictions on to his troubled wife: "The long winter misery has started. By this time tomorrow night I will be in the lines," he wrote. "Sometimes I've felt that I couldn't make myself go, but now that I'm here I want to take the plunge . . . I feel very strange and lonely here, as I always do in new places. I wonder about you and think about you and hate myself for ever having left you, and yet I suppose I would have hated myself if I hadn't come back . . ."[4]

Pyle ventured out to get the lay of the land. The roads between Naples and the Winter Line were thick with truck convoys, both British and American, "pounding" along at forty and fifty miles per hour. The nice macadam roadbeds paved by Il Duce prior to the war were fast being wracked into potholes by the traffic, and Allied engineers worked to repair them even as the trucks continued to roll.

Sycamore trees lined the entrance to the various Italian cities along the way, Pyle wrote, giving the sense of "driving through a beautiful tunnel"; but the towns and villages themselves had been mercilessly pounded first by Allied bombs and artillery, when they were occupied by Germans; then by German artillery when they were Allied-occupied. Street after street was stony rubble.

Pyle also saw "thousands of stenciled and painted signs" along the highway, "directing drivers to the numerous units," both American and British which dotted the landscape. At crossroads, the signs would be so thick that it was necessary to pull the jeep to the side of the road to decipher just where a destination could be found. It was like looking for a particular resort sign among dozens tacked to a tree at one of the Minnesota lakes, which Jerry had been raised among. Burma shave style signs were also popular, including one gently admonishing soldiers for their habit of discarding necessary gear to lighten their loads: "If you leave/good clothes behind/you may need them/some other time."

His initial impressions of the Italian landscape hailed the "uncommon beauty" of what he saw. Fertile valleys farmed up the steep slopes of hills until the rocky ridges left no soil in which to plant; stone farmhouses and sheds dotting the valley landscapes; distant mountaintops hidden in clouds; the Italians going about their business in the wake of the war passing through, hiding only when the German planes flew overhead.

But then as he delved further into the countryside, trod the path of invasion from Salerno northward, he found a countryside devastated by fighting. Every town that had been occupied by the Germans had consequently been shelled into heaps of rubble by the Allies, and still, day and night, the cannon fire rained down north of

Naples. Even the farm land, on closer inspection, revealed the ravages of war: "the limb of an olive tree broken off, six swollen dead horses in the corner of a field, a strawstack burned down, a chestnut tree blown clear out, roots and all, by a German bomb, little gray patches of powder burns on the hillside, scraps of broken and abandoned rifles and grenades in the bushes, grain fields patterned with a million crisscrossing ruts from the great trucks that had crawled frame-deep through the mud . . ."[5]

He ran into Dick Tregaskis, the war correspondent and author of *Guadalcanal Diary*, who had been at Salerno with Mark Clark and briefly visited 1st Battalion on the Sorrento Peninsula. Tregaskis was in a field hospital with a serious head wound inflicted by a German mortar while he was with the 3rd Infantry near the Volturno. He showed Pyle his helmet, which had a two-inch gash in its steel plating where the shrapnel had plunged into this head. Though he was on the mend, Tregaskis was not well. Pyle noted that he had trouble signing his name to a copy of his book when a wounded soldier asked for an autograph.

Ernie spent some time with an artillery unit back of the frontlines. He jeeped around the mid-section of Italy, visiting Pompeii and Naples, and spent time at Caserta at Allied Headquarter. He hooked up with *Stars and Stripes* cartoonist Bill Mauldin in Mauldin's little Naples studio. Mauldin was just a kid, twenty-two years old when Pyle profiled him, but his cartoons, which were like Pyle's writing in sketch-form, depicted a mature vision of the war. He drew GIs—grimy infantrymen, unshaven and rough, with both cigarettes and a sardonic line or two always dangling from their lips. As with Pyle, the guys on the frontline thought that Mauldin was getting things right, and appreciated him for it. A larger audience awaited: he was about to go syndicated at home which would soon bring his iconic characters, Willie and Joe, to readers across the country.

Pyle also visited a group of German POW's being held at a collection point behind Allied lines. There were Poles and Austrians in the group, as well as proud Nazis. He reported that the latter usually arrived feeling confident that Germany was still in control of its fate in this world war, but were immediately made uneasy at those prospects when they saw the collection of Allied supplies and equipment, jamming the roads south of the frontlines.

Pyle joined the 36th toward the end of November and saw, with a GI's eyes, what they were seeing. There was rain and more rain. "The country was shockingly beautiful, and just as shockingly hard to capture from the enemy," Pyle wrote. "The hills rose to high ridges of almost solid rock. We couldn't go around them through the flat peaceful valleys, because the Germans were up there looking down upon us, and they would have let us have it. So we had to go up and over. A mere platoon of Germans, well dug in on a high, rock-spined hill, could hold out for a long time against tremendous onslaughts."[6]

It was long evident by the time Pyle arrived that the Allies were not going to take Rome by Christmas. He tried to explain the difficulties faced by the troops in Italy to an audience back in the States, which had become accustomed to quick advances. It had been just three weeks from Salerno to Naples; now two months had passed and the combined efforts of the Allies had only pushed the Germans about forty miles from Naples, and the Germans were firmly entrenched in a mountainous line between the Fifth Army and Rome.

Pyle described the almost "inconceivable misery" in which the troops were fighting: "Thousands of the men had not been dry for weeks. Other thousands lay at night in the high mountains with the temperature below freezing and the thin snow sifting over them. They dug into the stones and slept in little chasms and behind rocks and in half-caves. They lived like men of prehistoric times, and a club would have been welcome more than a machine gun . . ."

Even if there had been no German fighting troops in Italy, Pyle said, just engineers to blow up bridges in the passes, the slog to Rome would have been slow.[7]

Who knew if any of this was registering with the folks back home? It was a hard truth that this was going to be a long arduous war. These mountains in Italy were like a promise of that fact. Yet who wanted to hear that?

14

Thanksgiving

GENERAL WALKER WAS PLEASED with the orderly fashion in which his division replaced Truscott's 3rd on the frontline. He was disturbed by the nature of the terrain and the fact that the Germans had assumed "very strong and well-coordinated defensive positions" all along the Bernhardt Line. Simply put, they held the heights at the center and flanks and had been fortifying the line for almost two months now. Defensive posts were well-concealed and well-constructed. The 36th, along with the British 56th Division on the left, would have to take them, hill by hill.

Walker set up his command post near four caves, which served as sleeping quarters for him and his staff. He entertained Clark and Major General Geoffrey Keyes soon after his division was in place, and again on the Tuesday before Thanksgiving. Keyes was the commander of the Army's II Corps, to which the 36th had just been reassigned. Both he and Clark, feeling pressures of their own from higher command, were anxious for Walker to prep his troops for the coming assault against the German line. Walker described them as "having ants in their pants" and was perturbed when Clark labeled Walker's division as "fresh," as if discounting the difficulties they encountered moving into the position and its hard fighting at Salerno.[1]

Walker's division was arrayed across a five-mile front. On the left, the 142nd was aimed at Mt. Camino and Mt. La Difensa, with an ultimate goal of sweeping beyond these first two mountains (both were more than 3,000 feet high) to Mt. Maggiore. Joining them in the attack on La Difensa was First Special Service Force, a joint Canadian-American outfit composed to a large extent of ex-lumbermen from the Canadian Rockies and Pacific Northwest, who had been specially trained in mountain warfare. As in the early November operation overseen by Truscott, the British—now in the form of 56th Division—would occupy the far left and again try to sweep around Camino.

The 141st's 1st and 2nd battalions were positioned on hills opposite one another: Mt. Lungo on the left, and Mt. Rotondo on the right. Smack dab between them was Via Latina. Lungo was still only partially occupied by the 36th and troops positioned in its southeast corner received a great deal of attention from enemy mortar and artillery fire because the mountain, unlike the brush-covered Rontodo, was a barren pile of rocks.

Camino, still occupied by the Germans, was to the southwest of Lungo and Rotondo, and gunners lobbed their shells and mortars at the 141st as it clung to the hillsides. To the north across the valley stood San Pietro and Mt Sammucro. Here, too, German artillery spotters were kept busy eyeing the activities across the valley and pointing gunners toward their targets.

On the far right of the 36th's position, the 143rd shared Rotondo with the 141st and occupied Mt. Cannavinelle on the distant right flank as well. No roads accessed Cannavinelle. The 143rd arrived there in the dark of night on November 15, with the 2nd and 3rd battalions of the regiment immediately moving out to relieve 3rd Infantry troops.

Lee Fletcher, a Bazooka man in Company I, recalled being driven as close as possible to the mountains above the Liri Valley from the bivouac northeast of Naples. There was still a far distance to go when they were dropped off. The trail up was narrow, slippery, rocky and incredibly steep, and made all the more arduous by the persistent rain, the fact that he was lugging a Bazooka, and that all this movement had to be done at night to avoid German shelling. It took two days just to get into position, in part due to the fact that daylight hours had to be spent hidden among the brush and vines that covered the hillsides. They finally reached the site vacated by the 3rd and occupied their foxholes. In the continuing rain, the holes quickly became muddy bathtubs.[2]

Mt. Cannavinelle overlooked the Liri Valley. About a mile across the valley to the northeast sat the tallest of the peaks in the area, Sammucro. Nestled into its side just above the valley floor was San Pietro, surrounded by terraced groves of olive trees. Down the road a few miles to the right of the 143rd was the village of Venafro.

Cannavinelle had been taken earlier by the 3rd Infantry in hard fighting and bodies of both Germans and Americans still littered the site. The nastiness of the battle was indicated by the continuing presence of some German corpses, who were garotted with piano wire strung around the necks.[3] Fletcher saw a mule on top of the mountain that had been wounded by artillery fire. Still living, its bladder extruded from its body and hung almost to the ground. A bullet from one of the 143rd GIs put the animal out of its misery.

The 36th outposts stretched along the ridgelines above the valley and from these positions forward artillery observers would spy German posts across the way, and phone them back to the gunners behind the lines. German spotters were doing the same. On both sides, the shells would crash down with the rain, severing the signal corps phone lines, which would then need to be replaced, prompting a flurry of movement, which would then prompt more shelling.

The absence of roads at the 143rd's position on Mt. Cannavinelle required a supply point be established at the terminus of the nearest highway. From there, 270 men and a pack of 30 mules were continuously employed in the process of hauling supplies up a treacherous mountain slope to the battalion position on top of the mountain. Every day, water, rations, clothing replacement, ammunition, and communication wiring was carried up a trail so rough and rock-strewn that according to after-action reports, a good pair of shoes could stand just three trips before falling apart.[4]

Meanwhile, the troops on top of the hill sent patrols out into the valley toward San Pietro, as well as up Mt. Sammucro, to gather as much information as they could about German positions and strength. Information about mines, observations posts, artillery positions and enemy installations, including command and supply posts, was collected. Company E from the 2nd Battalion got all the way to a stone house right next to the village and captured a German machine gun crew who provided valuable information about specific German army units fighting in the area.

German artillery fire was the gravest hazard to the 36th. Death could come in an instant and without warning. Company B, which initially had been stationed in reserve, had not been hit by any of the German shells until the morning of November 19. About 10 a.m., Jack Gordon, Hubert Ingram, and Jack Berry were talking about the coming holidays and how they used to spend them back in Texas. Gordon was showing off a new watch he had gotten from back home for Christmas. Ingram moved on to an errand down the hill from the Company's post. He was just on his way back when he heard a shell whistle overhead and land right in the midst of Company B. He rushed back toward his friends and saw immediately that someone had been hit. It turned out to be Gordon, the thirty-year-old former CCC man, who had found a job in the Mexia textile mill just prior to being called up to serve.

Ingram wound up writing the letter back to Gordon's mother, informing her of his death. He told her that Jack had a lot of friends in the company and elsewhere in the 36th. He wrote that her son had lasted about three minutes after the blast and that it had not been a horrible death. Ingram hoped that she received the watch that had been Jack's early Christmas present. He had seen someone from the mortuary team pack it up to send home with his other personal effects.[5]

It turned out that Jack had already written a letter home, in which he thanked his mother for the watch, and tucked $100 in the envelope for her to get presents for everyone in the family.[6]

When Company B moved from reserve to the top of ridge, it began the process of sending out nighttime rifle patrols, probing the valley and base of Sammucro in preparation for the move against the Germans. The bare hillsides above the tree line made the patrols obvious targets for German mortars and small arms fire. Bennett Palmer, the replacement infantryman from upstate New York, got his baptism of fire on these sorties. Years later, his fears were still vivid and he recalled shooting at anything that moved on those hillsides.

Palmer also recalled the freezing cold and snow on top of the mountains. He noted the sound of his own chattering teeth as it mixed with explosions from the incessant mortar and artillery fire.[7] Conditions were so awful up on the hilltops, that frequent relief was necessary and units would only spend a few days at a time up on the ridges before they were relieved and could go back down the hills. Unfortunately, the relief camps down below didn't provide much in the way of comforts; if the ridges were freezing cold and snowy, the valleys were damp, chilly and thick with mud.

Wet boots, never able to get completely dry, caused an outbreak of trench foot among the troops. The condition, which got its name during World War I because it was so prevalent in the sodden trenches of France, basically rots the feet. Left untreated, numbness from poor circulation is compounded by blisters, sores and fungal infections until necrosis settles in.

Riley Tidwell contracted the malady soon after arriving on the mountain and it would remain with him for much of the winter. The misery of the wet foxholes dominated Tidwell's recollections of the hilltop. The German artillery seemed to quickly zero in on the battalion's feeding schedule. With uncanny timing, the Germans shelled every time members of Company B rose from their wet foxholes to get something to eat. He also recalled eating Thanksgiving dinner while gazing out over a field still littered with dead Germans.

The rain was a constant, which made Tidwell and others grateful for the gas cakes. These were the gas masks issued to each of the infantrymen. Packaged in neat little cake-shaped squares, which gave them their nickname, they were never used except in the foxholes during the rain. In their misery, the guys learned they made good rain gear. By putting the masks over their faces, they could lean back against their packs in the foxholes, and look up into the sky, protected from the ever-present dripping sky—actually get some rest.[8]

For Thanksgiving, General Walker made certain that each man in the division was offered a turkey dinner, making sure cold storage was provided for the meals of those stuck on the frontlines until they were relieved and came down off the mountain. One soldier from the 142nd 1st Battalion was not assuaged by this measure. He recalled shivering in the rain on the top of Mt. Difensa on Thanksgiving Day, 1943. He and his comrades had been told about the turkey dinner and were expecting its arrival all day. From their position, they marked the progress of their meals through the course of the day, first watching as a mule train set out from a supply dump down in the valley and made its way halfway up the mountain. Then the dinner was transferred to the backs of company "mules"—infantrymen drafted into hauling where the mules could not go. With mouths watering, the men at the top of Difensa watched their turkey and stuffing slowly hauled up rope ladders on the backs of their fellow soldiers. Finally it arrived! The packets were unburdened and quickly opened: inside were gallon cans of chili con carne and the promise that their real Thanksgiving dinner awaited them down below. "It was many years before I developed a taste for chili con carne," said Alban Reid.[9]

15

Observers

PHOTOGRAPHER MARGARET BOURKE WHITE visited the 36th on
that same Thanksgiving. None of the GI's knew for sure who she
was, but the officers seemed to accept that she was someone important and made sure she was treated with deference. They gave
her use of a pigsty as a restroom because there were no other en-
closed buildings at the supply dump where they were congregated
and she needed privacy. No one said anything about the fact that
the sty was otherwise used as a gathering place for the battalion.
Later, she went up in one of the planes spotting German positions
for the artillery and took some great panoramic shots of the Liri
Valley.[1,2]

A few days after Thanksgiving, General Walker entertained a
whole slew of reporters, who were joining the 36th for the upcoming campaign. As with the infantry, the press corps had been delayed
by the terrain. They poured into the region. A war that had previously been spread out over pretty wide fronts had narrowed to the
limited territory fronted by the 36th. So Walker, not nearly as comfortable with the press as his Army commander, "Marcus Clarkus,"
now found himself answering questions from the cream of the correspondent crop. Robert Capa was back with the 36th, along with

John Lardner of *Newsweek*, H. R. Knickerbocker of the *Chicago Sun*, Homer Bigart of the *New York Herald Tribune*, Don Whitehead of Associated Press, and several others. The news people shuttled back and forth between the front and Allied headquarters at the palace in Caserta, where press offices were established and rooms—like Ernie Pyle's—were made available. There was also much to do and see in Naples, which is where John Huston had taken up quarters when he first arrived in Italy by way of Marrakesh.

HUSTON AND AMBLER had picked up a third filmmaker, Jules Buck, an old Hollywood production hand now in the Signal Corps, who Huston had asked for from London. Frank Capra had worked through Signal Corps command to see that Buck was assigned to Huston on the project, and Huston and Ambler met him in Morocco. With Huston wearing a pair of smoked aviator glasses that he'd acquired filming with the Army Air Corps on the Aleutian Islands, the trio flew first to Algiers, and then, after some delays getting a flight, on to Italy, where despite the rain, Huston continued to wear his dark glasses. He started to annoy Ambler in the process, who saw a touch of pretension in the look.[3]

Naples' port was still devastated and non-functioning. Cigarettes were the primary medium of exchange and packs of rats appeared in the streets, defiantly waiting to be shooed away. "The men and women of Naples," wrote Huston, "were a bereft, starving, desperate people who do absolutely anything to survive." He described Naples as looking "like a whore suffering the beating of a brute . . ."[4] Little boys offered their sisters and mothers for sale, he claimed. Typhus was everywhere and cholera was anticipated.

Yet at the same time, USO shows were taking place in city theaters to entertain the troops, including an Irving Berlin show at a downtown Naples theater, and allied troops, away from the front-lines, crowded the streets. Huston, upon arriving in the city, soon hooked up with his old friend, Robert Capa, for a bit of carousing before settling into his assignment.

Huston and company soon arrived at Allied headquarters in Caserta, where they reported to Colonel Melvin Gillette, commander of the Fifth Army Signal Corps photographic section. Gillette had arrived in Italy in late September and immediately set to work getting Signal Corps crews out into the field. Like Huston, Gillette had been given the War Department assignment to produce "first-rate pictures . . . to give the American people a visual accounting of the accomplishments of our soldiers overseas." It was his unit that was supposed to illustrate "the dangers and grimness of war."[5] And it was Gillette who had asked the War Department in Washington to send "qualified directors" and "recognized writers" to Italy in order to fashion the sort of films they were requesting. Yet when Huston arrived at Caserta, there was a question of who was in charge, the hotshots from Hollywood, or the Signal Corps?

Huston asked for personnel and equipment from Gillette's 163rd Signal Photo Company (SPC). He assumed he would be given assistance and autonomy to make the sort of documentary that he, Ambler and others had discussed in London. Gillette assumed Huston would be working for him, and was unimpressed with Huston's smoky glasses, Hollywood bona fides, his VIP friends, and the two pals he'd brought to Italy with him. Huston (and Ambler as well) was likewise unimpressed with Gillette, whom Ambler sarcastically characterized as someone who knew all about filmmaking "thanks to an eight-week guided tour of Hollywood studios" made "to prepare him for this mission."[6]

To make matters even more uncomfortable, Gillette, Huston, Ambler and Buck all wound up sharing the same sleeping quarters in Caserta, in a house next door to the grand palace. Huston complained about Ambler's loud snores. For his part, Ambler awoke one night late to hear Huston explaining "the subtleties of filmmaking to the colonel" including the differences between cutting from a scene and panning away from it.

Days passed during this awkward impasse. A message finally arrived from the War Department clarifying Huston's status in no uncertain terms to Gillette. A lot of trouble had been taken to get Huston to Italy, was its substance. He was to be given all necessary assistance in collecting combat footage for a documentary. It was clear that Huston was working with the blessing of some power in the War Department, and Gillette quickly assigned a camera and sound crew of five members of the 163rd to the Hollywood hotshot. Through no fault of his own, however, Gillette was still short of transportation to get Huston and his crew around the front.[7]

Buck, who had quickly learned to apply his jack-of-all-trades Hollywood skills to his work in the Signal Corps, was somehow able to secure a jeep for Huston and company. By early December, they were on their way to a unit on the right flank of the Fifth Army line, out by the village of Venafro. Like Ernie Pyle, Huston's film crew was meeting up with the 143rd Regiment.[8]

It had long since been obvious that the original plan for the documentary—filming the taking of Rome, and the triumphal entry of Allied troops into the city—was not going to happen anytime soon. The revised outline for a film was to create a documentary describing the difficulties Allied troops were facing in Italy with a focus on the infantry. Huston and company would follow American troops as they attacked the German Winter Line and captured the next Italian village on the path leading into the Liri Valley and onto Rome. This was the "dangers and grimness of war" angle which the War Department had been clamoring for since early September. The sense among all in the field was that realistic footage of infantry work would help explain why the Allied advance had bogged down north of Naples. It would show, in documentary form, the life of the GI, in much the same way that Ernie Pyle's writing was illustrating that life in the papers. It was time to let motion pictures lift the veil on the war experience of the typical infantryman.

Units of the 163rd Signal Corps had already been shooting film through October and early November, but their work illustrated some of the difficulties and dangers of meeting the request of the War Department for actual combat footage. As they would soon report to the War Department, it was possible to get a lot of film of the "grimness and dangers of war" variety—footage of the dead and wounded (both friend and foe); footage of burials, surgical operations, uprooted Italian refugees. As wells as human interest material—"material which will show how the ordinary soldier lives, works, rests and relaxes, fights, suffers; footage covering the various national and racial types of the men under arms in this theater." But for all this, combat footage of the "studio war" variety—explosions, sagging bodies, soldiers charging from their foxholes—remained missing. Despite "venturing so close to enemy lines that we draw fire, [camera crews] were unable to see, let alone photograph anything that is usually accepted as combat material." It was just too dangerous. A man trying to film in battle with his bulky camera had to expose himself to fire in order to get shots; he was just too obvious a target.[9]

Captain Huston and company heard of these difficulties from the Signal Corps crew that had been assigned to them, but Huston, who had filmed in precarious circumstances before on the Aleutian Islands, was not the sort of man who took it-can't-be-done for an answer. He kept his own counsel about his intentions, but fully intended to get the sort of footage that the War Department wanted.

16

Eve of Battle

ON DECEMBER 2, Walker met with Clark, Keyes, and all the ranking officers of his own 36th Division, to finalize plans for an assault against the mass of hills guarding the Liri Valley. Set to begin the very next day, the code name for the attack had an ironic ring to it. They called it, "Operation Raincoat."

This was the assault that was supposed to bring momentum back to the Allied cause and get them jumpstarted on a more effective path to Rome. Everyone recognized that the Germans held the high ground, but nothing seemed insurmountable that night. There were mountains, but they could be taken. There was a well-defended village and a string of solid defenses in the valley, but they could be destroyed. The rain remained relentless, but it fell on the Germans as well as the Allies.

The First Special Services Force, the combined American and Canadian woodsmen trained in the Rocky Mountains for just this type of warfare, was to start off the operation on the far left flank at Mt. La Difensa. Their assault was to be immediately followed by the 142nd against Mt. Maggiore to the right of La Difensa.

Both attacks were to be preceded by a massive artillery barrage that would rain shells from 900 guns down upon German positions on the mountaintops. The blasting, accompanied by bombing runs from the Army air force, would begin that night and continue for days, expending so much explosive fury on the hills to the south of San Pietro that Mt. Maggiore was soon dubbed "The Million Dollar Mountain" for the costs involved in its pulverizing.[1] Once the bombing began, the din echoing in the valleys was nonstop and so deafening that the commander of one German army corps said later that he had not witnessed a similar display of awesome firepower since the big battles of World War I.[2]

Attacking in the dark of the early morning on December 3, the First Special Services Force took La Difensa before dawn with relative speed. They watched, on the plateau down below, as the 142nd moved toward the slopes of Mt. Maggiore and a couple of smaller ridges that comprised the hill mass across the Liri Valley from San Pietro. The 142nd faced some vicious artillery fire from the Germans, but moved with alacrity over the plateau and into the hills. By evening of December 3, they held the ground just short of Maggiore, and by nightfall on the fourth, they'd taken the Million Dollar Mountain as well.

But it was the counterattacks against both the 142nd and the First Special Services Force where the bloodletting was wholesale. The top of La Difensa was a saucer-shaped rocky field rimmed by the men of the Special Services, but facing nasty mortar and machine-gun fire, as well as the ever-present rain. There were no available units to relieve the Special Services—every part of the 36th was dedicated to other areas along the front—which left Colonel Robert Frederick alone to deal with the brutal assaults against his command. There was nothing to do but stand and fight. Frederick grew so busy dealing with German counter assaults that he wrote in a dispatch that "[he had] stopped burying the dead." In all, his unit would sustain 511 casualties—a third of his force—including 73 killed.[3] But by the evening the Germans crept away from the area and the hill mass that ran from La Difensa to Maggiore was securely in Allied hands. The first hole was punched in the Winter Line.

The Germans were hardly going away, however. They still held the northern most peak of Mt. Lungo, which was actually a set of ridges that stretched northward from Mignano. The Germans still held the mile-wide Liri Valley, as well. Here defenses, anchored by a line of formidable pillboxes and interconnecting trenches, were arrayed from the terraced orchards that fronted San Pietro, west to the slopes of Lungo. Defensive posts were also arranged around the village and banked into the slopes of Mt. Sammucro itself. Near constant pounding by artillery and air support of the German bunkers and pillboxes had unfortunately done little damage.

Sammucro was the linchpin of the Bernhardt Line. It rose abruptly from the Liri Valley floor to several high, daunting peaks, but then stretched east in a lengthy series of ridges that swept toward the Italian interior as far as the eye could see. The bulk of the mountain loomed bare and rugged above the valley, with no vegetation above a tree line that extended just a third of the way up the mountain; it was all hard rock and jagged angles up to a height that seemed stratospheric from the floor of the Liri.

This was to be the next obstacle for Walker and the 36th, and simultaneous to its assault would be an attack on Mt. Lungo, undertaken by a portion of the Italian army in its first combat on behalf of the Allied cause. Keyes had notified Walker that he wanted Italian troops utilized in the battle, and suggested a target that was under-defended, which Lungo appeared to be. Though Walker was less than impressed with the Italian commander, he accepted the help and on December 7, the Italians moved into position for the attack.[4]

Meanwhile, the 143rd, situated at Mt. Cannavinelle on the right flank of the 36th Division position across the valley from Sammucro, was preparing to assault German positions on the higher mountain.

Its mission had already been assigned and battalions were moving into place, even as the Italians edged toward Lungo.

The evening of December 6, Colonel William Martin gathered all the officers of the 143rd to brief them on the upcoming operations.

The 1st Battalion would move under cover of darkness across the valley and up the spine of Mt. Sammucro on the right flank. It was to move west up the mountain and assault and conquer its peak, which overlooked the valley, San Pietro, and San Vittore to the north.

The 2nd Battalion would target San Pietro itself, on the left flank of the 143rd. One company was to secure the village by occupying the high ground to its northeast; the remainder would, as directed by 143rd Colonel William Martin, "quickly mop up the town and establish all-around security to the southwest and to the east."[5]

Trailing the 2nd Battalion at a distance of 700 yards would be the 3rd Battalion, whose assignment was to reinforce the 2nd on both flanks and to deal with "hostile elements on the south slopes" of the mountain. After the principal objectives were taken—the mountaintop in the case of the 1st, San Pietro and the mountain-side above the village in the case of the 2nd and 3rd—the 1st was to reach down the mountain, the 2nd, and 3rd to reach up, and together they would gather themselves in preparation for moving on toward Vittore, the next rock in the German defensive wall.

In support of these attacks, were mortar and antitank units positioned southwest of Mt. Rotondo, and also further to the west, on the road between Venafro and San Pietro. Two battalions of artillery, the 131st and 133rd, were in place to deliver supporting fire as directed by battalion commanders. Signal communications, including flares, were arranged between the artillery units and the infantry battalion commanders for those critical moments when concentration of fire was needed, or needed to be suspended.

In addition, the 3rd Ranger Battalion would be assaulting Hill 950, which was northeast of Sammucro and supplied flanking cover for German troops on Sammucro's summit.

D-Day was December 7; H-hour for the 1st Battalion, which would be leading off the assault up that long spiny ridge to the summit of Sammucro, was set for just after sunset. The next morning, the 2nd Battalion, followed by the 3rd, would head off toward San Pietro.

HENRY WASKOW'S thoughts after that meeting were both practical and spiritual. He needed to inform his men what was expected of them and to make sure they understood their assignments. There were close to 200 men under his direct command, and once they were on the mountain, it would be impossible to communicate with them on an individual or even a platoon basis at all times. Once the climb began, they would be spread out over the sides of Sammucro, and no matter how agile his runner, Riley Tidwell, might be, there would be gaps in communication. The best defense in combat was preparation, knowing what sort of chaos might be expected before it rained down.

Waskow felt prepared, but knew it was all well and good for a soldier to feel ready for combat, to know that he had experienced it already as Waskow had on the Sorrento Peninsula. It was another thing to see Mt. Sammucro looming out of the night sky across the valley and know that the same soldier was about to climb its heights and face German fire at the top. Calling it Hill 1205, labeling it 4000 feet high, was inadequate to describe how large it loomed. From anyplace down below, it was a giant mountain, as impressive to an infantryman like Waskow as Everest was to Mallory. It dominated San Pietro and the Liri Valley; it dominated the thoughts of the men who were about to climb it.

Which is probably one of the reasons Waskow had decided, in the last few days, to write a letter to his family that gave a sense of what he was thinking at this moment. He wanted to express all that he felt on the verge of this battle, wanted to make sure he got the language just right—nothing overly sentimental; nothing that would be anything but reassuring to his mother and family back home, but something that related the importance of what he was doing. He was an earnest and serious man, always had been, and now he was in the midst of the most serious business any man could imagine.

Waskow wanted his family to understand this and to know that for all his love for them back home, he was right where he was supposed to be. He wanted to reassure them of his sense of duty to his country, to let them see first and foremost that he understood precisely what George Marshall would have wanted him to know about his mission and the mission of his command here in Italy. He was deeply proud to serve his country and deeply proud of the fact that he had been placed in a position of command. He loved his men and hoped that they loved and respected him.

Waskow was a young man writing with emotion and sentiment, but he remained utterly sincere in his beliefs.

"Greetings," he wrote:

> *If you get to read this, I will have died in defense of my country and all that it stands for—the most honorable and distinguished death a man can die. It was not because I was willing to die for my country, however—I wanted to live for it—just as any other person wants to do. It is foolish and foolhardy to want to die for one's country, but to live for it is something else.*
>
> *To live for one's country is, to my mind, to live a life of service; to—in a small way—help a fellow man occasionally along the way, and generally to be useful and to serve. It also means to me to rise up in all our wrath and with overwhelming power to crush any oppressor of human rights.*

That is our job—all of us—as I write this, and I pray God we are wholly successful.

Yes, I would have liked to have lived—to live and share the many blessings and good fortunes that my grandparents bestowed upon me—a fellow never had a better family than mine; but since God has willed otherwise, do not grieve too much dear ones, for life in the other world must be beautiful, and I have lived a life with that in mind all along. I was not afraid to die; you can be assured of that. All along, I prayed that I and others could do our share to keep you safe until we returned. I pray again that you are safe, even though some of us do not return.

I made my choice, dear ones. I volunteered in the Armed Forces because I thought that I might be able to help this great country of ours in it's hours of darkness and need—the country that means more to me than life itself—if I have done that, then I can rest in peace, for I will have done my share to make the world a better place in which to live. Maybe when the lights go on again all over the world, free people can be happy and gay again.

Through good fortune and the grace of God, I was chosen a leader—an honor that meant more to me than any of you will ever know. If I failed as a leader, and I pray to God I didn't, it was not because I did not try. God alone knows how I worked and slaved to make myself a worthy leader of these magnificent men, and I feel assured that my work has paid dividends—in personal satisfaction, if nothing else.

As I said a couple of times in my letters home "when you remember me in your prayers, remember to pray that I be given strength, character and courage to lead these magnificent Americans." I said that in all sincerity and I hope I have proved worthy of their faith, trust and confidence.

I guess I have always appeared as pretty much of a queer cuss to all of you. If I seemed strange at times, it was because I had weighty responsibilities that preyed on my mind and wouldn't let me slack up to be human—like I so wanted to be. I felt so unworthy, at times, of the great trust my country had put in me, that I simply had to keep plugging to satisfy my own self that I was worthy of that trust. I have not, at the time of writing this, done that, and I suppose I never will.

I do not try to set myself on a pedestal as a martyr. Every Joe Doe who shouldered a rifle made a similar sacrifice—but I do want to point out that the uppermost thought in my mind all along was service to the cause, and I hope you all felt the same way about it.

When you remember me, remember me as a fond admirer of all of you, for I thought so much of you and loved you with all my heart. My wish for all of you is that you get along well together and prosper—not in money— but in happiness, for happiness is something that all the money in the world can't buy.

Try to live a life of service—to help someone where you are or whatever you may be--take it from me; you can get happiness out of that, more than anything in life.

—Henry T. Waskow [6]

Waskow carefully folded his letter and tucked it away in his kit. Chances were as good as not, that his family would never have to read this, that he'd come down from the mountain, and maybe forget that he'd ever had such sentiments. That would be a good thing. Even if all he wrote was true.

17

Sammucro

JUST AFTER FIVE O'CLOCK on the afternoon of December 7, 1st Battalion under the command of Lieutenant Colonel William Burgess began the long climb up the eastern slope of Mt. Sammucro.

Breaking off and heading to the right of the 1st was the 3rd Ranger Battalion, whose assignment was to take Hill 960, slightly to the north of Sammucro, toward San Vittore, which would be the next village to take on the road to Rome. All good-byes and good lucks were muted as the intensity of the operation mounted.

It was no easy task ascending the mountain in the dark. In the best of circumstances—daylight, dry, sunny weather—it was a three- or four-hour climb. This night in darkness and fog, it would take several hours more.

In the lead for Company A was commanding officer, Lt. Rufus Cleghorn of Waco, Texas and the Baylor University football team. He had been given the nickname "Rufus the Loudmouth" by members of his company, on account of his overly commanding voice.[1] Companies C and D were right behind, with Waskow's Company B bringing up the rear and providing supply-transport assistance.

The order given to Cleghorn by battalion commander Martin was a no-ifs-ands-or-buts: "Young man," he was told, "I want combat troops on that mountain by 8 o'clock in the morning."[2] So Cleghorn led with a determined pace. The mule trails on the slopes disappeared along with the scruffy pines at the tree line, leaving the men of Company A and the units following to continue by any means necessary, which at times meant on their hands and knees. There were moments, as well, when the climb grew so steep that the infantry was forced to chin themselves over sharp rocks; at other times, ropes were necessary to haul themselves upward. Company B was tasked with bringing supplies upward from where the mules left off at the tree line, which meant they were carrying ammo over these same rocks and ridges. The gentle hills of central Texas proved uneffective practice ground for this type of warfare, but the men of the 143rd soldiered on.

The fact that they were approaching the summit from the far right flank encouraged colonels Martin and Burgess to believe that the 1st Battalion would be striking with an element of a surprise against the Germans, whose focus was known to be toward San Pietro and the valley floor to the west of the peak. There was even some hope that the summit might be lightly, or not at all, occupied by the Germans.

That hope was quickly dashed. The mountain peak was indeed manned by Panzer units, but the good news was that they were, in fact, surprised to see American troops coming at them from the east. The 1st Battalion swarmed over the crest of the mountain, heaving grenades at pockets of Germans as they climbed. A fierce firefight followed the enemy's realization that they were being attacked. The battle quickly grew so intimate, that the Germans used loose boulders as weapons, trying to sweep 1st battalion troops off the mountainsides by knocking them over with rolling rocks. Cleghorn's stout voice helped guide his men toward the top, and like the Germans, he, too, began hurling rocks at the defenders—along with hand grenades and epithets.

The measure of surprise had its effect. The Americans made steady progress, and at six a.m., members of Company A, led by

Cleghorn, reached the top of Sammucro, just as Colonel Martin had ordered and hoped. A little after nine, platoons from Companies C and D joined Cleghorn and Company A in the lead and poured more fire on the Panzer forces at the summit, but a scribbled message to command said that "Ownership of Objective G [the summit] was still in question."

The 1st Battalion continued to fight and an hour later sent another message down the hill. While the Rangers on Hill 905 to the right flank were "having a pretty stiff fight . . . We are in supreme command of 1205."[3] Two hours after that, just after noon, the 1st was holding twelve German POWs on top of the mountain and catching its breath from eighteen hours of hard climbing and hard fighting.

Hard fought and hard won: it was a good way to start the battle for San Pietro and the Liri Valley. Not everyone involved would have such success.

WEARING FEATHERED caps to match their Alpine uniforms, two battalions of the 1st Italian Motorized Group set out that same morning from Mignano. A sharp American artillery cascade had preceded their move onto the hill, which occurred in the midst of the subsequent smoke and a fog that settled down in the valley. With vengeful spirit the Italians started to climb the ridges to the peak of Mt. Lungo boldly shouting challenges to the German troops above. Unfortunately, the Italians had failed to send out any recon the night before, and now blinded by the weather and smoky haze, they moved in tight units directly into a blast of German machine gun and mortar fire. The enthusiasm of the Italians was short-lived as the devastating fire quickly took a heavy toll.

A company of the 141st on nearby Mt. Rotondo set up firing positions to back up the Italians, and discourage the Germans from pursuing their advantage. But by noon, the 1st Italians were in a sorry condition, having already lost more than half of its original

1600 man strength, most of whom were missing, having high-tailed it off the mountain.[4]

Down below San Pietro, the 2nd Battalion of the 143rd was having a rough time of it as well. From their position on Mt. Cannavinelle, troops of the 2nd had headed out in the early morning darkness, moving down the three thousand foot mountain, where they'd been stationed in preparation for this attack. They headed toward the western slope of the Sammucro, just above San Pietro, but even their first steps were troublesome. Unlike Sammucro with its rock cover, Cannavinelle was blanketed in mud, which made footfalls treacherous. To prevent frantic sliding down Cannavinelle to the line of departure in the valley below, troops grabbed at roots, branches, tree trunks, anything that would catch their fall, all the while loaded with battle gear that included machine gun belts, mortar shells, boxes of hand grenades, and bazookas.[5]

White tape had been laid out the day before to mark the route, but rain that night had pretty well mucked up the markings. A bridge down below served as the point of departure, and the first troops of the 2nd—Companies E and F—set out from there at 6:20 after a booming display of "outgoing mail" from American artillery. Just two hundred yards into their trek into the valley below San Pietro, they hit a line of barbed wire backed by well-placed pillboxes armed with automatic weapons. Mines were also liberally laid in the field. All of which stopped the battalion in its tracks and allowed German mortar and artillery fire to zero in.

Efforts were made to move the troops back a hundred yards so that American artillery could safely pound the pillboxes; but when the guns started blasting the German posts, they did so to limited effect. The only openings in these fortresses were narrow slits designed for small arms fire, which served as great protection for the Panzer troops inside. More than one American lost his life trying to jump the barbed wire and roll a grenade through those narrow openings. Meanwhile, the artillery continued pounding away, creating an enormous echo chamber in the valley that reverberated with deafening explosions.[6]

Colonel Martin sent the 3rd Battalion swinging out to the right of the 2nd, in an attempt to flank the German line. Company L arced wide to the northeast, and headed back to the west, straight at San Pietro down the Venafro-San Pietro road. 600 yards into its westward advance it hit the same mix of mines, mortars, wire, and pillboxes that had stopped the 2nd. One Company L staff sergeant put it plainly, after all their efforts, "The Germans still held the high ground and had clear view of the valley."[7]

Martin committed two more companies of the 3rd Battalion, I and K, into the fight to the right of the rest of the battalion. "Texas cowhand and rebel yells pierced the air," according to one eyewitness account. "A German colonel leading his men was cut to pieces by a BAR. Other Jerries plopped down in a heap behind. The 'spang-spang' of the trusty MI's and rattle of our .30 caliber machine guns and BARs became more intense. Brave men were dying."[8] Again, however, the attack across what was about to earn the nickname, "Purple Heart Valley," made limited headway.

About four hundred yards into their trek, Companies I and K, were told to hunker down and dig in. Private Jack Clover, from Columbus, Ohio, and his digging buddy Jabe Curry chose the front edge of a gulley and quickly started to spade out a foxhole. They were waist deep in the project and hustling to finish when a giant shell landed nearby, burying them in their own hole. Clover clawed his way out of the would-be grave and waited a moment for Curry. He appeared "mole-like" beside Clover. They exchanged terrified glances, knowing there was no place for them to go.[9]

UP ON TOP of Sammucro, the situation was far better, but about to get dicey. The Germans were not willing to cede the summit of the

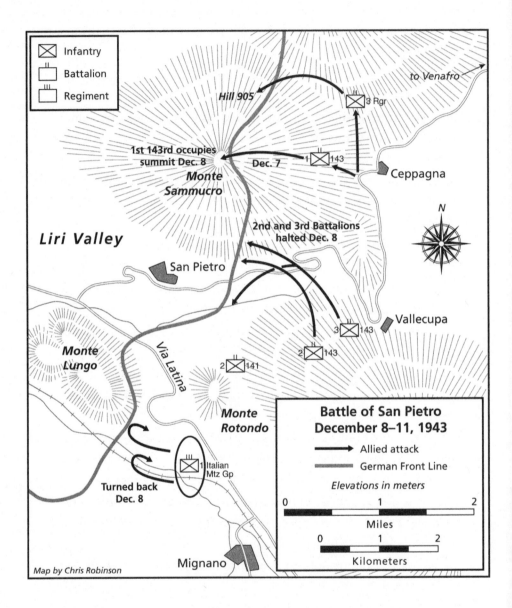

Infantry
Battalion
Regiment

to Venafro

Hill 905

3 Rgr

1st 143rd occupies summit Dec. 8

Dec. 7

1 143

Ceppagna

Monte Sammucro

N

Liri Valley

2nd and 3rd Battalions halted Dec. 8

San Pietro

Vallecupa

3 143

Monte Lungo

Via Latina

2 143

2 141

Monte Rotondo

1 Italian Mtz Gp

Turned back Dec. 8

Battle of San Pietro
December 8–11, 1943

Allied attack

German Front Line

Elevations in meters

0   1   2

Miles

0   1   2

Kilometers

Mignano

Map by Chris Robinson

hill so easily to the Allied advance. The first counterattack began at 6:30 a.m. the next morning and lasted for more than half an hour. Another assault hit from all sides at 8:10, wounding Lieutenant Roy Goad among others. A third came just after 10 a.m., and yet another hit just after noon, this one seriously wounding Lieutenant Colonel Burgess, who had to be evacuated and replaced by Major David Frazior of Houston, Texas.

The commanding officer of Company C, Captain Lewis Horton, attempted a probe of German positions to the west toward San Vittore with the idea of aiding the 3rd Rangers, which were having trouble taking Hill 960. Under heavy fire, Horton took his platoon leaders to a post where they had better vantage of enemy defenses. While devising a plan of attack, a sniper caught the company captain in his sights, killing him instantly.

So it went all day on the ninth of December. Counterattacks continued to a number that was either seven or eight—it was hard, under the circumstances, to keep an exact track. German prisoners later explained that they had been ordered to retake the mountaintop at all costs, which meant the nature of the fighting was often savage. Platoon leader Willie Slaughter of Company B saw one of his men engaged in a peek-a-boo style shootout with a German sniper. "They were crawling around in the rocks and every time one would stick his head out, the other would start shooting. They looked like a couple of lizards crawling in those rocks." From his "ringside seat" Slaughter could hear his man shouting, "Where is the son-of-a-bitch?"[10]

Using mortars that had been painfully hauled up the hill the day before, mainly by Waskow's company, the 1st Battalion was able to use its position to assist the 3rd Rangers on Hill 960. The Rangers were finally able to surmount the hill and thus relieve some of the fire heading up toward the 1st Battalion from the neighboring mountain.

As 1st Battalion battled counterattacks and assisted the 3rd Ranger Battalion, it also began to probe down the mountain toward San Pietro and San Vittore. As it did, the lines between Germans and American got crossed and intersected, particularly down the northwest side of the mountain toward San Vittore. Captain Jalvin Newell of Huntsville, Texas on the side of the mountain with three companies of the 143rd had his phone lines cut as he was trying to reach Lieutenant Richard Burrage, communications officer for the new commander, Major Frazior, who was at the top of Sammucro. Newell was afraid the Germans would intercept his radio messages to command, but he needed to pass on info and questions to Frazior. Companies A, B, and C were rapidly losing men. Should they head back up to the summit from their position or stay and fight down the hill?

To relay the communication, Newell resorted to a code that could be known only to Texas boys: he used references to Texas towns whose first letter coincided with Companies A, B, and C. A well-known Texas politician named Jerry Sadler became a stand-in for all the "Jerries" on the hill. There was talk about mail and numbers of letters addressed to each of the towns. It took a while for Burrage and Frazior to figure out what the hell Newell was saying. The numbers of letters to each town indicated the dwindling numbers of men in each company. The "Sadlers" were pressing hard meant the Germans were all around. Should the companies come back up to the summit?

After finally figuring out what was being transmitted, Burrage radioed back instructions—not necessarily happy news: Newell was asked to keep the battalion in place and hold on.[11]

Meanwhile, the wounded on the hilltop began to stack up. More than forty members of Company A were killed or put out of action in the two days of fighting; another dozen members of Companies B and C suffered similar casualties.

Some, like Ben Palmer, who took a hit of shrapnel to his right wrist from a German mortar, began to work their way down the hill on their own. Palmer made his way with a group of walking wounded. They were pretty quickly out of reach of small-arms fire, but the German artillery continued to drop shells all the way down. It took forever to reach the terraces that made more manageable steps of the base of the mountain, but Palmer did it. Ultimately, he caught a jeep ride all the way back to Naples.[12]

Many others were unable to make it down unassisted, and the perils of descending the mountain were nearly as great as heading up. Litters were carried over the same steep cliffs, inclines, and jutting rocks that were climbed on hands and knees, and with the aid of ropes on the way up. The wounded went down first, carried by others from their own units, who struggled against the hillside as they listened to the moans and cries of their comrades, essentially helpless to make the journey any easier. Still better than the dead, who came down when it was convenient, and then, most often, only to the way station at the tree line, where bodies covered in tarp and roped tight to the litters began to accumulate.

GIVEN ALL of the attacks and counterattacks, supplies of ammunition quickly began to dwindle on top of Sammucro. So did food, water, blankets, boots, and any sense of comfort. On the summit, snow took the place of the valley rain. The ground was all rock, which made foxholes impossible to dig; cold boulders and hard crevasses served as cover instead. Even without standing in muddy holes, boots remained constantly damp and feet were frozen. Trench foot was endemic.

Supplies going up the hill followed the path of 1st Battalion. There were about eighty mules in the train, led by Italian skinners who dressed, as had the Motorized Italian Army unit that had charged Mt. Lungo, in Tyrolean gear, including feathered hats. The mules were packed during the day and set out toward the mountain only after dark. According to Ernie Pyle, who had joined a 143rd supply unit a few days earlier, typical loads were 85 cans of water, 100 cases of K ration, 10 cases of D ration, about 1,000 rounds of mortar shells, a radio, telephones, 4 cases of first aid kits and plenty of sulfa. Also in the packs were cans of sterno, heavy combat uniforms (the men had originally gone up in regular gear), the "gas cakes" that Riley Tidwell had been using to cover his face in the rain, and what Pyle called the "most tragic cargo," the mail, which went up every night in what would turn out to be a long stay on the mountain.[13] Sometimes it would be received by dead men; sometimes by the wounded who were already heading down the mountain; sometimes it would be received with more than a little irony, as in the case of one corporal in Company B, who got a Christmas necktie in a package while up on Sammucro.[14]

The supply unit worked out of an olive grove near Venafro, and there Pyle shared quarters with about ten members of the unit in an old cowshed. Lem Vannata, a private from Valley Mills, Texas, who worked as a supply clerk at the post, remembered his arrival: An older man, relatively speaking, wearing a war correspondent patch on his shoulder and skinny as all get out. An officer told Vannata who the man was and said, basically, to leave him alone, that Pyle would contact them if he wanted to talk. His name, of course, was recognized by everyone in the theater, including Vanatta, who let him be until one day, Pyle caught him taking a nip from some bootlegged liquor that Vannata had stored near the dump. Turned out Pyle was just interested in taking a snort himself and there began a daily ritual between the two that lasted for the length of Pyle's stay.[15]

As noted, the Italian mules were unable to negotiate the full 4,000-foot climb up the mountain. It was just too steep and nasty. In fact, they were only able to haul about a third of the way up its sides. A whole column of assistants from supply, transport, and HQ stations down below would accompany the train each night, and when the mules gave out, the men would take over, strapping the loads to their backs and humping toward the battalion above.

Through the course of the battle, the battalion was forced into carrying its own supplies up the mountain. Carefully slipping down the mountainside, they would meet the ascending collection of cooks, truck drivers, and clerks who were hauling from the point where the mules gave out, and proceed to lift the cargo up to the summit, bringing their own K rations and mail to the rocky fortress on Sammucro. Company B had this assignment at the start of its time on the mountain.

Pyle, too, climbed up Sammucro, as much as anything else, to see the effort involved. He marveled at the strength of one packer, who could make it to the top with a full can of water in two and a half hours. Pyle's guide was a member of 1st Battalion, who had been at the top fighting, and was now supposed to be resting below. Instead, he was escorting Pyle on feet so sore from blisters that he walked only on his toes to save his sensitized heels from rubbing against the hard rock.

Pyle ran into a signal corps team of movie photographers—no doubt from the 163rd—as they bumped into a trio of German POWs being escorted down the hill by a lone GI. The signal corps camera operators asked the infantryman if he would go back up the hill fifty feet and come back down the trail so that they could get the shot of the POWs in action, descending down the trail. In the midst of war, reality was thrown in reverse to be captured on film. The Germans seemed only temporarily confused about what was happening. Soon enough they understood the filmmakers' needs and not only willingly repeated their march down the hill but took time to fix their collars and straighten their trousers.[16]

Pyle also happened across a regimental surgeon from the 36th who had been among the group that was captured and later released by the Germans at Salerno. Now he was at the medical station housed in an old stone building at the top of the mule trail and Pyle's arrival there prompted the doctor to break out a saved bottle of bourbon that had been waiting for the right company. Pyle later wrote Jerry about the visit, telling her that he and the doctor were talking in the loft of the station when German artillery started to land dangerously close, "but we felt so good by that time we didn't even pay any attention."[17]

He and the doctor, Emmett Allamon of Port Arthur, Texas, were talking about the "mental wreckage" of war—those soldiers broken by the dangers and stresses of the battlefield. The doctor took a pretty tough stance, saying that he thought the root cause for the number of breakdowns on the front line was societal, that too few American children were being given opportunities for self-sufficiency; and as a result, they crumbled now when faced with adversity. They simply hadn't faced enough tough times before. He thought ex-newsboys were best suited for war, because they'd been raised from early in life to fend for themselves.

Whether this conversation was an offshoot of what had happened in Sicily with George Patton and the slapping incidents, Pyle does not say. That story had finally been leaked by the press to the American public, and the subsequent outcry was making headlines. In any case, Pyle was much more sympathetic to the phenomenon than the doctor. "The mystery to me," he wrote, "is that there is anybody at all, no matter how strong, who can keep his spirit from breaking in the midst of battle."[18]

18

A Bad Day on the Mountain

A GERMAN COUNTERATTACK on December 11, left Rufus Cleg-horn wounded on Mt. Sammucro. He joined a growing number of officers and staff sergeants from Company A, who had been knocked out of action. Aside from losing Captain Horton, who was killed by sniper fire, and Lieutenant Goad to a wound, Company C was down two more officers and four staff sergeants by December 12. Waskow's Company B, which, because of the time spent hauling supplies was out of the most intense action, had lost only one officer killed in action.

Four days into the action, the battalion was down to half strength, with just 340 soldiers up on the ridge. The loss of men prompted General Keyes to reinforce the 1st on December 11, with the 504th Parachute Battalion. Also sent up top was Waskow's old Company I from Belton.[1] Revolving units of the 1st Battalion, including parts of Company B, were allowed to rotate partway down the mountain-side for temporary relief at the aid station, which had been erected where the mule paths ended.

Meanwhile in the valley, the Germans continued their tight hold over San Pietro. The 2nd and 3rd battalions remained stuck where they'd been since the attack on the eighth of December, about 1,000 yards shy of San Pietro. The Fifth Army might be holding Mt. Sammucro, but they couldn't go further without access to the Liri Valley—and the Liri Valley was controlled by the German forces surrounding San Pietro.

The pressures for moving on quickly mounted. On Walker. On Clark. On all their units. Already it felt like the army was stalled again, well south of Rome. It hadn't yet breeched the first of the Winter Lines; and the second, stouter line, the Gustav, still awaited. A plan for forcing the valley open was needed and Clark had one in mind. He bounced it off of Walker and Keyes: How feasible was it, Clark wanted to know, to mount a tank assault against the village?

Not very, Walker thought. A recon report suggested a number of formidable obstacles. Not only was the ground in the valley saturated by the incessant rain, but a series of streambeds and gullies ran along the southern base of Sammucro surmounted by a number of small bridges and culverts that could be easily destroyed by German artillery. Most daunting, however, were the terraces that fronted San Pietro to the south, east and up the mountainside. These were in the neighborhood of three to seven feet in height, all shored up by rock walls insurmountable to tanks. In addition, the snaking mule trails that led from one level to the next were simply too narrow for tanks to negotiate.

Nonetheless, Clark, supported by General Keyes, argued that heavy armor had made gains under more stressful circumstances and time was wasting. If it wasn't tanks doing the job, what would it be? In a few days, the 36th would be one full week stuck at San Pietro—one more week in which no progress had been made toward Rome. December 15 was the day chosen to mount the next assault against the village and tanks would lead the way.

A two-pronged attack was planned: a column of tanks would roar up the valley, sweep around the southwest corner of Mt. Sammucro and head straight for the village in a frontal assault. Meanwhile, forces from Sammucro would descend down the ridges to attack San Pietro from the hillside; and the 2nd and 3rd battalions would attack simultaneous to the tanks from the south and southwest of the town.

In preparation for the assault, the order came from Colonel Frazior on December 13 for Company B to edge out to the "nose of Sammucro"—the area of the summit on its west end overlooking the Liri Valley—to get into position to head down the summit by the next evening. Waskow's company was to take the lead in the attack of San Pietro from above, and to do so it needed to be on the west edge of the mountain, pointing down.

With a few hours of relief under its belt, Company B headed back up Sammucro from the east side of the mountain in preparation for its next assignment. On the way up, it ran into Company I coming down the hill.

It was not a moment for lingering reunion. In low voices, delivered around bobbing cigarettes dangling from mouths, the Mexia boys swapped stories with the Belton boys about what was happening up above and what was happening down below; who from their neck of the woods in Texas had been wounded, and who had been killed. There were even some laughs about the guy from Company B who had got a Christmas tie while up on the mountain. Waskow exchanged greetings with at least one old friend from the Belton unit, Marvin Splawn.[2] Then off they trudged in their opposite directions.

Riley Tidwell's feet were a mess. His trench foot had degenerated to the point where he could no longer put pressure on the soles of his feet, so covered in sores were they. Instead he dug into the hillside with his heels almost backing up the mountain. Down at the aid station, before Company B set out that day, Tidwell made coffee for his captain and pulled out his can of sterno. In the usual way, he stuck a piece of bread on the wire hangar that he always tucked into his kit for just this purpose. He proceeded to make toast for Waskow and listened as the captain told him once again how, when the war was over, he was going to get himself one of those fancy new pop-up toasters. "Smart Alec toasters," he always called them.

He also asked Tidwell about his feet[3] and Tidwell gave his captain an honest picture of his circumstances. Truth be told, he was having a hard time walking. He mainly had to stay on his heels. Waskow decided to send Riley back down to get treatment. What good was a runner who couldn't run? Tidwell heeled himself down to the aid station on the mountainside, where medics gently took off his boots, cleaned his feet, and wrapped them in gauze. It felt like heaven by comparison to how they'd been aching before. Tidwell felt chipper enough to rejoin Waskow and the Company as they were still ascending Sammucro.

Sergeant Willie Slaughter's platoon had broken off on a separate patrol to the west, to nearby Hill 570, where they were to make contact with a unit from the 504th Parachute, the unit that had initially served as a replacement unit for the 1st Battalion. As they walked the ridgeline, Slaughter spied a pair of heads poking up over a rock along his path. He inched his way forward, saw one of the men turn in his direction, caught the shape of a German helmet and then the sight of the Panzer rifleman turning a machine gun in his direction. Along with the rest of the platoon, Slaughter dove for cover as the Germans opened fire.

They had stumbled on a German observation post. Cooly, Slaughter took out a grenade and lobbed it in the direction of the two soldiers. Meanwhile Slaughter's old football buddy from Mexia High, Sergeant Jack Berry, was about to jump out from cover and help a member of the platoon who had been caught in the first burst of fire. Slaughter warned him against it, but Berry was gone before the words registered. Jack Berry was struck with gunfire and killed as he crawled over the rocks to his comrade.[4]

Slaughter and the rest of the platoon settled in for a firefight that would last for a couple of hours. In the end, seven Germans were killed, seven more wounded, and thirteen were captured. From the POWs came intelligence that U.S. artillery had knocked out the German command post down in San Pietro days earlier, that replacements coming into the village were generally older troops, thirty- and forty-year-olds, and that about 120 infantrymen were now in the town. All encouraging news.[5]

The rest of Company B heard the small arms fire and grenades of Slaughter's platoon as they moved along the summit of Sammucro. It was now deep into the evening on a misting, foggy night. As the company reached and then inched out over the "nose" of Sammucro, Waskow commented on the murky dark and the landscape: "Wouldn't this be an awful spot to get killed and freeze on the mountain?"[6]

With Tidwell and his first sergeant, John Parker, another Mexia man, Waskow eased down over the west edge of Sammucro. They'd gone just a few steps more when a shell came whistling in. Waskow picked up the sound of the screaming round a split second before Tidwell and gave him a shove, hollering at his runner to hit the ground. Tidwell did just that, as did Parker.

Waskow was too late. The shell burst above him and shrapnel tore into his chest, shredding heart and lungs. He was dead in a gasp.[7]

IT WAS A bad day for Company B on the mountain. The artillery fire continued intense all morning on December 14, sweeping the mountaintop and adjoining ridges. There wasn't much protection among the rocks when the German guns zeroed in.

The company continued down the southeastern face of Sammucro toward San Pietro moving in conjunction with 2nd and 3rd battalions, who proceeded on a line from the slopes to the west of San

Pietro, basically where they had left off a few days before during the first assault on the village.

Company B got pinned down in a German counterattack, and was asked to hold the position. All day long it fought and got punished for the effort. Both of the remaining officers in Company B—two first lieutenants—were killed. First Sergeant Parker was eventually wounded. Two staff sergeants, including Jack Berry, were also killed. Another Mexia man, Private Floyd Durbin, was dead, and yet another Mexian, Hulen Tackett was wounded. Scores of replacement soldiers—those who had arrived in October from all over the country—were also killed and wounded. Company B's casualties were now comparable to Company A's and C's. All units were down to about 30 percent of full. More than eight hundred of the men who'd climbed Mt. Sammucro on December 8, would be dead or wounded before the month was over.

Back where Henry Waskow lay, it was Tidwell who checked for signs of life and saw none. It was Tidwell who found Waskow's kit with its Bible, its postcard book from Capri meant for sister Mary Lee, with its last letter written and folded on a piece of rough field paper.[8] It was Tidwell who helped pick up the captain and took him down to the head of the mule trail.

There at the station, he lay Waskow down with the other dead bodies being collected. All were tied tight to their litters, waiting for their final leg off the mountain, when they would be draped over the sides of a mule and carried the last way down to the valley below.[9]

Tidwell went back up the mountain and reported to Frazior, the battalion CO, that Company B no longer had any officers. The unit was leaderless down at its end of the mountain, overlooking San Pietro.

Tidwell had known Frazior from his duties as company runner, going back and forth from Waskow to battalion headquarters. Frazior noticed the condition of the runner's feet. He asked Tidwell if he was capable of getting back to his unit. Tidwell guessed he was.

Tell one of the sergeants over there to take charge until I get someone to the company, Frazior told him, and then take yourself down the mountain to have someone look at your feet.

The company runner did as he was told, hobbling first to Company B, where he informed the first sergeant he saw of Frazior's order, then back down the mountainside again to the aid station, where his feet were again wrapped in cotton gauze. This time, he proceeded all the way to the base of the mountain, where he found a shed occupied by exhausted members of the 36th, leaning vacant-eyed against the rough walls. He sat himself down and breathed hard and deep.

Sitting off by himself scribbling in a notepad was a slight, middle-aged man, wearing fatigues and a rumpled knit cap. Ernie Pyle must have sensed that Tidwell wanted to talk and he slipped over in the tall man's direction.

In fact, the lanky private did have some things that he wanted to say about the captain he had left earlier that day at the end of the mule trail on the side of Mt. Sammucro. The man he had been trailing now for three and a half months through the mountains of Italy, and in North Africa before that, and Cape Cod, and all the way back to Camp Bowie in Texas. The man who drank his coffee, ate his toast, talked of smart alec toasters with him.

Pyle gently asked what had happened up there and Tidwell told him how his captain had just died on the mountain.

"He must have been a fine man," Pyle said.

Stunned by an awful day of war, feeling lucky to be alive and sick at what he had seen, Tidwell tried to frame his thoughts. "He was like a father to me," was the best he could do.[10]

19

Purple Heart Valley

As THE 1ST CONTINUED the fight on Sammurco, the 2nd and 3rd battalions began the assault on San Pietro, joined by a battalion of the 141st, which was given the assignment of attacking the village directly from the south, to the left of the units from the 143rd. Mt. Lungo, which had remained in German hands throughout the fight on Mt. Sammucro, was to be attacked as well, by the 142nd.

What was expected be the most powerful punch at the German line came steaming at San Pietro on a winding line down the Venafro Road. Starting from part way up the mountain to the east, then going down into the valley, and around the base of Sammucro, were Mark Clark's tanks, which jumped off at noon on December 15. The road itself left little room for error. To the right of the tanks loomed Mt. Sammucro; to the left was a steep drop-off down the hill. The road was only the width of two small cars and from the moment they arrived in the valley, they were in open view of German artillery.[1]

Eight tanks rumbled down the lane toward the village; eight more moved in conjunction with the 2nd and 3rd Battalions who were also sweeping around the mountain from the southwest in the wake of the first tanks. Neither component of the attack got very far. The Germans let the lead two tanks get near the town before they opened fire with anti-tank weaponry. The Panzer troops' aim was directed on the trailing tanks in the first group and it was accurate. In a matter of minutes, two American Shermans were destroyed. Those two effectively blocked any means of escape on the narrow road for the lead tanks, which meant Wehrmacht anti-tank guns could wreck them at their own pace.

The next three tanks were stopped and disabled by mines. Each was abandoned by its crew, halting the progress of the remaining tanks, which were left to take fire from German positions around the valley. In all, seven tanks were destroyed, five were disabled, and only four made it back to their original assembly area.[2]

The 2nd and 3rd battalions, moving in behind the tanks, were not having much better luck. They were hit by a wall of automatic weapons, mortar, and artillery fire coming from San Pietro, Mt. Lungo, and, most deadly, from the olive tree terraces that fronted the village. General Walker's assistant commander, Brigadier General Wilbur, ordered Company E of the 143rd to swing around to the right of the tanks, up the hill, in order to attack the village north to south, from above. Late in the afternoon, Company L joined them in the fight. They got near to San Pietro, but took such a severe pounding in the process that both companies were reduced to just a handful of rifleman as darkness fell on the 15th.[3]

Staff Sergeant Alvin Amelunke, Waco, Texas, attached to Company L, was in the midst of the fight when German artillery began to rain down. He was in a hole with a fellow sergeant from Company L when a shell hit a tree directly in front of them. A piece of shrapnel pierced his companion's helmet, killing him instantly.

The attack continued after dark, and Company L made some progress among the olive orchards and terraces, and even penetrated German lines. There they were met with heavy automatic fire, and

Amelunke's communications man went down in a heap. Without sleep, little food and water, and with heavy casualties, Company L was near the end of its rope.[4]

The 141st, coming at San Pietro from the south, had stopped along with the 143rd to regroup. The battalion mounted an attack from the valley side of the battlefield at about 5:30 in the afternoon. Artillery pounding San Pietro helped them get to the verge of the town, but there the stonewalls surrounding the village slowed them, as did the booby traps, mines, and barbed wire attached to the walls. German troops in buildings overlooking the barriers were also firing down from the upper floors, directly into the American forces. Once the attack had been slowed to a halt, the German mortars, planted in locales all around Sammucro and across the valley at Mt. Lungo, began to zero in on the 141st with pinpoint accuracy. The four companies from the 141st's 2nd Battalion involved in the attack were whittled down to a handful of officers and a few score riflemen by early the next morning, but a smattering of troops managed to break through the boundaries of San Pietro.

The one major success of the day's attacks was happening simultaneously—over on Mt. Lungo, the 142nd was lunging up the hill. One battalion attacked the northwestern side of Lungo, while another attacked the center. The Italian motorized brigade was once more involved and took the southern route against the Germans. The 1st Battalion on the right flank engaged in a number of fierce firefights. It knocked out more than a half dozen machine gun nests on its way to the top of the mountain. The 2nd Battalion likewise made a quick journey to the top, during which it was able to induce a newly captured POW into pointing out fifteen gun emplacements on the mountain. They were quickly zeroed in and subsequent fire saved American soldiers throughout the valley. Mt. Lungo fell by 1:35 on the morning of December 16, which proved vital to the capture of San Pietro as well.[5]

Come daybreak, the Germans tried to reinforce the village, but with the 142nd now on top of Lungo, exposing German posts in the town and valley, and with Sammucro still held by the 1st Battalion of the 143rd, the Panzer troops were now in a desperate position.

They acted accordingly. A fierce counterattack ensued on the afternoon of the December 16, focused on the American right flank, where the 2nd and 3rd Battalions of the 143rd were positioned. Here, Company I—the Belton guys, who'd been pulled off the top of the mountain and asked to join the assault against San Pietro—got caught in the first blaze of fire from the Germans. They were above the village, just to the northeast and they got smashed. The CO and second in command were both killed in the initial attack, forcing Company I to reel back. But the unit held its ground thanks in part to Private First Class Charles Dennis of Waco, who rallied the platoon with fierce machine gun fire.[6]

Company K was quickly drawn into the fight, too. Led by Captain Henry Bragaw of Southport, North Carolina, "a mild-mannered horticulturalist with a strawberry-colored handlebar mustache"[7] They were able to stop the counterattack, despite having lost its communication with the battalion command post.

A withering line of artillery fire was also essential to stopping the Germans. At the height of the fight, shells were landing within 100 yards of the American lines—a dangerous rain of fire, but so accurate that German troops could not penetrate it.

By one o'clock on the morning of the December 17, the fight was essentially over. The Germans began quickly withdrawing from the village, leaving just a smattering of troops to cover the retreat. What was left of Companies I and K proceeded into San Pietro and the area just to its north. In the process they collected ten German POWs not quick enough to escape the town.

San Pietro had been turned into a rough pile of stones. A few walls with window openings were huddled together, suggesting the

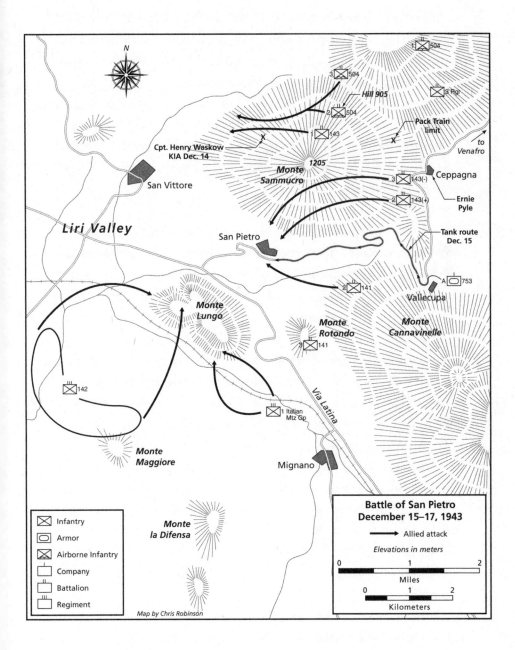

N

Hill 905

3 ⊠ 504

2 ⊠ 504

1 ⊠ 504

⊠ 3 Rgr

Pack Train limit

to Venafro

1 ⊠ 143

X

Cpt. Henry Waskow
KIA Dec. 14

X

Monte Sammucro 1205

3 ⊠ 143(-) **Ceppagna**

2 ⊠ 143(+) **Ernie Pyle**

San Vittore

Liri Valley

Tank route
Dec. 15

San Pietro

A ▭ 753

2 ⊠ 141 **Vallecupa**

Monte Lungo

Monte Rotondo

Monte Cannavinelle

3 ⊠ 141

⊠ 142

Via Latina

⊠ 1 Italian
Mtz Gp

Monte Maggiore

Mignano

Monte la Difesa

Legend	
⊠	Infantry
▭	Armor
⊠	Airborne Infantry
▯	Company
▭	Battalion
▭	Regiment

Map by Chris Robinson

Battle of San Pietro
December 15–17, 1943

➤ Allied attack

Elevations in meters

0   1   2
Miles

0   1   2
Kilometers

buildings from which they were derived and the shape of an ancient Italian village. The essential outline of the town's church, dedicated to St. Michael the Archangel, remained visible, but from a distance it looked like a sand castle kicked over and over again. Within one of the church alcoves, an armless statue of St. Peter looked out mournfully on what was left of the village.

Even as the 36th Division began sweeping through the remains, the German soldiers were racing away to their next line in the mountains, five kilometers away.

Up on the mountain, the weary 1st Battalion of the 143rd was relieved by a battalion from the 141st. Exhausted and unshaven, on wobbly legs and empty bellies, what was left of the outfit made a tired descent from Sammucro after spending the better part of ten days on its heights. Someone estimated that the 1st Battalion had pitched 2,000 hand grenades among the rocks of Sammucro in its stay up on the heights. That was more than a division would typically use in combat. Of course all of those grenades were lugged up to the top of the mountain by hand. Mortars, too, were used at a level three times the usual. They, too, were carried up on the backs of the human mules, who had scaled Hill 1205 time and again.[8]

Down below, Riley Tidwell was still waiting for his captain to come down off the mountain. It had been three days now that Henry Waskow lay wrapped in a tarp, still trussed up in the rope that had been used to secure his journey on a litter off the summit. His remains had lain with face covered, boots exposed, on bare ground, against yet another old stonewall in this land of old stone and mud.

Waskow was far from alone up at the station where the mule train ended. Many more dead were waiting to come down the mountain; and many more of the living congregated around them, resting themselves on the way, sitting among the dead bodies, as if they weren't dead, but simply dead-tired, like the soldiers of the 143rd seated around them.

That didn't ease things for Tidwell. It just wasn't right for the captain to be so long on the mountain. The company runner decided to take matters into his own hands. He "acquisitioned" a mule from one of the trains and took off by himself up the trail determined to fetch Captain Waskow. There was still sporadic gunfire on the hillside; still the persistent mortar fire from stubborn German troops, slowly retreating on the far side of Sammucro. But the slow process of bringing the dead off the mountain continued.

Riley Tidwell found his captain just where he'd left him. He draped Waskow over the mule like others were doing with the dead at the head of the trail. Tidwell pushed down his rigor mortis–stiffened legs on one side of the mule, bent Waskow's rigid waist over the mule's spine, and let his arms drape over the other side. He strapped his captain on the animal's back and headed down. For a time, the sporadic German fire focused on the mules coming down off the mountain and artillery came dangerously close. Tidwell was nicked by shrapnel: once across the back, once on the wrist, once by his left ear. The last wound left him bloody, but still upright as he neared the base of the hill. It was his feet that still were giving him the most pain.

"Here comes Riley," he heard someone from down below call, "and he's got Captain Waskow."

Several people helped him take the captain off the back of the mule and lay him down with the others who'd been brought down the mountain that day. His mission done, Tidwell went off to the field hospital, where they sewed fifteen stitches into the wound by his ear, and decided that his feet were bad enough to send him to the hospital.[9]

ERNIE PYLE was still at the shed below, watching the procession of mules and men, mingling with the living soldiers at the foot of the mountain, as the dead were placed among them. All day long the bodies were carried down the mountain on the backs of mules, according to Pyle, one at a time, as the exhausted men of 1st Battalion sat around talking in tired voices with vacant eyes. They would get quiet as each fresh body was laid next to the road that ran by the shed—convenient for taking the corpses away for their final disposition.[10]

Pyle saw the gangly Texas private he had run into in the shed a few days earlier, coming down the hill with a group of four other bodies on four more mules. He watched as they wound their way down the last few yards and got within earshot of the bottom of the hill.

Someone in the group said, "This one is Captain Waskow," and Pyle instantly noted a change in mood. What had been somber air became all the more heavy. A number of them stood up, tamped out cigarettes, and slowly sidled over to help him off the mule.

There he lay with all the rest, but Pyle could tell this death was a little different. This one was a little harder to take. One by one, the men from the company came over to pay their respects. Pyle carefully noted how they did so, catching the small gestures, the soft words. Later, he asked a few questions about the man who had just come down, listened for a while to the muted expressions of sorrow coming from the men who had known him best—the men who had served with him.

As the night continued in its black vein, Pyle slipped away, back to his bedroll in the cowshed to ponder this war and think on deaths like these. He shut his eyes and tried to get some sleep.

20

Aftermath

DON WHITEHEAD OF THE Associated Press and Homer Bigart of the New York Herald crossed "Purple Heart Valley" on December 18, heading toward San Pietro in the wake of the 143rd to view the aftermath of the battle—except the fight was not entirely over. German snipers were still hiding out in bunkers to the north of the village and enemy artillery was zeroed in on the town, which was empty of both German and American troops. Only the wounded and medical aid groups, like the one Whitehead and Bigart were joining in their dangerous sightseeing, remained in San Pietro.

They were warned not to enter, even as they crossed the valley. It wasn't only the hazards of the intermittent shelling and the snipers that made the village a dangerous place; it was also full of booby traps. The two journalists went toward the town anyway, passing the dead Americans who had charged across the open field toward the village terraces a couple of days earlier. "One boy lay crumpled in a shallow slit trench beneath a rock," wrote Bigart of the trip. "Another, still grasping his rifle, peered from behind a tree, staring with sightless eyes toward the Liri plain. A third lay prone where he had fallen."

This last dead body affected Bigart a little more than the others. "Evidently some fragment had killed him instantly, for there had been no struggle," he wrote. "Generally, there is no mistaking the dead—their strange contorted posture leaves no room for doubt. But this soldier, his steel helmet tilted over his face, seemed merely resting in the field. We did not know until we came within a few steps and saw a gray hand hanging limply from a sleeve."[1]

Like Pyle, Whitehead and Bigart had both spent some hours at the cowshed at the foot of the mule trail. Bigart was a bespectacled New Yorker with the look of a self-confident intellectual. Whitehead, a graduate of the University of Kentucky and in his mid-thirties, had a faint southern accent and a pencil-thin mustache. He was a buddy of Pyle's and when he went back to Caserta, in Pyle's room at the Palace, they were fond of sharing a drink or two or three.

As Bigart and Whitehead retraced the steps of the 143rd across the valley, they noted the debris of battle, the "abandoned rifles, cartridge belts, blood-stained bandages."[2] As they came to the first of the terraces fronting San Pietro, Whitehead nearly sprung a trip wire connected to a German Teller mine, but Bigart spotted it and shouted a warning, saving the Associated Press its correspondent.

They followed a mule path that widened into a cobbled alley and then came upon the first house in the village. Four dead Americans were sprawled within. They noted how "every approach to San Pietro, every ravine and sunken path offering shelter from machine-gun fire had been covered by German snipers."[3]

The was no discernible street pattern left within the village, all alleys and byways were heaped in rubble after being smashed by American artillery and bombed by American planes. Bigart noted the remnants of St. Michael and peeked inside to see the choir loft "hung crazily above an altar almost buried under the masonry." An inscription in a church alcove where the statue of St. Peter stood armless, read, "By the devotion of Americans from San Pietro." A young Italian woman emerged from one of the caves in the hillside, which had been home during the battle to scores of the villagers.

She explained to the reporters that many San Pietrans, including her own uncle who now farmed near Syracuse, New York, had emigrated to the U.S. and sent back donations.[4]

Further along in the village they saw sandbag bunkers with roofs made of rock. There were dead mules and hogs on the edge of town, along with the burned out remains of two American tanks that had made it as far as the village limits. There were a number of wounded Germans left behind by their comrades. They asked for food and water as the American medics arrived.

As the day advanced, more Italian villagers emerged from the caves—about twenty middle-aged men, according to Bigart, some women and children "all very dirty and unkempt, but showing no signs of hysteria."[5]

Whitehead's prose was more muscular than Bigart's. "American doughboys have won one of their bloodiest, bitterest and toughest battles of World War II on this one hundredth day of the Fifth Army's invasion of Italy," is how he opened his report when he sat down to write it that night. "In all the fighting from the beaches of Salerno to the Garigliano River, none has been so packed with drama and heroism as that of this forty-eight hour span, nor has any been so costly in American lives as the battle for San Pietro, which ended today shortly before we walked through 'Death Valley' to reach this pile of misery and rubble that once was a town."

Americans had entered "this battered, filthy, stinking little town at the bottom of Mt. Sammucro to find that the enemy had pulled back toward Cassino . . ."

"We picked our way with a patrol and first aid men through fields ripped by mortars and shells and strewn with the still bodies of doughboys who fell in the bloody, savage fighting," Whitehead wrote, "the fierceness of the fighting was written in those fields and in jagged piles of masonry in the town. Neither Tobruk nor Bizerte nor Battipaglia nor Toina were as ripped and torn and pulverized by explosives as this gray, little town, overlooking the approaches of Cassino. The Americans call it "Death Valley" because death was on the rampage . . ."[6]

BIGART AND Whitehead weren't the only journalists to venture into San Pietro, nor were they the first.

On the afternoon of December 17,[7] John Huston, Eric Ambler, Jules Buck, a crew from the 163rd Signal Corps, and an interpreter set out in a pair of jeeps for San Pietro, approaching the village directly from the valley floor, rather than sweeping around Sammucro on the Venafro Road from the east. They were armed with a large tri-pod camera, able to record sound, and an Eyemo, which was a handheld 35-mm favored by newsreel photographers.

As they headed toward the village, they ran into General Mark Clark being driven in a jeep below San Pietro. Clark was getting photos taken near the edge of the battlefield, looking "alert, determined, fighting fit," according to Ambler. Pictures taken, the commander was quickly back in his vehicle and whisked away to safer ground.

Huston's jeeps proceeded up the road to a point just short of the terraced olive groves. A group of tank men worked to rescue the Shermans that had failed to breech the village outskirts, and which still blocked access to the village. Huston and his people climbed out of their jeeps and were warned by the tank guys to stay in the tracks that their machines had made so as to avoid anti-personnel mines laid by the Germans. Sound advice.

A little further down the road, they ran into a party of litter bearers, who were lining up dead bodies and checking them for identification. Dead for a day or two, they were already becoming "awkward to handle," in Ambler's words. "One had an arm raised and a finger with signet ring on it pointing rigidly at the sky."[8]

The sergeant heading the 163rd camera unit lingered to talk further with the stretcher-bearers, and then raced to catch up to Huston, who had proceeded on up the road. The sergeant said that he had been strongly advised not to continue into San Pietro. There were a lot more casualties up ahead, both dead and wounded, and the Germans were still quite active. Snipers were firing on the medics; mortar and artillery fire was still coming in.

Huston ignored the warning, though he acceded to a request that they all move in single file rather than massed in a group. As they reached the first olive grove, they came upon a unit of T-Patchers, sitting under the trees, who confirmed that medics were being fired upon in the town. When they saw the cameras, they asked if they could get filmed and be in the newsreels back home. Jules Buck, who was manning the Eyemo, took some footage of the soldiers, who were relaxed and smiling in the shots.

Just two days earlier, Huston had had Buck film another group of T-Patchers, these from the 143rd, just prior to the attack on December 15. They were in a reflective mood at the time, and talked, according to Huston, about what they were fighting for, "what the future might hold for them, their country and the world. Some of the bodies of these same soldiers were now scattered around the trail to San Pietro.[9]

Huston's crew continued on and found another platoon of T-Patchers closer to the village. These GI's were crouched in a drainage ditch and were surprised to see the filmmakers walking upright and uncovered toward San Pietro. They told Huston that they were waiting for orders to move into the village and expressed concern about the safety of Huston and his men. Again, Huston ignored the warnings.

Two hundred yards further on, the director hesitated as he lead the group around a bend in the grove. There was a T-Patcher around the corner, kneeling beside a tree with his rifle at his shoulder as if frozen in a combat position. It was only when they moved closer that they could see why he'd paused: the GI's face had been peeled off by mortar. His corpse was simply propped up by the tree.

The dead infantryman had many companions and the land around them told the story of their demise: it was pockmarked with craters where mortars and artillery shells had fallen. "Scattered about among the dead were their possessions," Ambler recorded, "their tubes of toothpaste and their shaving kits, their toilet paper and their girlie magazines, their clean socks and their letters from home . . ."[10]

They could see now into the village of San Pietro, and the interpreter took the opportunity to tell Huston that it didn't look as if there were any living Italians in the town for him to interpret. The hint was left untaken. The interpreter soon decided he had had enough and vamoosed. After some consideration, so did the camera crew from the 163rd. Huston, Buck, and Ambler continued on, with Buck still manning the Eyemo.

They were less than 200 yards from the town now and had a choice: they could either follow the road into the village, which presented a blind entrance as it swung around the mountain and into town; or they could cut across a field that had open access to San Pietro. The second avenue was undoubtedly mined and would expose them to enemy machine-gun fire. The Germans helped them reach a quick conclusion. A machine gun opened fire from the hillside sending them scurrying for cover by a retaining wall. Mortars started to rain down showering them with dirt and bits of stone. Huston asked Buck to take some shots in the midst of this action, but ultimately he was only able to shoot the sky, reeling above, as he dove for cover. Fortunately for the filmmakers, the dust and debris kicked up by the mortar explosions created enough cover from the machine gun for them to escape their predicament. One at a time they raced back to relative safety at their jeeps, fully aware of the dangers and frustrations of combat photography.[11]

HUSTON, AMBLER, and Buck returned the next day. They had been reassured that the village was now fully "taken" by the Allies.

The three of them drove their jeeps along the road from Venafro carefully skirting the disabled tanks. They headed right into San Pietro this time, up to the town piazza, where rubble lay all around them. "There were one or two stumps of wall still standing," Ambler wrote, "but nothing, not even the church, that could be identified as a particular building."[12]

An American engineering crew in the village warned them to watch for land mines and booby traps. In particular, if they saw a German pistol lying around, they were not to pick it up; it was certain to be a trap. The engineers said that they had found a couple of Italian families in cellars, buried within the rubble. There were no doors left; the people came and left through holes in the destruction.

Huston had Buck set up the camera in the piazza and directed him to focus back over the valley behind them to create an establishing shot for the village. He should slowly pan from the landscape below, up a full 180 degrees back to the destruction of San Pietro. Buck started to film just as the first of several German artillery shells came whistling into town.

Leaving the tripod camera behind, Buck, Huston, and Ambler scrambled with the engineering crew to a nearby cave for cover, but soon Huston wanted to check out one of the cellars, where the Italian villagers were cowering. He and Buck made a dash for it. Ambler, who was growing annoyed by Huston's risk-taking (and expressed it through snide reference to Huston's smoky aviator glasses), ultimately followed suit.

Once they were in the cellar, the shells started to fall heavy on the piazza, thundering in and shaking the ground and rubble above. The thought of being entombed within the destruction of San Pietro crossed everyone's mind.

The three filmmakers shared the cellar with "a skinny old man, two-exhausted middle-aged women and three quiet and very dirty children."[13] The old man offered Ambler a rickety, wicker chair, but visible on its seat were a host of scampering lice and he declined.

When the shelling lightened, Huston, Buck, and Ambler decided to make a run for it. They ran first to the camera, where Huston had Buck make another establishing pan of the valley and then they quickly got back into the jeep and headed down the road.[14] An American command car was coming in their direction and paused briefly on the open road. Huston and company yelled a warning, but in an instant, a German .88 artillery shell hit the car and in Huston's words, "It simply disintegrated."[15]

There was one more terrifying moment: a pair of I-beams had been placed along the road to serve as a bridge across a gulley. Their width was more appropriate to a truck than a jeep, and in their haste to get out of area, Buck, who was driving, had caught one of the jeep tires up on the raised edge of the I-beams. For several horrifying moments, as they imagined the German artillery zeroing in, the jeep remained stalled over the gulley. Huston swore a blue streak at Buck, who finally was able to get traction again and steer the jeep and its passengers back out of harm's way.

21

New Year

"The downtrodden G.I. as suffering servant: this was the symbol of the new heroism of World War II. It was largely the creation of Ernie Pyle, and the key work was done during what he called 'the long winter misery' of the Italian campaign."

—James Tobin[1]

THERE WAS NO LETUP for the 36th Division. The village of San Vittore remained occupied by Germans just two miles from San Pietro and beyond it was the next, even more formidable line in the German Winter defense centered at Mt. Cassino, a few kilometers passed San Vittore.

General Wilbur of the 36th devised a plan for a nighttime attack against Vittore; and on December 20, the 141st's 1st Battalion, and 143rd's 3rd Battalion inched around the western edge of Mt. Sammucro at its base toward the village. Meanwhile the 2nd Battalion of the 143rd moved up the mountain to attack from higher ground.

More fighting among the rocks ensued. Again the 36th was stymied. The 143rd was finally relieved on the morning of December

23 by the 1st Special Forces unit—the mountain troops who had taken Mt. La Difensa at the start of the assault. The special forces were reinforced by the 504th Parachute Infantry and a battalion of the 141st. They coordinated a successful attack against San Vittore, and by Christmas Eve, the village was finally in Allied hands.

Still it was apparent the enemy would contest every inch of ground. Nothing would be easy, a fact that General Walker felt was not evident to his immediate superiors, Clark and Keyes.

They had come to his command post on December 19, two days after San Pietro had been taken, this time with Eisenhower and Major General Bedell Smith. After lunch, Walker took them along Highway 6 to get a clear view of Mt. Sammucro and the village of San Pietro. Eisenhower surprised Walker by asking him to lay down some artillery fire on the village, which was obviously a pile of rubble already. Just what this shelling was supposed to accomplish, Walker had no idea. He was trying to figure out how to deal with the suggestion, when Bedell Smith whispered to him that he ought to simply ignore it. Meanwhile, Clark and Keyes were wondering, in less than subtle fashion, why it had taken so long to render the village.[2]

Walker was already deeply discouraged by the Italian campaign. "[It] will not be finished this week, nor next," he confided to his diary. "Our wasteful policy or method of taking one mountain mass after another gains no tactical advantage, locally. There is always another mountain mass beyond with Germans dug in on it, just as before. Somebody on top side, who has control of the required means, should figure out a way to decisively defeat the German army in Italy, instead of just pushing, pushing."[3]

Two days before Christmas, his thoughts were with his soldiers. "This is about as miserable a day for the troops as one can imagine," he wrote. "Several units are moving to new positions this afternoon. I regret the hardships they must endure tonight. Wet, muddy, cold, and hungry, they will go into a camp in the mud and rain without rest or sleep. They have been going for thirty-five days."

The Germans were defending every mountain, but the high command seemed to be paying little attention to the toll this was taking on his men. "They set up schedules of progress to be made from day to day, but they do not consult the German soldiers, who are defending the positions in our front . . ."[4]

Christmas was not very merry for him or his men. Walker spent it visiting his three infantry regiments and handing out Silver Stars and Distinguished Service medals. Some troops got a very nice Christmas dinner complete with roast turkey, dressing, gravy, mashed potatoes, cauliflower, fruit salad, rolls, butter, cake, coffee, and three kinds of pie, apple, custard, and chocolate.

As with the Thanksgiving turkey, those still on the front lines were promised this same meal as soon as they were relieved.

Walker's quarters were in a mountain near the village of Presenzano. Next door in a larger cave slept his aides and others in the general staff. The offices of the command post were housed in tents down the hill from the caves; and each morning, Walker and his staff would take the trails down, and each evening, they'd head back up. On Christmas Eve, Walker received a visit to his command cave from some carolers who sang a number of Christmas melodies. As the songs echoed on the mountainside, his neighbors stepped from their caves, too, to listen and dream of better days to come. When the music died down, a general wish was expressed that next year's Christmas be conducted under peaceful skies and circumstances.[5]

ON CHRISTMAS Day, bazooka man Lee Fletcher of Company I and Jack Clover of Company K helped the Graves Registration teams pick up battalion dead along the hillside of Mt. Sammucro near San Pietro. Fletcher never forgot the sight of two men from that grim duty. Both were found within feet of each other on one of the terraces. A single mortar shell had killed them in the same instant. The first body was riddled with shrapnel. The second body left Fletcher numb. It had both legs and an arm blown off. The man's intestines had gushed out onto to the terrace and had to be scooped up into a mattress cover and carried off the mountain. "Not a pleasant thing to do," he wrote later. When he got back to that Christmas Day party, turkey with all the trimmings held no appeal to him. He couldn't eat.[6]

Clover was working the terraces, too. He was exhausted, having just been pulled from the front lines at San Vittore, for this duty. Clover and the burial team he was working with came upon one G.I. lying facedown on a terrace. The dead man was wearing a raincoat with just one leg sticking out from beneath. The other leg, with its foot in a muddy combat boot, was just behind and to the left of the rest of the man's body. They covered the man's head, torso, and one leg in a blanket and lashed it to a litter for the hike down the mountain, placing the detached limb next to its partner, making a pair of muddy combat boots once again. Then they kept on with their work.

The detritus of war was everywhere: the stone terraces were smashed and ruined; olive trees were torn literally, limb by limb; burned up M 1 rifles and scattered back packs and cartridge belts lay all around. Two soldiers were killed against a stone wall, clutching their rifles as a mortar hit and took their lives. All the while he worked, those two muddy combat boots stayed in Clover's mind.

Back in the bivouac area, he found himself slowly getting into the holiday spirit. There were fires around the tents and some members of his platoon were singing Christmas carols. "Mail from home had arrived and a turkey dinner was upcoming. The late afternoon sun shone brightly in the Italian sky as it sawed its way into the massive snowcapped peaks above," he wrote.[7] Yet those muddy combat boots still haunted him.

On New Year's Eve, a storm blew down from the mountains, whipping tents and dumping snow all around the bivouac and headquarters, reminding one Texan of "a Blue Norther, blow[ing] in cold and fierce . . ."[8]

Up on Sammucro, a part of the 142nd Infantry was given the assignment of guarding the summit for one last night. Newcomers to the top, they tried to set up tents but had little luck securing a substantial shelter in the rock. They took two tent halves and tied one to a boulder and staked the other side in a patch of thin soil, then tried, with little success to fix the two halves together with buttons.

The rain and wind came with the evening. The shelter leaked like a sieve. Water ran down the rocks and soaked them to the bone. They huddled under blankets until the wind blew their shelter off the rock to reveal that the rain had turned to snow inches deep. Sleep was impossible.

In the morning, they got their hands on a Coleman stove and huddled as close as they could. It was New Year's Day 1944. Before it was through, all elements of the 36th were relieved of duty and sent into bivouac. The battle of San Pietro was over.

22

The Death of Captain Waskow

ERNIE PYLE RETURNED to his room at Caserta to get some writing done in the aftermatch of the battle for San Pietro. He was housed in the castle in a large room that he shared with a couple of other reporters, though eight cots were available for those times when the press corps filled the place. The room was "big and bare and cold," he wrote to Jerry. "Several of the windowpanes were blown out; the door was blown out; the place was cold and dirty."

An Italian "houseboy" just showed up one day and started tidying the room and running errands for the reporters. He got the windows fixed, found some wood for the stove, and did laundry for the correspondents. He even brought in flowers and tables for them to work on. "He looks over my shoulder when I'm writing," Pyle wrote to Jerry, "and sits in the room all day trying to anticipate our wants . . ."[1]

Pyle told another correspondent that his plan in Caserta was to catch up on his work with about five days of writing before heading back to the front "which means I'll spend Christmas in the mud . . ." But he had a hard time getting the columns out and wasn't particularly satisfied with what he was doing.

Don Whitehead returned to Caserta just before Christmas as well. He described visiting with Ernie in the big castle room. "Usually he would be huddled in his bedding roll with only his head sticking out, looking like a pixie in that knit cap."

Whitehead and the other reporters had grown protective of Ernie. He was so frail and got sick so often. "I suppose we sensed that war was a heavier strain on him than on most of us," Whitehead wrote later, "because he was more sensitive to cold and hunger and pain and the shock of seeing men killed and wounded." Ernie told Whitehead that he'd grown depressed after his time at the frontline, and heard complaints from Ernie about "losing his touch" and writing "stuff" that "stunk."[2]

He was working on columns about the artillery and the mule trains that he had visited, and a third story, a piece about the captain who had been brought down off the mountain on the back of a mule. He showed this last column to Whitehead, who said to Ernie, "If this is a sample from a guy who has lost his touch then the rest of us had better go home."

The Captain Waskow piece couldn't be printed until the family itself was notified of Henry's death. Regardless, Pyle's work was done and he took his columns to an office in Naples to be transmitted to the United Press in New York. Pyle decided that in the interim, instead of returning to the front, he would have a few drinks. Those few drinks turned into a lot of drinks.

There was a bar at the Caserta palace, and that Christmas Eve Pyle began drinking cognac. He was soon joined by a member of the Special Forces unit, who was heading out for an assignment in the next few days. Together they went on a days' long bender that ended just before New Year's Eve when the chief public relations officer of the Fifth Army sent a young doctor to Ernie's room at the palace to wake Pyle up and give him a shot of B-1 vitamins for his hangover.

The next day he wrote a letter to Jerry in which he told about the drunk, but added, "I'm not sorry, for I guess we had to relax somehow, and I was more than a week ahead with the columns, and also we stayed in our room most of the time and didn't bother anybody . . ."[3]

A couple of days earlier, Henry Waskow's family having been notified of his death, Pyle's story was transmitted via the Signal Corps to United Press in New York for distribution. Staff Sergeant Wallace Irwin's job was to read one news article after the next into a microphone, each to be sent by short-wave radio across the ocean for transcription and publication. Suddenly Irwin found himself struggling to finish the copy that was in his hand. Ernie Pyle's story, soon to be published across the country under the title, "The Death of Captain Waskow" had that sort of effect.[4]

Who knows where the power of the piece came from? It was obviously built out of the miseries, frustration, and horrors of the previous month's engagement in the mountains and valleys of Italy, but Pyle had seen other hard moments in this war. He had never met Henry Waskow in life, but Pyle knew him in the way that he knew hundreds of other brave young men who were climbing this war's mountains, only to be carried home on the backs of mules.

Regardless, its impact was deep and immediate. Simple, stately, steeped in respect and empathy—of all the stories Pyle wrote during World War II, none would have a greater force than this one:

At the Front Lines In Italy—

In this war I have known a lot of officers who were loved and respected by the soldiers under them. But never have I crossed the trail of any man as beloved as Capt. Henry T. Waskow, of Belton, Texas.

Captain Waskow was a company commander in the 36th division. He had been in this company since long before he left the States. He was very young, only in his middle 20s, but he carried in him a sincerity and gentleness that made people want to be guided by him.

"After my own father, he comes next," a sergeant told me.

"He always looked after us," a soldier said. "He'd go to bat for us every time."

"I've never known him to do anything unkind," another one said.

I was at the foot of the mule trail the night they brought Captain Waskow down. The moon was nearly full at the time, and you could see far up the trail, and even part way across the valley. Soldiers made shadows as they walked.

Dead men had been coming down the mountain all evening, lashed onto the backs of mules. They came lying belly down across the wooden packsaddle, the heads hanging down on the left side of the mule, their stiffened legs sticking awkwardly from the other side, bobbing up and down as the mule walked.

The Italian mule skinners were afraid to walk beside dead men, so Americans had to lead the mules down that night. Even the Americans were reluctant to unlash and lift off the bodies, when they got to the bottom, so an officer had to do it himself and ask others to help.

The first one came early in the morning. They slid him down from the mule, and stood him on his feet for a moment. In the half light he might have been merely a sick man standing there leaning on the other. They laid him on the ground in the shadow of the stone wall alongside the road.

I don't know who that first one was. You feel small in the presence of dead men and ashamed of being alive, and you don't ask silly questions.

We left him there beside the road, that first one, and we all went back into the cowshed and sat on water cans or lay on the straw, waiting for the next batch of mules.

Somebody said the dead soldier had been dead for four days, and then nobody said anything more about him. We talked for an hour or more; the dead man lay all alone, outside in the shadow of the wall.

Then a soldier came into the cowshed and said there were some more bodies outside. We went out into the road. Four mules stood there in the moonlight, in the road where the trail came down off the mountain. The soldiers who led them stood there waiting.

"This one is Captain Waskow," one of them said quickly.

Two men unlashed his body from the mule and lifted it off and laid it in the shadow beside the stone wall. Other men took other bodies off. Finally, there were five lying end to end in a long row. You don't cover up dead men in the combat zones. They just lie there in the shadows until somebody else comes after them.

The uncertain mules moved off to their olive orchards. The men in the road seemed reluctant to leave. They stood around, and gradually I could sense them moving, one by one, close to Captain Waskow's body. Not so much to look, I think, as to say something in finality to him and to themselves. I stood close by and I could hear.

One soldier came and looked down, and he said out loud: "God damn it."

That's all he said, and then he walked away.

Another one came, and he said, "God damn it to hell anyway!" He looked down for a few last moments and then turned and left.

Another man came. I think he was an officer. It was hard to tell officers from men in the half light, for everybody was grimy and dirty. The man looked down into the dead captain's face and then spoke directly to him, as though he were alive: "I'm sorry, old man."

Then a soldier came and stood beside the officer and bent over, and he too spoke to his dead captain, not in a whisper but awfully tenderly, and he said: "I sure am sorry, sir."

Then the first man squatted down, and he reached down and took the captain's hand, and he sat there for a full five minutes holding the dead hand in his own and looking intently into the dead face. And he never uttered a sound all the time he sat there.

Finally he put the hand down. He reached up and gently straightened the points of the captain's shirt collar, and then he sort of rearranged the tattered edges of his uniform around the wound, and then he got up and walked away down the road in the moonlight, all alone.

The rest of us went back into the cowshed, leaving the five dead men lying in a line end to end in the shadow of the low stone wall. We lay down on the straw in the cowshed, and pretty soon we were all asleep.[5]

23

Finishing Up

JOHN HUSTON'S DOCUMENTARY film was in trouble. The order from the War Department and the president himself that real combat footage be included in the making of quality documentaries about the war—documentaries that would exceed the quality of filmmaking efforts from "our allies"—was proving more easily demanded than done. In spite of their harrowing journey to the village of San Pietro and back as the battle pulled away to San Vittore, Huston, Buck, Ambler and the camera crew from the 163rd had failed, like many other filmmakers in this war, to get actual combat footage.

The difficulties of gathering the sort of Hollywood-style war film that was hoped for and anticipated, were delineated in a long report from the Signal Corps in Italy to the War Department in Washington, written just days after San Pietro had ended. To get combat scenes, it was "not enough" for camera crews "to risk life and limb" by getting close enough to the action, said Major Herbert Freeland of the 163rd in the report. That had been done. One of many problems in shooting combat was that the war was in many ways "invisible." Troops in this war were spread out over wide areas, worked often at night and in small patrol units. Much of the action was centered on artillery, mortar, and air fire, which, by the nature of its unexpectedness, made it impossible to get the sort of combat footage that was anticipated by viewers wanting to see a war movie. "From a photographic standing, the enemy is most perverse and unaccommodating."

"Recently we spent time with cameras set up behind rocks on Mt. Lungo overlooking the town of San Pietro and San Vittore," Freeland continued in the report. "Our lines and those of the enemy were less than half a mile away, and shells were often landing within one hundred yards of us, yet all that could be photographed were our own shells landing in San Vittore, and those of the enemy dropped into San Pietro. We shot these shellings under adverse conditions and the quality of the material is questionable."[1]

In addition, the white phosphorous shells, which emitted a photogenic puff of white smoke, were being used less and less in the war. And large cameras, easily spotted as they were poked out of foxholes, were quick to draw enemy fire, making many combat groups "allergic" to being accompanied by such units.

What Huston and company were able to shoot was a lot of "after the fact" footage: the ruins of San Pietro, scenes of battle destruction, blown-out bridges and tanks, etc. They also had footage of the landscape—ravaged olive trees and holes made by shells in the valley—and shots of the two units of the 36th that they'd made near the olive grove on the way into San Pietro. They got background footage of artillery units rapidly loading and firing howitzers. They had the footage of German prisoners, coming down off Mt. Sammucro that Ernie Pyle witnessed and reported on. They had a number of long shots of artillery fire and some tanks moving in toward San Pietro. They shot several powerful images of dead bodies, German, Italians (in white sheets being tossed in the back of a truck), and even some Americans. Someone had also gotten very dramatic footage of one of the tanks being destroyed by the Germans.[2] There was more incidental footage gathered in their days with the 143rd. But much more was needed in order to tell the blow-by-blow story of the battle for San Pietro.

Scenes of combat could be reenacted, but given the strictures placed on film crews at the front to produce the most realistic movies possible, to pursue re-creations was not a thing done lightly. In fact, Huston sought Frank Capra's advice in Washington before deciding to do so. He, Ambler, and Buck took a few days off and went to Naples, where Huston wired Capra explaining the circumstances and asking for counsel.

By coincidence, his old friend and colleague Humphrey Bogart was in the city with wife Mayo on a USO tour. As Huston waited for Capra's response, he had "a grand reunion" with Bogart, who threw a party in his hotel room to toast the occasion. The festivities got out of hand and ended, according to Huston, with Bogart telling a complaining general from across the hall "to go fuck himself."[3]

Meanwhile, word came back from Capra to get the film done any way that Huston could.[4] Huston returned with Buck to the 143rd in the Liri Valley (Ambler had received orders to head back to England for a new assignment with the British Film Unit in the interim). Though Huston would never confess to doing so in later descriptions of the filming, they proceeded to use troops from the unit to reenact moments of the battle that the battalion had just fought.

The recent University of Texas law school grad, newly married on Cape Cod, and son of a Texas Democratic Party bigwig, Captain Joel Westbrook, operations officer for the 143rd, who also happened be an old friend of Henry Waskow, was asked to facilitate Huston's work. The two men would go over maps together and Westbrook would describe the battle action to the filmmaker—which units were where, the various areas and landscapes in which they worked, the weaponry they would have been using, how the fighting ensued.

Beginning in late December and working together until mid-January, Huston and troops from the 143rd returned to the different corners of the battlefield to re-enact action from the fighting. Westbrook was able to secure concussive, rather than the more dangerous fragmentation grenades for the shoots, allowing Huston to get dramatic footage of GI's popping up out of crouched positions to heave their ammo.[5]

They went back to Sammucro on December 31 and shot images of infantrymen cautiously and laboriously trudging back up the mountain among the rocky rubble. They took shots of riflemen from the mountaintop, shooting downward toward the valley, and shots of riflemen among the rocks on the way to the top, shooting up the hill.

On other days, in December and early January, they shot a variety of scenes: wounded soldiers being carried down the hillside on a litter, a medic treating a wounded GI, an officer taking a phone call in the field, infantrymen carefully advancing through the olive groves, and over the valley directly to the south of San Pietro, soldiers passing smokes to one another, and men of the 143rd soldiering in the various terrains associated with the battlefield.[6]

Shots of the destroyed town were also collected, with images of infantry cautiously entering the village and checking inside its many downed buildings, as well as footage of the Italian refugees, emerging from their caves in the wake of the fighting. A scene with General Walker and his staff overlooking a map of the battlefield, pointing here and there at various positions, was shot, so were images of the 143rd post-battle, clustered in repose at the foot of a hill. A haunting shot of Italians digging neatly lined graves in a cemetery, and pounding dog tags and names on grave markers was also made.

Meanwhile, Huston worked on the script in the evenings, crafting a powerful and straightforward description of San Pietro and the battle in elegant language, tightly focused on the infantry, the action, and the consequences to the village. Huston offered no great triumphal message to the taking of San Pietro; instead he wrote a salute to the bravery, determination, and sacrifice of the men who waged war in the Liri Valley. His narration was a deep and moving bow.

Huston lost his re-enactors in the middle of January, when the 36th moved out to the next hard fight on the way to Rome—the Rapido River, at the German Gustav Line. He finished up shooting through the end of the month, picking up shots of tank maneuvers, landscapes, and more Italian citizens.

By the end of February, Huston was back in the States, already beginning the editing of a film that would one day be considered one of the greatest documentaries produced during the war.

RILEY TIDWELL was hurt badly enough on his walk down the mountain with Captain Waskow that he was sent to a hospital in Naples, and from there, a C-47 transport plane took him to further medical care in Bizerte. The plane took off and as luck would have it, hit some turbulence en route. Tidwell was in a row of litters stacked to the side of the plane; he was not strapped down. When the C-47 hit an air pocket, Tidwell bounced up off the canvas and hit his head on the litter above, breaking open the stitches on his wound near his left ear. There was lots of blood, but the company runner was none the worse for wear when the plane was forced down in Sicily.

A two-day stay on the island followed before Tidwell finally got to Bizerte, where he promptly caught pneumonia. It wasn't the pneumonia, nor the wounds, however, which were the primary concern of his doctors. The trench foot that he'd contracted in Italy was threatening his feet. Without the proper care and without him "working" the circulation by walking the hospital hallways, there was a good chance he could lose his toes. To reinforce the message, he was shown a jar full of digits in formaldehyde—pickled toes, he and his fellow trench foot victims called them—as an object lesson in the benefits of exercise.

He spent two months in Bizerte before getting his discharge. From the hospital, he was sent to a replacement camp outside of the city, where he was expected to get back into shape for further service. While there, he was told to expect to be shipped to England. From England, he would probably be shipped back to the U.S. and then quickly to the Pacific.

Less than thrilled at the prospect of leaving his Company B comrades in Italy, Tidwell simply decided to head back to Naples and join up with his old division. As soon as he felt sufficiently mended, Tidwell went AWOL from his replacement camp, hitched a ride on a plane bound for Naples, and soon after landing, reported himself to an MP. The military police were so surprised at an AWOL soldier heading toward the frontlines, that they simply told Tidwell to return to his unit. He got back with Company B in mid-February, just in time to witness the bombing of the monastery at Cassino.

Riley Tidwell would spend another year and several months in the Army with stints in the 36th at Anzio, and briefly in the south of France, before heading back to the States in the fall of 1944.

Once home, he would surprisingly find that his ties to his old captain were not yet severed.[7]

MARY GOTH WASKOW was born in MacGregor, Texas, in 1877 to a sheepherder named George Goth, and a young German immigrant, also named Mary, who died just five years after her daughter's birth.

Twenty- years later, young Mary Goth married a neighbor boy—another child of German immigrants—named Frank Waskow, and the two of them proceeded to have eight children, the youngest two being Henry Thomas and Mary Lee.

The Waskows farmed a few central Texas homesteads before settling onto a place in Bell Country between the towns of Temple and Belton. The home they inhabited teemed with children and young adults, whose ages spanned a full twenty years. They kept some livestock and grew cotton; they nurtured a pecan tree in the front yard. The boys slept on a porch kept open in the hot Texas summers, and tied off with tarp in the cold winter winds. Mary made her children's clothing out of flour sacks and it was expected that a pair of shoes would last until they were outgrown, at which time they would be passed down from one sibling to the next.[8]

She baked bread, encouraged a close reading of the Bible, and raised a troupe of honest and hard-working children, six of whom were still living around Belton at the end of December 1943.

Mary was sick in bed quite often that winter. She suffered from high blood pressure and had been feeling a little woozy and worried about Henry. All of this fighting in Italy only added to her anxiety. It was enough to be concerned about her son, August, who had come home on December 16, ravaged by war wounds and soon to depart to a hospital in Atlantic City, New Jersey, for more rehab. Having barely survived Altavilla, August was now about to spend his third month in a hospital—first on a ship in Naples harbor, then in Bizerte, now this new one in Atlantic City, New Jersey[9]—with no telling when he'd be better.

And she hadn't heard any news from Henry in weeks. He was always the most punctual one in the family. Up to that time, his letters had arrived faithfully every three weeks, the last one arriving at the end of November. Where was his new cablegram? Why hadn't she heard from Henry?

She couldn't keep her mind off pending disaster and it was wrecking her own constitution. Her children were so concerned about their mother's health that they worked out a plan if anything happened to Henry. They didn't want to think about such things themselves, but just in case, Mary Lee, the youngest in the family, knew the women who worked in Belton's Western Union Office. If they were to get a telegram about Henry, she arranged to have them contact her, instead of her parents. She would pass the word on to her mother.

That very thing happened on the twenty-ninth of December. The women from Western Union called Mary Lee, who was doing volunteer work at the hospital, and told her there was a telegram. The military had been holding news of fatalities until after Christmas, which is why word was so slow getting to Belton. After a good deep cry on her own behalf, Mary Lee got ahold of her older brothers.

Together they drove to the Waskow home, where they found their father and mother together. Mother was in bed. She saw them all coming in with those faces and knew in an instant what had happened. Her youngest son, her dutiful boy, was dead.[10]

THE WAR news in Texas that January was nothing but grim. The toll from the fall and winter campaigns in Italy continued to resound in headlines of death and injury in the ranks of the 36th. There were so many wounded Texans waiting for an opportunity to recuperate at home, that for the first time ever, the army organized a mass evacuation by transport plane of Texas patients from a hospital in South Carolina, where they had originally been flown from North Africa. Instead of being loaded on trains for a two or three-day trip, seventy-five soldiers, including Jack White of Belton, were flown to McCloskey General Hospital in Temple to resume their treatments.

Amid these headlines, news of Henry Waskow's death appeared on the front page of the Belton paper a week after his family got word of the same. The story had no details of what had happened in

Italy, but told of Captain Waskow's early life in Belton, his gradua-tion from Belton High and Temple Junior College. It said he had earned a bachelor's degree from Trinity University and that he had been a member of the Belton National Guard since he was a teen-ager. It mentioned that another son of Frank Waskow, August, had been seriously wounded in Italy in the fall, and was just finishing a visit at home in Belton, before heading off to a hospital stay in New Jersey. The article was simple and brief, but its placement on the front page suggested there was more to be said.

That happened four days later, on January 10, when Ernie Pyle's column was published for the first time.

PYLE'S EDITORS knew they had something special from the mo-ment the piece arrived. Without giving the story a headline, the *Washington Daily News*, Pyle's old daily and the flagship newspaper of Scripps-Howard, ran the story in large type across its entire front page, using that striking first paragraph to grab the reader's atten-tion: *In this war I have known a lot of officers who were loved and re-spected by the soldiers under them. But never have I crossed the trail of any man as beloved as Capt. Henry T. Waskow, of Belton, Texas . . .*

The edition sold out. Pyle's story was likewise placed on the front pages of his syndicators across the country, often under the title, "The Death of Captain Waskow." It was picked up by other news-papers in Texas—Laredo, El Paso, Brownsville, Paris, Port Arthur, Anson, Abilene, Lubbock and elsewhere. Newspapers in Reno, Ne-vada; Kingsport, Tennessee; Helena, Montana; Troy, New York; Madison, Wisconsin; Long Beach, California and scores more fea-tured the piece. *Time Magazine* asked Scripps-Howard if it could reprint the column; the *Readers Digest* published it whole; Arthur Godfrey read it to his CBS radio audience.

From the moment it appeared, "The Death of Captain Waskow" was acknowledged not only as a masterful piece of writing, but one of those stories that catches the essence of the times. For months now, it seemed that something was not quite right with the U.S. Army in Italy; it hadn't been moving toward Rome as it should have, as it had through Sicily. It was one thing to read of the difficulties the GIs faced in the mountains and valleys of Italy, and another to have that terrible effort boiled down to the death of one soldier brought down off the rocks and saluted by his comrades. Americans understood immediately that Henry Waskow stood for thousands of others who had already perished, and thousands more whose deaths were yet to come. At home, mothers, fathers, family, and friends read Ernie Pyle's story and thought not only of their own sons and daughters serving in harm's way overseas, but of each other, and the awful toll of war.

The *Belton Journal* ran the column on January 13 and was instantly flooded with letters from people saddened by the death of Henry Waskow and deeply moved by Pyle's account of it. Many readers from outside the area sent clippings of the story from their own newspapers, as if the news might not have arrived yet in tiny Belton; these included Texas Congressman William Poage, sending the front page from the *Washington Daily News*, and a man from Chicago, who had served with Waskow before the war. "It was my pleasure to know and serve under this outstanding young leader while with the 36th Div. in Camp Bowie, Texas, in 1941," wrote Sgt. Edgar F. Kirby, Jr. "It grieves me deeply to learn of this loss to your community and his very dear loved one."[11]

The editor of the *Belton Journal* understood the power and impact of the story but worried on behalf of the Waskow family. "We will not bother to suggest that you read Ernie Pyle's story on page 1 today about Captain Waskow," he wrote. "If you have not already read it, we suspect that some of your friends will urge you to do so.

"What we are thinking about is the effect of this dispatch on Captain Waskow's own people here at home. We doubt that they can read it without tears, and for any accentuation of their grief, we are most regretful. But did ever a sorrowing family receive a more moving testimonial to the affection with which a brave man was regarded, in death as in life, by his comrades-in-arms?"

At the Waskow home, condolences flowed freely. Stacks of cards and letters came in, none of them, unfortunately, enough to console the grief of Mary Goth Waskow. She remained bedridden. Included in the post, was Henry's last letter home, written sometime on the eve of his final battle: "If you are reading this, I will have died for my country and all that it stands for . . ." It was too close, too dear for the family to share. In fact, the Waskow family would hold on to it and keep it unpublished for the next fifteen years.[12]

Back in Italy, Ernie Pyle decided to continue his R & R in Naples. He got sober, found a room in a house maintained by the Air Force press corps right in the city, and continued to catch up on his column writing. He found out his North Africa book, *Here Is Your War,* was maintaining its status on bestseller lists and his reporting from Italy was receiving unprecedented acclaim for a war correspondent.

One reporter declared the "three great discoveries of this war are the jeep, the Red Cross girl, and Ernie Pyle." The *Saturday Evening Post* called him "the most prayed-for man with the American troops"; and *Life* said that his work "occupied a place in American journalistic letters which no other correspondent in this war has achieved." An editor for the *Toledo Blade* called Pyle's "story of the dead men coming down the hill . . . the most beautifully written newspaper story I have ever read."[13]

The president of the United Press wrote of the story, "I'm going to hang it up and look at it every once in a while just to make me glad that . . . there are still men in [the business] like Pyle who can write stuff like that."[14] The story was used as a means to sell war bonds all across the country, including in the city of Belton itself. Above the masthead on the very day it published Pyle's column, the

Journal ran a banner that read, CAPTAIN WASKOW GAVE HIS LIFE * The Least You Can Do Is Buy Bonds!

Praise from members of the press was echoed by soldiers in the theater. In a little more than a year's time, Pyle had gone from a fairly anonymous reporter to one of the most recognized and famed figures of the war. His skinny frame, clothed in hanging fatigues; his knit cap, with its little bill edging down toward his brow; his sad eyes, as doleful as an old dog, were now as recognizable as Eisenhower's bald head or Patton's ivory handled pistols to GIs all over North Africa and Italy.

To crown his achievements for the year and validate his new-found fame, Pyle was awarded with the Pulitzer Prize for Correspondence in the spring of 1944—presented for the quality of his war reporting in the previous year. Lee Miller nominated him, but Pyle didn't think he had a chance "because my stuff just doesn't fit their rules."[15] He even made a $100 bet with his editor that he wouldn't win. Pyle was in London, preparing for D-Day, when word of the award came. Don Whitehead phoned him with the news. "Well I'll be goddamned," Pyle said. "Now I lose a hundred dollars."

Ernie Pyle remained a guy with a myriad of aches, pains, and insecurities. He was still an Indiana guy who wanted to be liked by the people he met along the way. He was still escaping a bad marriage (Jerry was once again back in the hospital in New Mexico, and more tribulations were to come) by risking life and limb on the front lines of a world war. He would ultimately spend another year leading this dual life that combined fame and uncertainty, acclaim and heartache, fraternity and loneliness, all without ever finding simple happiness.

His time would finally come far from North Africa, or the Italian mountains, or the beaches of Normandy, where he was soon headed. Even far from the infantry that he so admired. Instead, Ernie Pyle would die on an island in the Pacific, almost as an afterthought to the ground war, as the fighting wound down in April 1945.

For now, however, back in Italy in the third week of January 1944, Pyle had had enough of the comforts of Naples, and the notes from Lee Miller telling him of his successes back in the States. It was time to return to the frontlines, to follow the troops as they butted heads, once again, with the German Panzer divisions on this slow and agonizing journey to Rome. He decided to skip, for the time being, the Allied landing at Anzio, and instead join the 34th Division as it contemplated an attack on the Gustav Line.

He barely missed the prelude to this assault, which once again featured the 36th Division, in a disastrous attempt at crossing the Rapido River.

24

Rapido

THERE WAS ONE MORE STORY to be written about the 36th Division in the Liri Valley, one more tragedy.

After almost three weeks bivouac, during which replacement troops poured into the division to fill the enormous number of slots vacated by all the casualties inflicted on the Texas Division at San Pietro, the unit made ready to advance against the next of the Winter Lines constructed by the Germans in the Liri Valley, the formidable Gustav Line.

Extending down from the famed monastery on top of Monte Cassino and through the town of Cassino, which, much like San Pietro, was tucked into the foot of the mountain near the valley floor, the solid defenses of the Gustav ran right across the Liri on the north side of the Rapido River. The 15th Panzer Grenadiers had had months to build and perfect the interlocking system of defenses along and above the river. They constructed concrete bunkers, embedded tanks in the landscape, planted mines along approach routes, cut down trees to open lines of fire and set up artillery pointed at every possible approach to the Rapido.

The river itself presented difficult challenges. It was eight to twelve feet deep and forty to fifty feet wide. There were steep banks leading into and out of the water, the flow of which was rapid, and, in January, freezing cold. In a word, the Rapido was unfordable. It also had no bridges. The only means across were assault boats and pontoon walking bridges, which would need to be erected by troops operating under the well-placed guns of the German forces arrayed before them. Only four of these bridges were available for use by the 36th.

Approaches to the river were almost all uncovered, leaving German artillery and small arms fire with wide-open views of the American attack from the surrounding hillsides. And finally, once across the river, infantry would be greeted by the ubiquitous barbed wire that seemed to be everywhere in the valley.

Since the battle at San Pietro, General Clark had decided that the only way to break the German Winter Lines in the Liri Valley was to go around them by means of an amphibious assault. He had been mulling over such a plan since late October. The idea for that attack had advanced to the point where it was now scheduled to take place at Anzio in the third week of January. But to ensure its success, he would need to pin down German troops in the Liri Valley, to keep them from hindering the planned amphibious assault at Anzio. Enter the 36th: as part of his Liri Valley strategy, General Walker and his division were ordered to advance across the Rapido on January 20.

Walker's 141st and the 143rd regiments drew the short straws. More than 1,000 enlisted replacement troops and ninety officers had been plugged into their ranks, yet both regiments remained undermanned, particularly the 143rd. The Rapido crossing would be the first action for the great majority of the new troops, including many of the officers, who were largely fresh from officers' training school.

Walker smelled a disaster in the works and voiced his trepidations to Clark. He was told, essentially, that Clark knew this would be a difficult fight, but it was a military necessity for the larger success that would come at Anzio. Victory at Anzio, it was understood, would open the door to Rome.

Walker's World War I experience included a battle on the Marne, where he had commanded American troops against a German attack similar to the one that he was about to undertake with the 36th. "On that day, in my battalion sector, a German division of about 10,000 men made an attack across the river," Walker wrote later. "In good defensive position along the Marne, my battalion of 1,200 solders turned the Germans back, disorganized, confused, and slaughtered them."[1] Now he feared the same thing would happen to his own troops.

As with earlier attacks in the mountains and valleys of Italy, the British X Corps led off the assault on the left side of the front, nearer the coast. On January 17 the Brits had some initial successes, crossing yet another river blocking the way north, the Garigliano, and establishing a beachhead on the opposite side. The Tommies were soon stalled, however, which left the left flank of the Americans uncovered as January 20 approached.

The focal point of the American attack was a village on a bluff on the north side of the river called Sant'Angelo. Another thunderous barrage of artillery preceded the 36th's advance, which began at 7 p.m. the night of the twentieth. Darkness had fallen and a heavy fog blanketed the valley but neither prevented the Germans from detecting the movement and almost immediately opening fire with mortar, small arms and artillery.

The 141st took the lead, but confusion reigned from the start. Inexperienced troops wandered off the paths markeds to crossing points and into heavily mined areas. Of the pontoon footbridges to be employed in the crossing, one turned out to be defective; one was destroyed by a mine as it was being carried to the river; and a third was lost to artillery fire.[2] Assault boats were sunk or damaged, drowning a number of infantrymen in the process. Just before dawn a few score men of 1st Battalion had crossed on the only functioning bridge, but they were soon left to their own devices as other members of the battalion and regiment continued to be stymied on the southwest side of the river.

Meanwhile the 143rd, which had set out at 8 p.m. the evening before, was having similar bad luck. Companies B and C—far different creatures from a month and a half earlier, with almost all new personnel—had made it across the river, but most of their boats were wrecked in the process, which meant that few others could get across the Rapido to assist. The two companies were pinned down and taking a terrific pounding, when Colonel William Martin, still in command of the regiment, ordered them back to their starting point across the river from Sant'Angelo. A third and fourth crossing never even got off the ground due to intense enemy fire.

Keyes ordered General Walker to do it all over again on January 21. More boats were found, and now the 3rd Battalion took the lead. But again the 36th butted into a hard enemy wall of fire. Starting in the late afternoon of the twenty-first, the 3rd, the 1st, and eventually the 2nd battalions were all able to make it across the river, but because of heavy enemy fire, they couldn't shore up their gains by constructing any bridges across the river that would allow armored reinforcement. They were ordered to withdraw by early afternoon the next day.

To the south, the 141st was likewise able to get a couple of battalions over the river, and likewise was unable to secure those gains with bridgeheads. They could also find no remnants of Companies A, B, and C, who'd been left on the far side of the river that morning. Soon the 2nd and 3rd battalions were themselves trapped on the wrong side of the river. When the 143rd completed its withdrawal, German forces concentrated their attack on the two trapped battalions, moving to within yards of them. In the end, just forty men from the two battalions were able to escape by swimming across the Rapido. Everyone else was either killed, wounded, or taken prisoner.

Unbelievably, Keyes wanted Walker to take one more try at the river, but this time the commander of the 36th balked. It just could not work, he argued. The 36th had taken too much punishment and they could not make any gains. Keyes argued that the Germans had taken a hard blow, that their morale was probably low. But as Walker wrote later, "This was wishful thinking."

Keyes spoke with Clark about Walker's misgivings and after some back-and-forth, Clark agreed to call off the third assault. He would continue to pursue the Gustav Line from a higher position, near the village of Cassino with the 34th Division taking the lead.

Meanwhile the 36th withdrew with an agonizing toll. In 48 hours of fighting, they suffered more than 2,100 casualties, including 155 killed, more than 1,000 wounded and more than 900 captured. Battered and bruised, needing to rebuild itself one more time, the Texas Division was, in the words of an historian "for all practical purposes, no longer an effective combat unit."[3]

Recriminations followed quickly. Walker knew that someone would pay for the disaster at the Rapido and he fully expected that someone to be himself. It was not in Clark's makeup to fall on his own sword. Two weeks after the battle, Walker's staff was dismissed by Clark, including: General Wilbur, Colonel Martin, and Walker's son, Fred, Jr. Walker was not even given the opportunity of naming his own replacement officers.

Privately to Walker, Clark acknowledged the failure of the Rapido attack, but never fully accepted that an error in judgment—his own—had occurred. He continued to suggest that the assault had been a necessary component of the Anzio action. In years to come, Clark never mentioned the battle at the Rapido and he failed to write anything about it in his memoirs.

Though he had obviously lost Clark's confidence (a mutually felt sentiment from Walker towards Clark), Walker was told that he would not be dismissed until he had a chance to rebuild the 36th and lead it one more time into successful combat. This would happen in early June at the village of Velletri, where Walker led the rebuilt division in a breakthrough that would help get the Fifth Army finally to Rome.

Soon afterward, Walker was sent home to serve as commandant of the U.S. Army Infantry School at Fort Benning, Georgia. Walker had made it to Rome, but that was as far as he would go. As he arrived in the city on June 26, 1944, and took up a brief residence in a villa before his departure from Italy, his remaining officers arranged for a dinner at which he was saluted. It was, Walker confided to his diary "The only real reward I receive[d] for my past three years with the division . . ."[4]

25

A Final Posting

WORKING FROM THE ARMY Pictorial Services production facilities in Astoria, New York, John Huston edited an initial version of a documentary film that he wanted to call *San Pietro* (Frank Capra preferred *Foot Soldier* or *The Foot Soldier and San Pietro*)[1].

A first showing that spring elicited a strongly negative reaction from the Army brass who saw it. According to Huston, one unnamed three-star general walked out about three-quarters of the way through the movie and was followed by a string of officers, taking their lead from the general in descending order of rank.[2] Huston got the message through the Pictorial Services that the War Department wanted no part of the movie.

San Pietro languished through the summer, the subject of debate in the conference rooms of the Pentagon, and in editing suites at the offices of Hollywood branch of the Signal Corps, where Huston had taken the movie for more editing. But in early August, Capra was able to get the film a viewing with George Marshall and its fortunes soon changed.

Marshall knew at a very personal level the hardships of this long war. He had recently lost his stepson to a sniper bullet near Velletri in Italy. He was working with Capra on a new set of documentaries intended to prepare the American public for the ongoing battle with the Japanese after the war in Europe was over. He thought *San Pietro* was too long, and could be judiciously edited, but he was not about to stifle its release. In fact, he said "this picture should be seen by every American soldier in training. It will not discourage but rather will prepare them for the initial shock of combat."[3]

Huston cut the movie down from five reels to three. He added a prologue from General Mark Clark, who stands stiffly in front of the camera and intones a brief message acknowledging the hard fighting at San Pietro, but proclaiming its value to the Allied cause. The film needed further vetting and feedback from an array of viewers at the Signal Corps and in the War Department.[4]

Finally, in March 1945, the film got a preview with a general audience at Twentieth Centry Fox studios in Hollywood. "I can't say it was a joyous evening," Huston later wrote in a thank you note to Darryl Zanuck, head of Fox. "*San Pietro* is a dolorous goddamn picture, full of hacked up towns and tanks and bodies, but the response from the two hundred assorted people present was very gratifying. In other words, I succeeded in making everyone of them utterly miserable which is the purpose of this picture."[5]

San Pietro opened with a long shot of the Liri Valley and its surrounding mountains, describing the history of the region and its agricultural roots. Footage of denuded olive trees are followed by the first close-ups of the destruction in the village of San Pietro, ending on a shot of the shell-racked walls and a roofless chancel of the Church of St. Michael the Archangel, and its statue of St. Peter, the village's patron saint.

There follows a straight-forward description of the battle from its opening moments at the muddy Volturno River, to its conclusion at San Pietro, with Italian refugees coming out of the caves in the hillside. What was shocking to many were the images of death and suffering littered throughout the film: stacks of dead bodies were seen being tossed into the back of a truck; dead soldiers, both German and American, were shown on the battlefield; a body strapped to a litter, much like Henry Waskow, was shown being carried down the mountainside. In conjunction with images of smiling Texas infantrymen, shown gathered on the eve of battle at the start of the film, the implications were startling. This was an Army film, intended to be shown to a large audience of recruits and even the general public, telling a story that did not shirk from the horrors of war. Huston was told that he'd made an "anti-war" film, and his initial response was to say that if he ever made a pro-war film, he hoped someone would take him out and shoot him.[6]

The movie was released in April 1945 and got largely glowing reviews, particularly from film critic James Agee in *Time* who named it one of the two best films of 1945. Despite the fact that much of the combat footage was actually reenacted, the documentary was seen as one of the most realistic portrayals of the life of a foot soldier ever put on film. Even though it was released as the war in Europe was coming to an end and a year and several months after the battle itself, *San Pietro* remained a vivid and truthful description of the cost of battle.

Photographs of dead Americans on the battlefield had been published before in World War II (beginning in the fall of 1943), but *San Pietro* put those images in an ongoing narrative context that remains haunting to viewers almost seventy years later. As Huston panned the aftermath of the fight, including images of the men of the 143rd weary, resting after the battle, some smiling in a measure of relief at having survived the fight, many just gazing off with their own thought, Huston' narration intones: "Many among those you see alive here have since joined the ranks of their brothers in arms who fell at San Pietro. For ahead lay San Vittore and the Rapido River and Cassino. And beyond Cassino more rivers and more mountains and more towns . . . more San Pietros . . . greater or lesser . . . a thousand more."

In 1991, *San Pietro* was chosen to be preserved in the National Film Registry by the National Film Preservation Board. It was picked ten years later to be one of fifty films included in a boxed DVD set compiled by the National Film Preservation Foundation.

The film has not grown old without controversy. Some in the film community have criticized the army for insisting upon the cuts that reduced the length of the feature from about fifty to thirty-two minutes. Others have chided Huston for never coming totally clean about the fact that he used re-creations in the making of the film. But the last word on the subject rightfully belongs to Joel West-brook, the 143rd Battalion captain who helped make the filming possible. Not only did Westbrook think it was an accurate depiction of the battle, he actually promoted its showing when he returned to Texas after the war.[7,8,9]

THE OTHER film named by James Agee as the best of the year in 1945 was *The Story of G.I. Joe*, the movie that Ernie Pyle had worked on with Arthur Miller back in the fall of 1943. Miller had long since been detached from the production but it had contin-ued in the Hollywood pipeline and came out in the fall of '45. Essentially it followed the story of Pyle's reporting in North Africa and Italy, with the dramatic conclusion centered on a version of Henry Waskow's death. Like Huston's *San Pietro*, *The Story of G.I. Joe* was lauded for its realistic and unsentimental portrayal of U.S. infantrymen.

The Pyle character was played by Burgess Meredith, who later starred in Sylvester Stallone's *Rocky* movies, as the trainer. The Waskow character, renamed Lieutenant Walker for the film (at the insistence of the Army), was portrayed by Robert Mitchum. Di-rected by William Wellman, the film garnered four Academy Award nominations, including Best Supporting Actor for Mitchum; it was proclaimed one of the ten best films of the year by the National

Board of Review; and it was nominated by the New York Film Critics Circle for Best Picture of the Year. Like *San Pietro, The Story of G.I. Joe* was chosen in 2009 for preservation by the National Film Preservation Board.

Just as the movie was being completed in the late spring of 1945, and between Ernie Pyle's death in the Pacific and the release of the movie, Riley Tidwell was tapped by the War Department public relations people to take an active role in a joint Army-Hollywood promotion of the movie. Tidwell, stationed at Camp Lee in Virginia after his European tour, had done an interview about his role in the Henry Waskow story for the public relations arm of the War Department in September 1944. His story of Waskow's death in the battle for Hill 1205 and his part in getting Waskow's body down the hill was picked up in a number of Texas newspapers.[10]

Almost a year later, Tidwell, now stationed at Fort Dix in New Jersey, was once again contacted by the War Department promotional people, who ordered him to take the train to Indianapolis for the premier of the movie *The Story of G.I. Joe.* There followed a whirlwind press tour for Tidwell and others involved in the movie.

Tidwell was photographed with Pyle's father and an aunt of Ernie's. He made an appearance on Ed Sullivan's radio program (called *Vox Populi*), which was being broadcast from Indiana. He went to Washington, D.C. and did a program at the National Press Club with Burgess Meredith.

He was finally discharged from the Army but continued to promote the film back home in Texas. He traveled around the state with Robert Mitchum, including to Belton and Temple, as well as to Houston and Dallas. He met Mary Lee Waskow and others in the Waskow family, while in Belton.

Riley Tidwell settled down in Houston after the war, where he became a truck driver and faithfully attended reunions of Company B in Mexia, held annually for many years. He died in 1995.

THE LAST chapter of Ernie Pyle's World War II saga was written in the Pacific. Pyle was not wild about going. It was too far away, he was too tired, he'd been doing war correspondence for far too long, and he had plenty of business to take care of on the home front. Still, he felt an obligation to see this war to its conclusion, just as so many others involved were doing. The plus side, he told *Life* in an early 1945 article was that unlike in Europe, where he was always cold and miserable, "I'll be damned good and stinking hot . . ."[11]

Pyle had spent the summer of 1944 following the Allied armies through France, winding up in Paris in the fall of '44. He came home on the *Queen Elizabeth* to more applause from the reading public, more book business, numerous requests for appearances and interviews, movie production questions (for Pyle's two cents, Walter Brennan would make a better Ernie Pyle than Burgess Meredith),[12] and life with Jerry.

His next book *Brave Men*, which covered Sicily, Italy (including the Captain Waskow story), and France, came out in late fall to more praise and rave reviews, including a "Dear Ernie" note from Dwight D. Eisenhower, in which Eisenhower praises Pyle's ability to "tell the truth about the infantry combat soldier . . . what the infantry soldier endures. . . I get so fighting mad," writes Eisenhower, "because of the general lack of appreciation of real heroism—which is the uncomplaining acceptance of unendurable conditions—that I become completely inarticulate."[13]

Pyle thanked "Dear General Ike," and responded, in part: ". . . I've found that no matter how much we talk, or write, or show pictures, people who have not actually been in war are incapable of having any real conception of it. I don't really blame the people. Some of them try hard to understand. But the world of the infantryman is a world so far removed from anything normal that it can be no more than academic to the average person."

Jerry had a monumental breakdown as Pyle was on the verge of leaving for the Pacific theater. She had been running through manic-depressive mood swings for a few days prior to the incident, but a live-in nurse had been carefully monitoring her condition and things seemed to be under control. One morning, Pyle was visiting the dentist's office in downtown Albuquerque. When he returned, he found the nurse outside the house, screaming and frantic. Jerry was within, soaked in her own blood. In his absence, she had taken a pair of scissors and repeatedly plunged them into her neck.

The nurse had already called for a doctor and got the scissors from Jerry. Though she had stabbed herself numerous times, no arteries had been nicked and she survived. Ernie and the nurse found a hospital in Albuquerque that would admit her that day for another lengthy stay, including shock therapy. As they waited for the ambulance, a doctor came and Jerry was sewn up and cleaned up. She asked for a cigarette from Ernie as they waited, once again, for her to be taken to the sanitarium.[14]

On January 15, 1945, Pyle took a Navy plane to Oahu and began reporting on the war in the Pacific. It was a different sort of combat and Pyle had trouble adjusting to its rhythms. He joined a carrier out of Guam, which was part of the fleet attacking Iwo Jima, but Pyle wasn't involved in the landing and saw none of the fighting there. He returned to Guam and wrote a series of stories about the carrier; the articles pleased him not at all.

He made himself ready for the invasion of Okinawa as the war in Europe was coming to a close. On Easter morning, he went ashore on that island with a group of Marines who saw little action in the few days that Ernie was with them.

He returned to the ship in time to hear the news that FDR had died and then prepped for yet another landing, on a small island near Okinawa called Ie Shima. He wrote a letter to his father the night before he was to go ashore on April 17 and started a column about the end of the war in Europe, to be published as soon as that event happened. He stuck the story in his pocket, where it stayed the next day as he climbed into a Higgins boat to head into the island.

Pyle came in after the initial landing on Ie Shima and saw evidence of the fight in the form of landmined vehicles and dead Japanese. He spent the night on the island in the company of the 305th Regiment of the 77th Division of the U.S. Army—back with his beloved infantry.

The next morning, Pyle took a jeep ride with three officers of the 305th toward the village of Ie Shima. They were in a column of vehicles traveling on a road that paralleled the beach along the East China Sea. A handful of trucks and another jeep led the way up the road. Suddenly, a Japanese machine-gunner opened fire on Pyle's ride. All four men dived out and headed for a ditch beside the road. When the shooting died down, Pyle stuck his head out to locate the others. "Are you all right?" he called.

Those were his last words.

The gunner opened fire once again, and Ernie Pyle was dead, a bullet to the left temple.[15]

MARY GOTH WASKOW died on February 21, 1944, a little more than three months after her son, Henry. Her heart just gave out on her.

Mother and son were celebrated together at a memorial service at the First Baptist Church in Belton three days later. The Reverend Lonnie Webb, lifelong pastor of Henry, officiated and a handful of members from the 36th, all recovering from wounds and on leave from nearby McCloskey General Hospital served as honorary pallbearers. They included Captain Judson Skiles, Sergeant Jack White, Lieutenant Warren Klinger, Sergeant Lawrence Dahlberg, and Sergeant A.J. McDonald.

Mary Goth was survived by her husband, Frank, and seven children. August, still recovering in the hospital in New Jersey, was able to make it back for the funeral.

The Reverend Webb remembered both Mary Goth and Henry to the folks at the service. He told of the letter that Henry had written on the eve of battle and mentioned its haunting opening line: "When you read this, I will have been killed in action." The reverend said that in the letter Captain Waskow had asked that in their prayers his family, "remember also my men."

Lieutenant Klinger, from Company A, who had been wounded on the last day of Naples campaign way back in early October, gave the eulogy for Henry Waskow. Klinger, whose arm was still in a sling, remembered being comforted by Waskow as he was being carried from the field that day five months earlier. He had spent a good deal of time with Waskow before that and knew him well.

They had served in camp together, crossed the ocean on the same ship and went into Italy together. They had lived and fought together, one in Company B, one in Company A.

"He was a captain really and truly," Klinger told the congregants, "Men under him wanted to follow him. He never gave an order. He asked his men to follow him and they did. And they all loved him.

"Very few men have had the standing Captain Waskow had with his men. I am happy to have known him, to have served with him, to have been his fellow officer."[16]

Henry Thomas Waskow missed his own funeral. Or at least his remains did. They were buried in a the Sicily-Rome American Cemetery, established at Nettuno, Italy first as a temporary wartime burial ground, then as a permanent home and memorial for the bodies of the nearly 8,000 Americans who were killed in Sicily and Italy during World War II.

Back home in Belton, even before the war was over, the town named the VFW post for Henry Waskow. They also named one of the public schools for him and both still hold his name. In 1959, the family released the full text of Waskow's last letter home and its contents added to the continuing memory of the man. He was periodically recalled at reunions of the 36th and Company B in years to come, either in conjunction with that letter or Ernie Pyle's column.

As the years since the war have passed and those who knew Henry Waskow as a young man have themselves advanced into old age and death, the number who remember him have naturally diminished.

Still Ernie Pyle's words have resonance.

On November 11, 2000, at the groundbreaking for the long sought Word War II Memorial in Washington, D.C., one of the guest speakers at the ceremony was actor Tom Hanks. Hanks interest in World War II extended from his role in the *Saving Private Ryan* to ongoing efforts at producing a number of exemplary documentaries on the war. One of the chief fundraisers and supporters of this monument, it was only natural that he should be asked to speak at the ceremony. When it came time for him to come to the microphone and honor all those who had sacrificed so much during the war, he did a simple reading from Ernie Pyle:

"In this war I have known a lot of officers who were loved and respected by the soldiers under them," Hanks began, "but never have I crossed the trail of any man as beloved as Henry T. Waskow, of Belton, Texas . . ."[17]

NOTES

CHAPTER 1

1. Pyle, *Brave Men*, p. 20.
2. Knightley, *The First Casualty*, p. 326.
3. Boomhower, *The Soldier's Friend*, p. 18.
4. Ibid p. 32.
5. Coyne, *Columbia Journalism Review*, Jan.–Feb., 2012.
6. Tobin, *Ernie Pyle's War*, pp. 51, 53.
7. Ibid, p. 54.

CHAPTER 2

1. Walker, pp. 107–109.
2. Ibid, pp. 1–5.
3. Les Leggett, 36th Division chatroom notes, November 2, 2006.
4. Ibid, p. 12.

CHAPTER 3

1. Pyle, *Here Is Your War*, p. 172.
2. Desmond, pp. 296–300.
3. Knightley, p. 316.
4. Pyle, *Here Is Your War*, p. 28.
5. Ibid, p. 61.

6. Ibid, p. 102.

7. Ibid, p. 168.

8. Ibid, p. 83.

9. Ibid.

10. Tobin, p. 89.

11. Tobin, p. 54.

12. Pyle, *Ernie's War: The Best of Ernie Pyle's World War II Dispatches,* edited by David Nichols, pp. 42-44.

13. Tobin, p. 57.

14. Boomhower, p. 57.

15. Tobin, p. 62.

16. Miller, p. 191.

17. Pyle, Here Is Your War, p. 200.

18. Pyle, *Here Is Your War*, p. 241.

19. Ibid, p. 241.

20. Ibid, p. 242.

21. Pyle, *Here Is Your War*, p. 245.

22. Ibid, p. 303 (1943 edit).

CHAPTER 4

1. Walker, p. 114.

2. Interview with Bernita Peeples, Belton (Texas) newspaper, February 13, 2013.

3. Ibid.

4. Michael Lanning, "Goodbye to Captain Waskow," Veterans of Foreign Wars, May 1981, p. 9.

5. "I Was the Captain's Runner," *The Houston Post*, April 12, 1958, clip (original page unknown).

6. "In the Services of their Country," Belton Journal, p. 1, 7/29/43.

7. Section 6, Sweeney, Michael, Ph.D, Appointment at Hill 1205: Ernie Pyle and Henry T. Waskow, Texas Military Forces Museum, Austin (submitted as a paper at Ohio University, 1995).

CHAPTER 5

1. Pyle, *Brave Men,* p. 32.

2. Tobin, p. 107.

3. Pyle, *Brave Men,* p. 50.

4. Ibid, p. 56.

5. Tobin, p. 110.

6. Pyle, *Brave Men*, p. 71.

7. Ibid, p. 75.

8. "Fed Up and Bogged Down," Ernie's War: The Best of Ernie Pyle's World War II Dispatches, edited by David Nichols, pp. 166-67.

CHAPTER 6

1. Walker, p. 230.

2. Blumenson, pp. 1–10.

3. Ibid, p. 10.

4. Ibid, p. 74.

5. Wagner, p. 8.

6. Baedeker, p 195.

7. Citino, Robert, "Mark W. Clark: A General Reappraisal," *World War II Magazine*, June 8, 2012 (online).

8. Wagner, p. 53

9. Glenn C Clift, "A Letter from Salerno," October 22, 1943, 36th Infantry Division Association, texasmilitaryforcesmuseum.org/gallery/36div. htm.

10. Walker, p. 234.

11. Ibid.

CHAPTER 7

1. Tidwell interview.

2. Jack White, "Company I, 143rd Caught Hell Near Altavilla," radio interview transcript, KTEM, Temple, Texas, January 14, 1944, texasmilitaryforcesmuseum.org/gallery/36div.htm.

3. Walker, p. 240-241.

4. White, "Caught Hell," radio interview.

5. Wagner, p 36. Kelley received the 1st Congressional Medal of Honor in Europe for this action.

6. Ibid, p. 37.

7. Ibid, p. 38.
8. Ibid, p. 55.
9. Ibid, p. 52.

CHAPTER 8

1. For more on how the 1st 143rd got this assignment, see Burrage, p. 16.

2. Burrage, p. 14.

3. Ibid, p. 15.

4. Tidwell interview.

5. See for example, Klinger quote in *El Paso Herald*, 2/24/44.

6. See for example, Ray Goad, pg. 19, Waskow Legend.

7. Tidwell interview.

8. Burrage, pp. 20–21.

9. Ibid, p. 20.

10. Ibid, p. 25.

11. AAR Report, p. 5.

12. "Half Mexia's Two-Man Army Comes Home From Italy's Rains," *Mexia Weekly Herald*, May 5, 1944 (no byline).

13. Burrage, p. 23.

14. Ibid., pg. 22.

15. Some have speculated that he took the name because it sounded like Frank Capra—short and punchy; Richard Whelan, p. 81

16. Kershaw, p. 33.

17. Ibid, p. 107.

18. "Capt. Waskow's `Runner' Tells His Battle Story," *Belton Journal* 9/21/44 (no byline).

19. Burrage, p. 31.

20. Walker, p. 265.

21. Burrage p. 33.

22. Walker, p. 236.

23. Burrage, p. 33.

24. Humphrey, Walter, "Home Town, Comrades Pay Tribute to Hero," *El Paso Herald Post*, Feb. 24 1944.

25. Burrage, p. 34.

CHAPTER 9

1. Sweeney, section 9.
2. "Is Assigned to McCloskey," *El Paso Herald,* June 1944.
3. 143rd After Action Report Copy No. 3, pp. 12–14.
4. Jack White, KTEM interview, Jan 14, 1944.
5. Tidwell interview.
6. Sweeney, section 7.
7. "Capt. Waskow Says We Can Lick Nazis Any Time Anywhere," Belton Journal, Nov. 4, 1943, p. 1.
8. "Willie B. Slaughter Gets His German," Mexia Weekly Herald, 12/10/43, p. 2 (no byline).
9. "Billie Sunday Tells of Action," Mexia Weekly Herald, 11/5/43, p. 8 (no byline).
10. Baedeker, p. 186.
11. Steinbeck, p. 167.
12. *Life* Magazine, Oct. 18, 1943, p. 33.

CHAPTER 10

1. Huston, p. 102.
2. John Huston interview with R. Hughes.
3. Capra, p. 314.
4. Capra, *The Name Above the Title,* pp. 325–327.
5. Marshall interviews 466, Feb. 14, 1957.
6. Marshall 463, Feb. 14, 1957.
7. Capra, *The Name Above the Title,* p. 327.
8. Capra, p. 329.
9. McBride pg. 467.
10. McBride 467; Capra p. 334.
11. Capra, p. 340.
12. Maslowski, p. 80.
13. Report on Photographic Activities, p. 3.
14. Ibid.
15. Ibid.

CHAPTER 11

1. Tobin, p. 115.
2. Miller, p. 282.
3. Ibid p. 117.
4. Tobin, p. 122.
5. Ibid p. 128.
6. New York Times 1/25/42.
7. Huston, p. 87.
8. Ambler, p. 190.
9. Report on photographic activities, p. 1.

CHAPTER 12

1. Atkinson, p. 302.
2. Ibid, p. 298.
3. Blumenson, p. 166.
4. Ibid, p. 183.
5. Ibid, pp. 186-187.
6. Atkinson, p. 303.
7. Ibid, p. 334.
8. Ibid, p. 312.
9. Blumenson, p. 232.

CHAPTER 13

1. Walker p. 268.
2. Wagner, p. 53.
3. Palmer, p. 15.
4. Miller, p. 294.
5. Pyle, *Brave Men,* p. 117.
6. Pyle, *Brave Men,* p. 141.
7. Ibid, p. 141.

CHAPTER 14

1. Walker, p. 278.
2. 36th Historical Quarterly, winter 1990, Lee Fletcher.

3. 36th Historical Quarterly, spring 1981, Jack Clover.

4. AAR, Operations in Italy, 143rd Infantry, November 1943.

5. "Friend Writes to Mexia Family of How Son Killed," Mexia Herald, 2/11/44 p. 4.

6. "Jack B Gibson Is Reported Killed in Italian Action," Mexia Herald, 12/10/43.

7. Palmer, p. 20.

8. Tidwell interview.

9. Alban Reid, Thanksgiving 1943, Nov. 23, 2002 from 36th memo board.

CHAPTER 15

1. Les Leggett, Thanksgiving 1943, Nov. 24, 2005, 36th memo board.

2. See photos in "They Called it Purple Heart Valley," Bourke-White.

3. Ambler, p. 192.

4. Hustion, *An Open Book*, p. 107.

5. Maslowski, p. 83.

6. Ambler, p. 193.

7. "Report on Motion Picture Progress," 12/31/43 p. 27.

8. Ambler, p. 194.

9. "Report on photographic activities," 12/31/43, pp. 1-2.

CHAPTER 16

1. Wagner, p. 68.

2. Ibid, p. 68.

3. Atkinson, p. 339.

4. Blumenson, p. 276.

5. AAR Op. Dec. p. 2.

6. Various sources, including the *Mexia Daily News*, 5/4/74. The complete Last Will and Testament was held by the family until 1959, when it was given to the Temple Telegram for publication.

CHAPTER 17

1. Whitehead, p. 83.

2. Wagner, p. 74.

3. Journal 143rd CT 12/8/43.

4. Atkinson 341.

5. AAR p. 4.

6. Clover, Jack, "San pietro do you read me?" 36th Division Association, texasmilitaryforcesmuseum.org/gallery/36div.htm.

7. Alvin Amelunk, Personal Account of the B of San P, spring 1993, 36th H. Quarterly.

8. Clover, "San Pietro, Do You Read Me?"

9. Ibid.

10. AAR p. 5.

11. "Texas Doubletalk," San Antonio Express, Dec. 31, 1943, p. 3 (no byline).

12. Palmer, p. 21.

13. Pyle, *Brave Men*, p. 142.

14. AAR p. 5.

15. Vannatta, Lem, "Lucky #13," 36th Historical Quarterly, undated.

16. Pyle, *Brave Men*, p. 152.

17. Miller, p. 295

18. Pyle, *Brave Men*, pp. 153–154

Chapter 18

1. Sweeney, Sec. 10.

2. "The Waskow Legend," Winter 1984, Michael Lanning, 36th Military History Quarterly.

3. Tidwell interview.

4. Mexia Weekly Herald, Slaughter to reporter, May 5, 1944.

5. 143rd Journal CT, Dec. 13.

6. Lanning 36th Quarterly.

7. Tidwell Interview.

8. Tidwell, *The Galveston News*, Monday April 13, 1959.

9. Tidwell interview to end of chapter.

10. Tidwell interview.

Chapter 19

1. Huston, p. 110.

2. Wagner, p. 81.

3. AAR pp. 7-8.

4. Amelunke, Alvin, "Personal Account of the Battle of San Pietro, Italy," 36th Historical Quarterly, Spring 1993.

5. Wagner, pp. 82–83.

6. AAR, p. 8.

7. Bigart, Forward Position, p. 33.

8. Ibid, p. 34.

9. Tidwell interview.

10. Pyle, Brave Men, p. 155.

CHAPTER 20

1. Bigart, p. 28.

2. Ibid, p. 28.

3. Ibid, p. 29.

4. Ibid, p. 29.

5. Ibid, p. 30.

6. Whitehead, p. 82.

7. There is some dispute about when Huston first shot footage of San Pietro and the battlefield. Though sketchy on specific dates, his autobiography suggests that Huston and his team followed the tanks on December 15, when they ". . . crept forward and photographed the disastrous results . . . These shots were in the original uncut version of the film." (Huston, *An Open Book*, p. 110.) Ambler, also sketchy on the dates, implies that their first trip into San Pietro was at least a day after the Germans had left the village.

8. Ambler, p. 200.

9. Huston, p. 110.

10. Ambler, p. 202.

11. Huston, p. 111.

12. Ambler, p. 206.

13. Ibid, p. 209.

14. Huston, p. 112. Ambler suggests otherwise—that the camera was just grabbed and taken directly to the jeep.

15. Ibid.

CHAPTER 21

1. Tobin, p. 132.
2. Wagner, p. 288.
3. Walker, p. 290.
4. Ibid, p. 289.
5. Ibid, p. 292.
6. Fletcher, Lee, "San Pietro Memories," 36th Historical Quarterly, Winter 1990.
7. Clover, Fall 1981.
8. Wagner, p. 90.

CHAPTER 22

1. Miller, p. 295.
2. Ibid, p. 297.
3. Miller, p. 302.
4. Tobin, p. 137.
5. Pyle, *Brave Men*, pp. 154-156.

CHAPTER 23

1. Report on Motion Picture Progress, 12/25/43.
2. There is some question about whether or not this footage was recreated, too. See Armed with Cameras, p. 90.
3. Huston, p. 114.
4. Ambler, p. 211.
5. Bertelsen, section 3.
6. Archives shot lists, "Captain Huston's Team Coverage," San Pietro, Italy 12/31/1943, National Archives RG 111: Records of the Chief Chief Signal Officer.
7. Tidwell interview.
8. Sweeney, section 3.
9. Belton Journal, Jan 6, 1944, p. 1.
10. Sweeney, section 11. Sweeney interviewed Mary Lee and got the story of her mother's reaction to Henry's death. Mary Lee Waskow Barr passed away in 2012.
11. Editorial Column, Belton Journal, Jan 21, 44, p. 2.

12. Not until 1959 would the family allow it to be published in full.
13. Miller, p. 305.
14. Ibid.
15. Ibid, p. 312.

CHAPTER 24

1. Walker, "General Walker's . . . Rapido Crossing" 36th Historical Association, texasmilitaryforcesmuseum.org/gallery/36div.htm.
2. Ibid.
3. Clayton Laurie, Mil. History, The Rapido River Disaster, 2000.
4. Walker, p. 404.

CHAPTER 25

1. John Huston collection, Academy of Motionn Picture Arts and Sciences, Margaret Herrick Library, Los Angeles, CA, August 5 1944 memo
2. Huston, *An Open Book*, p. 119.
3. Ibid, p. 119.
4. Office of the Chief Signal Officer memo (from Huston collection in LA) Dec 22. 1944.
5. Huston Collection LA March 14, 1945 letter to Zanuck.
6. Huston, Open Book, p. 119.
7. See Bertelsen for discussion of San Pietro and Westbrooks thoughts
8. See Armed with Cameras for criticism of Huston.
9. San Antonio Express, May 7, 1948.
10. Abilene Reporter News, Sept. 22, 1944.
11. Miller, p. 369.
12. Ibid, p. 327.
13. Ibid, p. 400.
14. Miller, pp. 373–379.
15. Miller, p. 425.
16. Humphrey, Walter, "Home Town, Comrades Pay Tribute to Hero," El Paso Herald Post, Feb. 24, 1944, p. 1.
17. See "National World War II Monument Groundbreaking," Nov. 11, 2000 http://www.c-spanvideo.org/program/160418-1.

Sources

Atkinson, Rick, *The Day of Battle: The War in Sicily and Italy, 1943–1944*, Henry Holt and Company, New York 2007

Ambler, Eric, *Here Lies*, Weidenfeld and Nicolson, London 1985

Baedeker, Karl, Baedeker's *Southern Italy and Sicily*, Chas. Scribner's Sons, New York, 1930

Barzini, Luigi, *The Italians*, Atheneum, New York 1964

Bertelsen, Lance, "San Pietro and the Art of War," Southwest Review, v. 24, no. 3, Spring 1989, pp 230-256

Bigart, Homer, *Forward Positions: The War Correspondence of Homer Bigart*, ed. Betsy Wade, The University of Arkansas Press, Fayetteville, 1992

Blumenson, Martin, *The United States Army in World War II: The Mediterranean Theater of Operations: Salerno to Cassino*, Center of Military History, Washington, D.C. 1993

Boomhower, Ray E. , *The Soldier's Friend: A Life of Ernie Pyle*, Indiana Historical Society Press, Indianapolis, 2006

Bourke-White, Margaret, *They Called It "Purple Heart Valley": A Combat Chronicle of the War in Italy*, Simon and Schuster, New York, 1944

Capra, Frank, *The Name Above the Title*, The MacMillan Company, New York, NY 1971

Coyne, Kevin, *Columbia Journalism Review*, Jan.–Feb., 2012.

Desmond, Robert W., *Tides of War: World News Reporting 1940–1945*, University of Iowa Press, Iowa City 1984

Sources

Huff, Richard A., Staff Sergeant, *The Fighting 36th: A Pictorial History, The Texas Division in Combat,* ed. Ray Merriam, Merriam Press, Bennington, Vermont 2012

Huston, John, *John Huston: An Open Book*, Alfred A. Knopf, New York 1980

Kershaw, Alex, *Blood and Champagne: The Life and Times of Robert Capa*, Thomas Dunne Books, New York, 2002

Knightley, Phillip, *The First Casualty: From the Crimea to Vietnam: The War Correspondent as Hero, Propagandist, and Myth Maker*, Harcourt Brace Jovanovich, New York 1975

Mander, Mary S., *Pen and Sword: American War Correspondents, 1898–1975*, University of Illinois Press, Urbana, Chicago, and Springfield 2010

Marshall, Katherine Tupper, *Together, Annals of an Army Wife*, Tupper and Love, Inc. New York, Atlanta 1946

Maslowski, Peter, *Armed with Cameras: The American Military Photographers of World War II*, The Free Press, New York, 1993

McBride, Joseph, *Frank Capra: The Catastrophe of Success*, Simon & Schuster 1992

Miller, Lee G., *The Story of Ernie Pyle*, The Viking Press, New York, 1950

Palmer, Sr., Bennett J., *The Hunter and the Hunted: A Combat Soldier's Story*, Bennett J. Palmer, Sr., Holland, NY (undated)

Poague, Leland, ed., *Frank Capra Interviews*, University of Mississippi Press, Jackson 2004

Pyle, Ernie, *Brave Men*, University of Nebraska Press, Lincoln 2001

Pyle, Ernie, *Here Is Your War*, Henry Holt and Company, New York, 1943; Pyle, Ernie, *Here Is Your War: The Story of G.I. Joe*, University of Nebraska Press, Lincoln and London, 2004.

Snyder, Louis L., ed., *Masterpieces of War Reporting: The Great Moments of World War II*, New York, 1962

Steinbeck, John, *Once There Was a War*, Viking Press, New York, 1958

Sweeney, Michael, Ph.D, "Appointment at Hill 1205: Ernie Pyle and Henry T. Waskow," Texas Military Forces Museum, Austin (submitted as a paper at Ohio University, 1995)

Tobin, James, *Ernie Pyle's War: America's Eyewitness to World War II*, The Free Press, New York, NY 1997

Wagner, Robert L., *The Texas Army: A History of the 36th Division in the Italian Campaign*, State House Press, Austin, Texas, 1991

Walker, Fred L., *From Texas to Rome: A General's Journey*, Texas Publishing Company, Dallas, Texas, 1969

Whelan, Richard, *Robert Capa*, Alfred A. Knopf, New York 1985

Whitehead, Don, *"Beachhead Don": Reporting the War from the European Theater, 1942–1945*, ed. John B. Romieser, Fordham University Press, New York 2004

Oral History Interview with Riley Tidwell, March 28, 1994, int. Jane Purtle, Cherokee County [Texas] Historical Commission, 1994

36th Division Historical Quarterly, various authors, The Texas Military Museum, Austin

36th=Infantry Division, Italian Campaign of World War II, September 1943 – June 1944, [originals at the National Archives and Records Administration], Microfilmed in 1965 by author Robert Wagner, now reposing in the Archives Division of the Texas State Library, Austin, Texas

Burrage, Richard, See Naples and Die, unpublished manuscript, 1988 (from the archives of the Texas Military Museum, Austin)

Designated here as 143rd Infantry Regiment AAR (After Action Reports) Operations Avalanche; Operations in Italy, November 1943; Operations in Italy, December 1943

George C. Marshall: Interviews and Reminiscences for Forrest C. Pogue, 1956–1957, Marshallfoundation.org

Hughes, Robert, ed., "The Courage of the Men, an Interview with John Huston," from Film Book 2, Grove Press, New York 1962

APS, "Report of Photographic Activities" (Signal Section, Headquarters Fifth Army, Dec. 31, 1943), Records of the 163rd SPC, NA. 51 pp. RG407, Entry 427, Box 18365, Folder SGCO-163-0.1.

APS, "Report on Motion Picture Progress" (Signal Section, Headquarters Fifth Army, Dec. 25, 1943), Records of the 163rd SPC, NA. 5 pp. RG407, Entry 427, Box 18365, Folder SGCO-163-0.1.

ACKNOWLEDGMENTS

Thanks to my agent, Farley Chase, who has been a stellar representative and advocate of my work from the day my writing first arrived on his desk. It's always been a pleasure working with you, Farley, and I deeply appreciate your hard work and help.

Thanks to Bob Pigeon at Da Capo Press, a thorough, encouraging, and knowledgeable editor of this book. It's been a thoroughly enjoyable process.

Thanks to Kevin Morrow, whose work on my behalf at the National Archives in Maryland, has been excellent and crucial to a pair of books.

Thanks to Lisa Sharik, Deputy Director the Texas Military Museum at Camp Mabry, Austin, Texas, for all of her help before, during, and after my visit to the museum. And thanks to the museum itself for offering such a wonderful archive for the 36th Division.

Thanks to Megan Cooney, Reference Archivist at the Texas State Library and Archives, for her help and guidance at this rich repository of information and materials.

Thanks to John Brady for his work digging through the John Huston collection at the Margaret Herrick Library at the Academy of Motion Picture Arts and Science.

Acknowledgments

Thanks to the Scripps Howard Foundation for permission to print Ernie Pyle's column, "The Death of Captain Waskow."

Thanks to the many authors whose work I used for this book, most particularly James Tobin, for his excellent biography of Ernie Pyle; General Fred L. Walker, whose diary offers a crucial perspective on the invasion of Italy; and Robert Wagner, whose extensive research on "The Texas Army," collected at the Texas State Library and Archives, is a first stop for anyone interested in the actions of the 36th Division in Italy.

Thanks, of course, go to Ernie Pyle himself, a magnificent writer and journalist. I hope I've done your work some justice.

Thanks to Sam and Hannah for being the best children ever.

Thanks to my wife, Susan, always my first and best reader—I can tell by the look on her face if a passage is working or not. And she is unerring in her assessment. Ti amo.

Thanks, finally, to all the GIs from whose stories, letters, and reminiscences I have borrowed to tell this story. Your sacrifice and service has been extraordinary and heroic.

INDEX

Photo section is indicated by *p1–p8*

Absent without leave (AWOL), 228
Academy Award, 246
Across the Pacific (film), 131
"After the fact" footage, shot by
    Huston, 224
Agee, James, 245, 246
Alcoholics Anonymous, 16
Alexander, Harold, 141
Allamon, Emmett, 186
Allied assault, in Mediterranean
    theater, 61–62
Altavilla
    battles around, 82–83
    as command post, 81–82
    leveling of, 87
    patrols along, 81
    Texas Division and, 85
Ambler, Eric, 134
    on Clark, 206
    gunfire and mortars experienced
        by, 208–210
    on San Pietro destruction, 209
    on soldier's remains, 208
Amelunke, Alvin, 196
American Mercury (magazine), 132

American Office of War
    Information, 134
Amphibious assault
    at Rapido River, 238
    training for, 22, 26, 49
    in Volturno River, 145–146
Appenine terrain, 144
Army Air Corps, 162
Army Pictorial Service, 243
Army Port of Embarkation, 23
Army Signal Corps, U.S., 119, 131,
    162
    arrival of, in San Pietro, 206
    on photographic coverage, 128
Arsenic and Old Lace (play), 122
Associated Press, 162, 203
Astor, Mary, 132
Auto racing, Pyle's fascination with,
    12
AWOL. *See* Absent without leave

Baedeker's, 66, 67, 114
BAR. *See* Browning Automatic
    Rifle
Barron, Gaines, 81

Battle of Britain, 33
"Battle of Chiunzi Pass," 116
Battlefield fever, 52
Belden, Jack, 101
Belton, Texas
    Army correspondence to get to,
        230
    casualties reported to, 113
    Christmas preparations in, 2
    war news in, 50
    Waskow, Henry's, death
        announcement at, 230–231
Belton Journal (newspaper), 232
Berlin, Irving, 2, 162
Bernhardt Line (first Winter Line),
        138, 142
    Mt. Sammurco as linchpin of, 169
    success of, 143, 153
Berry, Jack, 47, 96, 113, 156
    death of, 190, 192
Best Supporting Actor award, 246
Bigart, Homer, 162
    on body retrieval, 203–204
    San Pietro aftermath viewed by,
        203
    on war death, 204
    Whitehead's life saved by, 204
The Black Cat Band, 2
Blue Grotto, 114
Body retrieval
    Bigart on, 203–204
    Clover on, 214
    Fletcher on, 213–214
    of Waskow, Henry, 201
Bogart, Humphrey, 132, 133, 225
Book-of-the-Month Club, 129
Bragaw, Henry, 198
Brave Men (Pyle), 248
Brazil (ship)
    accommodations on, 23–24
    pin-up style sketches and, 24

British Film Unit, 225
British Ministry of Information, 134
British X Corps, 90
Brooke, Alan, 62
Broun, Heywood, 15
Browning Automatic Rifle (BAR),
        83
Buck, Jules, 162, 206, 207
    gunfire and mortars experienced
        by, 208–210
    jack-of-all-trades skills of, 164
Burgess, William, 175
    wounding of, 181
Burrage, Richard, 47, 89, 182

Camp Bowie, 18
Camp Edwards, 18
    36th Division at, 49
Capa, Robert, 98–99, 112, 161–162
    big news break of, 99
    Capri travels of, 116
    with Company B, 101–102
    filmmaking procedures and, 121
    Huston and, 163
    Naples documented by, 115–116
    photographs captured by, 99–100
    war action sought by, 100–101
Cape Cod, Texas Division influence
        on, 21–22
Capra, Frank, 22, 119
    failure of, 122–123
    Huston consulting, 225
    Marshall and, 121–122
    successes of, 122, 126–127
    training film made by, 125–126
Capri
    Capa's trip to, 116
    description of, 114
    trip to, 114
Chennault, Jack, 133
Chesterfield cigarettes, 10, 129

Chicago Sun (newspaper), 162
Chicago trip, by Pyle, 12
Chiunzi Pass, 91, 93
  rocky trek on, 103
  stone house at, 94, 96
Christmas
  caroling, 213, 214
  at Company B and Company I's
    home front, 2
  dinner for, 213
  mail from home received on, 214
  Walker on, 212–213
Churchill, Winston, 62, 122
  Roosevelt's meeting with, 61
Civil Service Commission, 13
Clark, Mark, 17, 25, 60, 67, 74–75,
    90, 135, 212, *p7*, *p8*
  admiration for, 68
  Ambler on, 206
  casualty report by, 102–103
  nervousness of, 79
  photographic coverage of, 206
  as Salerno invasion commander,
    69
  San Pietro advancement pressure
    on, 188
  tanks of, 195
  Walker and, 68–69, 86, 145–146,
    153
Cleghorn, Rufus, 175
  wounding of, 187
Clift, Glenn, 71
Clover, Jack, 179, 213
  on body retrieval, 214
Cocoanut Grove fire, 22
Cole, Walter Roy, 113
Combat photography. *See*
    Photographic coverage
Combat scenes re-created
  Huston filming, 225–226
  at Mt. Sammurco, 226

  with Walker, 226
  Westbrook helping with, 225–226
See also Photographic coverage
Combined Chiefs, 63
Commando Hill, 102
Company A
  casualties of, 187
  Cleghorn leading, 175–176
  Mt. Sammurco climbed by,
    175–176
Company B, 89
  Capa's time with, 101–102
  castle fight and, 104
  casualties of, 187, 192
  Christmas on home front of, 2
  Company I interaction with, 1–2,
    189
  formation of, 47
  German command post knocked
    out by, 190–191
  as leaderless, 192
  locals interaction with, 106–107
  members of, 47
  Mt. Sammurco climbed by,
    175–176
  nighttime rifle patrols of, 157
  Palmer joining, 147
  Salerno beach landing of, 2,
    77–78
  supply-transport assistance given
    by, 175
  tank assault lead by, 189
  Thanksgiving and, 158–159
  325th Glider Infantry Regiment
    helped by, 97
  Waskow, Henry's, tribute to,
    97–98
Company C
  casualties of, 187
  Mt. Sammurco climbed by,
    175–176

Company D
  Mt. Sammurco climbed by,
    175–176
  Waskow, Henry's, tribute to,
    97–98
Company I
  battle of, 83–84
  Christmas on home front of, 2
  Company B interaction with,
    1–2, 189
  injuries and, 85
  organization of, 45
  as reinforcements, 198
  retreat by, 84–85
  Salerno beach landing of, 2,
    78–79
  from Texas, 45
Company K, 198
Company L
  casualties of, 196–197
  communication lost by, 197
  San Pietro assault and, 196–197
Council on Books for Wartime, 129
Curry, Jabe, 179

Dahlberg, Lawrence, 250
Daily Student (Indiana University
    newspaper), 12
  Pyle as editor-in-chief, 13
Darby, William, 69, 90
  debriefing by, 91
  heroic action of, 94
  operation overseen by, 93–94
Davis, Bette, 2
Dawley, Ernest, 17, 69, 74–75, 135
  as Corps Commander, 145
D-Day
  artillery and mortar fire during,
    90
  for Pyle, 51
  See also Salerno invasion

"The Death of Captain Waskow,"
    219
  other soldier's memories
    resounding with, 232
  popularity of, 231
  reader's response to, 232–233
  soldier's response to, 234
  United Press on, 233–234
  war bonds sold due to, 233–234
"Death Valley," San Pietro as,
    205–206
Dennis, Charles, heroic action of,
    198
Der Spiegel (Capa), 99
Distinguished Service medals, 213
Dos Passos, John, 100
Durbin, Floyd, 192
Durbin, Flynn, 47

Earhart, Amelia, 14
Eisenhower, Dwight, 54, 64, 102,
    135, 148, *p7*, *p8*
  artillery fire requested by, 212
  on Pyle, 248
  San Pietro tour given to, 212
Empire Theater, 23
ETOUSA. *See* European Theater of
    Operations U.S. Army
Europe, cross-channel invasion of,
    61
European Theater of Operations
    U.S. Army (ETOUSA), 134

Fifth Army, commander choice
    questioned for, 67–68
Fifth Army, U.S., 2
Fifth Army Headquarters, 87
Films
  documentary form, 164–165
  footage for, 165
  real combat footage for, 223

soldier training, 123, 125–126
of war coverage, 119–120
War Department on, 128, 164
See also Photographic coverage
First Baptist Church, 2
First Special Service Force, 154
1st Armored Division, 17
1st Battalion
deadly day for, 107–108
first casualty of, 92
marching orders for, 90
Mt. Sammurco climb by, 175
1st Italian Motorized Group
casualties suffered by, 177–178
Mt. Lungo climb attempted by,
177
recon not done by, 177
504th Parachute Battalion, 187
Fletcher, Lee, 154
on body retrieval, 213–214
Ford, Henry, 12
Fort Benning, 19
Fort Dix, 247
Fort Hood, 45
France, cross-channel invasion of,
63–64
Francis, Kay, 29
Frazior, David, 181, 182, 189,
192–193
Frederick, Robert, 168
Freeland, Herbert, 223
Freeman, Douglas Southall, 24

Gavin, James, 105
Gellhorn, Martha, 100
German propaganda, 127
German Winter Line, 138, 148, 164
Germans
anti-tank weapons used by, 196
army of, waiting at Salerno, 65
artillery fire of, 156

Company B knocking out
command post of, 190–191
counterattack by, 187
defense for Italy, 139–140
Liri Valley controlled by, 188
pillboxes used by, 178–179
POW revealing gun emplacements
of, 197
Rome invasion resistance by, 136,
139–140, 142–143
San Pietro held by, 187–188
San Pietro stripped by, 141
San Vittore occupied by, 211
Slaughter killing, 97
two-front war fighting by, 61
unit identification confusion by,
96
war resources and, 62
winter lines constructed by, 138
withdrawal of, 198
Gibson, Jack, 47
Gillette, Melvin, 163
Goad, Ray, 45, 109, 111
wounding of, 92, 187
Goad, Roy, 45, 91, 108, 181
Golden, Herbert, 147
Goldwyn, Samuel, 132
Gonzales, Manual, 70
Gordon, Jack
death of, 156
letter home sent by, 157
Grapes of Wrath (Steinbeck), 115
Graves Registration team, 213
Great Depression, 45
Great Lakes Naval Training Station,
12
Greely, Orlando, 92
Greenstreet, Sidney, 132
Guadalcanal Diary (Tregaskis), 98,
150
Gulf of Naples, 112

Gustav Line (German Winter Line), 138, 227, 235
  Rapido River and, 237

Hanks, Tom, 252
Hemingway, Ernest, 36, 100
Here Is Your War (Pyle), 40, 56, 129, 233
Hersey, John, 99
Hewitt, Kent, 69, 74–75
High Sierra (film), 133
Highway 6, 138
Hill 1205, goal of, 3
Hitler, Adolph, 34, 137
"Hoosier Vagabond," 15
Hope, Bob, 120
Horton, Lewis, 181
  death of, 187
Hospital
  incidents reported to Eisenhower, 54
  Patton's incidents at, 53–54
  Pyle's stay at, 52–53
Hotel Savoy, 33
Huston, John, 119, 128, 206
  "after the fact" footage shot by, 224
  biography of, 132
  Capa and, 163
  Capra consulted by, 225
  criticism received by, 245
  documentary film by, 223
  film editing by, 227
  films by, 131–132
  gunfire and mortars experienced by, 208–210
  on Naples, 162
  re-created combat scenes filmed by, 225–226
  risk-taking by, 209
  screenwriting career of, 133

soldier warnings ignored by, 207
status of, 164
tenacity of, 133

Ie Shima, 249–250
Indiana University, 12
Indianapolis 500, 12
Ingram, Hubert, 113, 156
Irwin, Wallace, 219
It Happened One Night (movie), 121
Italy
  defensive line running across, 137
  destruction of, 150
  German defense on, 139–140
  mainland assault for, 63–64
  surrender of, 64–65, 77
  terrain of, 138–139, 142, 149

Jenkins, Lou, 77, 89
Journal (newspaper), 113

Kasserine Pass, 31
Kelly, Charles, 83
Kesselring, Albert, 137
Keyes, Geoffrey, 153, 169, 212, 240
  reinforcements ordered by, 187
  second Rapido River crossing suggested by, 241
"The Khaki Parade," 23
KKK. *See* Ku Klux Klan
Klinger, Warren, 107, 250
  Waskow, Henry, eulogy by, 251
Knickerbocker, H.R., 162
K-ration, 10, 184
Kratka (Captain), prisoners of war aided by, 110–111
Ku Klux Klan (KKK), Pyle threatened by, 13

Land, James, 108
Landis, Carole, 29

Lang, Will, 101, 112, 117
Langford, Frances, 120
LaPorte Herald (Indiana), 13
Lardner, John, 162
Lee's Lieutenants (Freeman), 24
Leibling, A.J., 100
Life (magazine), 112, 248
 photos shared by, 116
Lindbergh, Charles, 14
Liri Valley, 3, 137, 138, 169, 227, *p4*
 German control of, 188
 tragedy in, 237–242
Logan, James, 70
London, Pyle's travel to, 32–33
"The Lost Generation," 100
Lucas, John, *p7*

Maiori, *p2*
 battle at, 98
 command base at, 93
The Maltese Falcon (film), 131–132
Marshall, George, 20, 62, 63, 172
 Capra and, 121–122
 need to inform of, 124
 on *San Pietro* (film), 243–244
 as strategist, 123
 training film concerns of, 123,
  125
 troop education and, 124–125
 on young recruits, 123–124
Martin, William, 82, 170, 175–176,
  179, 240
Mauldin, Bill, 150
Mayfair, Mitzi, 10, 29
McCloskey General Hospital, 250
McCreery, Richard, 69
McDonald, A.J., 250
Mediterranean theater
 Allied assault in, 61–62
 goal of, 61
 island-hopping campaign for, 62

Pyle influenced by, 10
 transport barge and sub-chaser
  encounter in, 8–10
Mencken, H.L., 132
Meredith, Burgess, 246, 247
Meuse-Argonne, 43
Mexia, Texas
 Army correspondence to get to,
  230
 Christmas preparations in, 2
 war news in, 50
Mexia Weekly Herald (newspaper),
  113
Miller, Arthur, 130, 246
Miller, Lee, 33, 52
 Pyle and, 11, 13, 30, 234
Miller, Mallory, 113
"The Million Dollar Mountain," 168
Mills, John, 120
Miranda, Carmen, 23
Mitchum, Robert, 246, 247
Mobley, William, 81
Mojave Desert, 120
MOMA. *See* Museum of Modern
  Art
Monte Soprano, capture of, 79
Montgomery, Bernard, 69
Morgan, Charles, 113
Morocco, Walker's stay in, 25
Mr. Deeds Goes to Town (movie), 121
Mr. Smith Goes to Washington
  (movie), 121
Mt. Cannavinelle, 154, 169
 carnage on, 155
 mud hindering climb of, 178
 supply point on, 155–156
 white tape marking trail for, 178
Mt. Cassino, 211
Mt. Lungo
 attack on, 169
 success at, 197

Mt. Sammurco, 138, *p4*
  as Bernhardt Line linchpin, 169
  boulders used as weapons on, 176
  climbing feat of, 175
  combat scenes re-created at, 226
  mule trails and, 176, 184
  Pyle's climb of, 185
  rock cover of, 178
  size of, 171
  terrain of, 1
  troop collection area at, *p6*
  Waskow, Henry, on, 191
  wounded descending, 183
Mt. Sammurco battle
  ammunition and supplies
    dwindling during, 183
  casualties suffered during, 182
  communication during, 182
  Company A, B, C, and D
    climbing, 175–176
  counterattack for, 181
  efforts thrown at, 178–179
  element of surprise hoped for, 176
  firepower used in, 181
  1st Battalion climb of, 175
  German defense at, 4
  Germans defending, 175–186
  Germans ordered to fight with all
    costs, 181
  limited headway for, 179
  at peak of, 4, 177
  sniper peek-a-boo style shootout,
    181
  supplies for, 183–184
Murrow, Edward R., 16
Museum of Modern Art (MOMA),
  125

Naples, *p3*
  Capa documenting, 115–116
  destruction of, 115

Huston on, 162
  rain hindering advancement north
    of, *p3*
  triumphal entry into, 105–106
Naples campaign
  casualties of, 136
  success of, 135
National Board of Review, 247
National Film Preservation Board,
  246, 247
National Film Preservation
  Foundation, 246
National Film Registry, 246
National Guard, 2
National Press Club, 247
Naval Reserve, U.S., 12
New Years Eve, San Pietro storm
  and, 215
New York Herald Tribune
  (newspaper), 115, 162, 203
Newell, Jalvin, code created by, 182
Newsweek (newspaper), 162
North Africa
  countryside of, 29
  Texas Division journey to, 23–24
November operation, strategy for,
  154

Of Mice and Men (Steinbeck), 115
Ohio National Guard, 19
Ohio State University, 19
141st Regiment of the 36th Infantry
  Division, 43, 44
143rd Regiment of the 36th Infantry
  Division (Texas Division), 2
  casualties of, 146
  replacement troops for, 146
  Salerno Bay landing of, *p1*
Operation Raincoat
  casualties of, 168
  communication gaps in, 171

counterattacks during, 168
firepower used in, 168, 170
strategic meeting for, 167
strategic moves during, 170
Operation Torch, 8
goal of, 61
Walker's meetings for, 24–25
war correspondents in, 27
Otto, Henry T., 45
ambitions and talents of, 46–47
honors and rewards of, 46
military service of, 47
Otto, John, 45

Pacific war, Pyle reporting on, 248,
249–250
Paestum, 73
aerial view of, *p2*
historic conquering of, 67
Palace of Caserta, 139
Palmer, Bennett, 193
Company B joined by, 147
description of, 146
on hillside conditions, 157
as replacement, 147
training of, 146
Parade march, by Texas Division,
17–18
Parker, John, 191, 192
Patton, George, 36
hospital incidents by, 53–54
Pyle and, 54
troop speech by, 21
Walker meeting with, 18–19
Pearl Harbor, 121
Pederson, Ray, 108
Pershing, John "Black Jack," 19
Peterman, Joseph, 91, 108
Photographic coverage
"after the fact" footage and, 224
Army Signal Corps on, 128

of Clark, 206
dangers of, 208
Freeland on, 223
as incidental, 224–225
problems with, 223–224
re-creation of, 120, 185
Roosevelt on, 127–128
of shells, 224
War Department on, 128
Poage, William, 232
Pompeii, Texas Division passing
through, 103–104
Port Lyautey airfield, 17, 49
Post, 14
POW. *See* Prisoner of war
Prelude to Victory (movie), 124
Prelude to War (Capra), 22
Prisoner of war (POW), 198, 205
evacuation of, 111
interrogation of, 137, 197
medical aid for, 110
rescue of, 111
Waskow, August, as, 109–110
White, Jack, as, 110
Pulitzer Prize for Correspondence,
234
"Purple Heart Valley"
limited headway in, 179
See also San Pietro battle
Pyle, Ernie, 5, 164–165, 184, *p7*, *p8*
alcohol and, 218–219
auto racing fascination and, 12
aviation and, 14
battlefield fever of, 52
bravery of, 31
castle room used for writing by,
217–218
cautionary note by, 39–40
childhood Chicago trip by, 12
childhood of, 12
college degree of, 12–13

Pyle, Ernie (*continued*)
 cross-country tour of, 14, 15–16
 D-Day for, 51
 death of, 234–235, 250
 depression of, 35, 148, 218
 description of, 10, 234
 on destruction, 149
 Eisenhower on, 248
 embeddedness of, 30
 employment of, 13, 14
 fame of, 36, 129–130, 148, 234,
  248
 family of, 12
 First Lady and, 131
 goal of, 10–11
 higher causes and, 11
 on hospital stay, 52–53
 identifying with soldiers, 53–54
 insecurities of, 11
 on Italian landscape, 149
 KKK threatening, 13
 London travels of, 32–33
 marriage issues of, 35–36, 37,
  131, 234
 Miller, Arthur, and, 130
 Miller, Lee, and, 13, 30
 mother's death influencing, 34–35
 Mt. Sammurco climb by, 185
 mule and men procession watched
  by, 201–202
 nickname of, 12–13
 Pacific war reporting by, 248,
  249–250
 Patton and, 54
 prose and contradictions used by,
  34
 Pulitzer Prize for Correspondence
  received by, 234
 reader response to stories by, 32,
  34
 refocus of, 56–57

 reporting style of, 11, 13, 28–29,
  33–34
 rest and relaxation of, 130, 233,
  235
 settling down of, 16
 in Sicily, 51–57
 on slow military advancement,
  150–151
 on soldier's spirit, 186
 spine-tingling war story told by,
  29–30
 stay in Tunisia, 30–31
 story of Waskow, Henry, by, 231
 Tidwell interviewed by, 193
 Tobin as biographer for, 35
 transport barge and sub-chaser
  encounter witnessed by, 8–10
 traveling itch of, 16
 U.S.S. Biscayne stay by, 10
 on view of war, 7, 248
 war influence on, 10, 41, 56–57
 Washington Daily News
  employment, 13
 on Waskow, Henry's, death,
  219–222
 Whitehead on, 218

Quick, Quint, 32

Rapido River, 227
 crossing of, 238
 Gustav Line running along, 237
 second crossing suggested for,
  241
Rapido River assault
 casualties from, 240–241
 confusion during, 239
 disaster of, 241
 hesitation for, 238–239
 recriminations following, 241
 troop separation during, 240

Walker taking responsibility for, 241

withdrawal from, 240–241

Ray, Martha, 29

Recriminations, following Rapido River assault, 241

Reid, Alban, 159

Riefenstahl, Leni, 125

Rocky (movie), 246

Rome invasion, 135

  by Christmas, 142

  German resistance and, 136, 139–140, 142–143

  Kesselring's fight for, 137

  mountains inhibiting, 143–144

  plan for, 136

  slow advancement toward, 150–151

Rommel, Erwin, 8, 136

Roosevelt, Eleanor, 131

  death of, 249

Roosevelt, Franklin D., 119

  Churchill meeting with, 61

  memorandum from, 127

  on photographic coverage, 127–128

Sadler, Jerry, 182

Salerno, 59–75

  description of, 66–67

  Germany Army waiting at, 65

  terrain of, 3

Salerno Bay, *p1*

  bombardment at, 59–60

  Company B landing at, 2, 77–78

  Company I landing at, 2, 78–79

  strategic landing importance at, 60–61

  36th Division landing at, 66

  Walker landing site adjustment at, 60

Salerno invasion, 64, *p1*

  army forces for, 69

  bravery during, 71–72

  command post for, 74, *p2*

  commander choice for, 67–68

  dangers of, 87–88

  general plan for, 69–70

  head count after, 86

  landings of, 95

  medics around, 82–83

  perimeter formed during, 75

  radio communication during, 74–75

  resistance encountered in, 70–71

  targets missed in, 70

  3rd Battalion and, 85–88

  Walker's experience of, 72–73

  Walker's plan for, 70

  waves of, 71

San Pietro

  advancement pressure felt by Walker and Clark, 188

  Army Signal Corps arrival in, 206

  battle aftermath of, *p5*

  capture of, 198

  casualties in, 206–207

  as "Death Valley," 205–206

  German's hold on, 187–188

  German's stripping of, 141

  medical detachment heading into, *p7*

  New Years Eve storm in, 215

  ruins of, 198, 200, 204–205, 209, 224, *p6*

  villagers emerging from hiding in, 205

  villagers immigrating to U.S., 204–205

San Pietro (film)

  Capra on film name, 243

  debate regarding, 243

San Pietro (film) (*continued*)
    destruction footage as shock in,
        244–245
    editing of, 243, 244
    film critic on, 245
    Marshall on, 243–244
    opening shot of, 244
    perceived as "anti-war" film, 245
    preserved by National Film
        Registry, 245
    re-creations used in, 246
    strong negative reaction on, 243
    as training video, 244
    War Department on, 243
    Westbrook on, 246
San Pietro battle, 195
    aftermath of, 203–210
    boundaries broken during, 197
    Company L and, 196–197
    end of, 215
    firepower used in, 196, 200
    map of, 180, 199
    by tank, 188–189
San Vittore
    German occupancy of, 211
    nighttime attack of, 211–212
Saturday Evening Post (magazine), 233
Saving Private Ryan (movie), 252
Scripps-Howard, 14, 16, 32, 33, 231
Sergeant York (film), 133
Shattuck Academy, 19
"Shoot and scoot" tactic, 96, 98
Sicily
    countryside of, 52
    global forces for invasion of, 8
    invasion meeting on, 62–63
    Pyle in, 51–57
    rock blocking highway in, 55–56
Siebolds, Geraldine "Jerry," 13–14
    alcohol problem of, 15–16,
        34–35, 131

attempted suicide by, 249
    as "That Girl," 15
Signal Photo Company (SPC), 163
Silver Star medals, 213
Skiles, Judson, 250
Slaughter, Willie, 47, 181
    Germans killed by, 97
    heroic actions of, 190
    on war, 113
Smith, Bedell, 212
Soldiers
    Christmas enjoyed by, *p5*
    "The Death of Captain Waskow"
        response from, 234
    deceased, *p6*
    female longing by, 40
    filming requested by, 207
    gear of, 65, 184
    hillside conditions affecting, 157
    home-sick, 39
    Huston warning by, 207
    letters sent home from, 113
    life detail of, 11
    mail from home and, 214
    necessities of, 29
    photos sent home of, 116–117
    pragmatism of, 31
    property regard of, 40
    Pyle identifying with, 53–54
    Pyle on, 11
    questions of, 39
    reflective mood of, 207
    regarded as heroes, 103, 105–106,
        113, 211, *p5*
    spirit of, 186
    Thanksgiving dinner for, 158–159
    Tobin on, 211
    trench foot and, 157
    Waskow, Henry, respected by,
        202, 231
    on Waskow, Henry, 220–222

Sorrento Peninsula
  assembly points in, 91
  mountains of, 105
  oddity fights on, 94
  raids on, 96
  resort in, 94
  securing of, 90
SPC. *See* Signal Photo Company
Splawn, Marvin, 189
St. Michael the Archangel, 200, 244
Stars and Stripes (Mauldin), 150
Statue of Liberty, 39
Steinbeck, John, 100
  travels of, 115
Stevens, George, 128
Stevenson, Coke, 23
Stone house, at Chiunzi Pass, as
  command post, 94, 96
The Story of G.I. Joe (film)
  Academy Award nominations for,
    246
  Agee on, 246
  realistic and unsentimental
    portrayal by, 246
  rewards and nominations for,
    246–247
  Waskow character renamed
    Walker in, 246
Street of Abundance, 103
Strong, George, 63
Sub-chaser, helping transport barge,
  8–10
Sultan Guard, 17
Summers, Elaine, 23
Sunday, Billie, 113

Tackett, Hulen, 192
Tank assault
  Company B leading, 189
  failure of, 196
  logistics of, 188–189

preparation for, 189
  recon suggesting against, 188
  on San Pietro, 188–189
Taro, Gerda, 99
Temple Junior College, 231
Texas Division
  Altavilla and, 85
  amphibious training and, 22, 26,
    49
  call to duty for, 22, 23
  Camp Edwards stay, 21–22
  Cape Cod influenced by, 21–22
  good impression from, 18
  North Africa journey of, 23–24
  parade march by, 17–18
  photos sent home of, 116–117
  Pompeii passed through by,
    103–104
  reorganization of, 86
  Texans reduction in, 146
  See also 143rd Regiment of the
    36th Infantry Division
Thanksgiving dinner, 158–159
"That Girl," Siebolds as, 15
3rd Battalion, Salerno invasion and,
  85–88
36th Division, 17
  active duty of, 18
  at Camp Edwards, 49
  casualties of, 146, 241
  formation of, 43–44
  German artillery fire and, 156
  infantry regiments of, 43
  inventive groups within, 20
  landmark for, 64
  no break for, 211
  replacement troops for, 146
  Salerno Bay landing of, 66
  service history of, 43–44
  soldier background and ethnicities
    within, 44–45

325th Glider Infantry Regiment, 97
Tidwell, Riley, 47, 77, 89, 101, 158,
  184, 200
  AWOL, 228
  body recovery by, 192
  as communication runner, 92–93,
    171
  enlistment of, 48
  fame of, 247
  medical treatment received by,
    190, 201, 227
  Pyle interviewing, 193
  at replacement camp, 228
  travels of, 247
  trench foot and, 189–190,
    192–193, 227–228
  War Department interviewing,
    247
  war public relations and, 247
  Waskow, Henry, and, 48, 92–93
  Waskow, Henry's, body retrieved
    by, 201
  Waskow, Henry's, death
    experienced by, 193
  Waskow, Mary Lee, and, 247
Time (magazine), 34, 112, 231, 245
Tobin, James
  as Pyle's biographer, 35
  on soldiers, 211
Toledo Blade (newspaper), 233
Toro del Greco, 104
Tortilla Flats (Steinbeck), 115
T-Patchers. *See* Texas Division
Transport barge, engine breakdown
  of, 8–10
Tregaskis, Richard, 98, 150
Trench foot
  soldiers and, 157
  Tidwell and, 189–190, 227–228
Triumph of the Will (Riefenstahl), 125
Truscott, Lucian, 51, 69, *p7*

engineering challenges facing,
    140–141
Tunisia
  battle of, 37–38
  Pyle's stay in, 30–31
Tunisian Victory (movie), 119, 128,
    133
  British collaboration for, 120
  film ventures represented by, 134
  re-created footage for, 120

United Press, 219, 233
University of Illinois, 12
University of Kentucky, 204
University of Texas, 225
U.S.S. Biscayne, 8, 27
  Pyle's stay on, 10
U.S.S. Chase, 59, 72, 89
U.S.S. Stanton, 78

Vannata, Lem, 184
Volturno River, 137
  amphibious assault in, 145–146
  crossing of, 140
  floods of, 141
  practice crossing of, 147–148
Vox Populi (radio show), 247
Vu (French magazine), 99, 100

Wadle, Arthur A., 47, 97
Walker, Fred Livingood, 17, 169, 238
  appointment in Texas Division,
    19–20
  army service of, 19
  on Christmas, 212–213
  Clark and, 68–69, 86, 145–146,
    153
  combat scene re-created with, 226
  company discipline problems
    faced by, 22–23
  description of, 19

on destruction, 104–106
dinner rewarding, 242
Italian campaign influencing, 212
Morocco stay and, 25
officer characteristics of, 20
Operation Torch meetings and,
   24–25
Patton's meeting with, 18–19
on Patton's troop speech, 21
Rapido River assault responsibility
   accepted by, 241
Salerno invasion plan by, 70
San Pietro advancement pressure
   on, 188
San Pietro tour given by, 212
Silver Stars and Distinguished
   Service medals handed out by,
   213
on Sorrento mountains, 105
Thanksgiving dinner served by,
   158–159
on war games, 20–21
War
   debris of, 214
   doubts surrounding, 127
   entertainment tour for, 29
   film coverage of, 119–120
   Pyle on view of, 7, 248
   romance to, 100
   Slaughter on, 113
   understanding of, 248
   Waskow, Henry, on, 112
   as wasteful, 40
War bonds, 233–234
War College, 19
War correspondents
   arrival of, 98–99
   Italy invasion and, 100–101
   job duties of, 27–28
   leadership disagreements among,
      163

in Operation Torch, 27
   presence of, 161–162
War Department, 223
   on photographic coverage, 128,
      163
   on *San Pietro* (film), 243
   Tidwell interviewed by, 247
War Munitions Building, 121
Warner, Jack, 133
Warner Bros. Studios, 133
Washington Daily News (newspaper),
   13, 14, 231
Washington-Hoover airport, 14
Waskow, August, 50
   as German prisoner, 109–110
   rehabilitation of, 229
   reunited with Company I,
      109–110
   wounding of, 89, 109
Waskow, Henry, 77, 171
   Army service of, 4–5
   biography of, 219–222
   buried remains of, 251
   Company B and D tribute from,
      97–98
   condolences regarding death of,
      233
   death of, 191, 217–222
   description of, 4–5
   eulogy for, 251
   home dreams of, 93
   leadership style of, 93
   letter sent home from, 112–113,
      172–174
   misinformed on brother's
      whereabouts, 111–112
   mountain descent of body,
      200–201
   on Mt. Sammurco, 191
   mule carrying, 220–221
   noble responsibility of, 5

Waskow, Henry (*continued*)
  Pyle on death of, 219–222
  relaxing trip to Capri, 114
  remembrance of, 251–252
  sincerity of, 172
  soldier's recall of, 220–222
  soldier's respect for, 202, 231
  telegram regarding, 230
  Tidwell and, 48, 92–93
  Tidwell experiencing death of, 193
  Tidwell retrieving body of, 201
  VFW post and school named
    after, 251–252
  on war, 112
Waskow, Mary Goth
  biography of, 228–229
  concern for her children, 229–230
  death of, 250
  grief of, 233
  health problems of, 229
  memorial service for, 251
  as Waskow, Henry and August's,
    mother, 229
Waskow, Mary Lee, 229
  telegram received by, 230
  Tidwell and, 247
Watch on the Rhine (movie), 2
Wehrmacht anti-tank guns, 196
Wellesley, Henry, 102
Wellman, William, 246

Westbrook, Joel, 23
  combat re-creation with, 225–226
  on *San Pietro* (film), 246
Westbrook, Lawrence, 23
Western Taskforce of Operation
  Torch, 18
White, Jack, 45, 109, 162, 230, 250
  as German prisoner, 110
  wounding of, 110, 113
White, Margaret Bourke, 161
"White Christmas" (Berlin), 2
Whitehead, Don, 54, 65, 217, 234
  Bigart saving life of, 204
  prose of, 205
  on Pyle, 218
  San Pietro aftermath viewed by,
    203
Why We Fight (documentary series),
  126
Wilbur (General), 196, 211
Winter Lines
  constructed by Germans, 138
  evaporation of, 139
  success of, 188
Winterstellungen (winter positions),
  137

Yates, Bill, 78, 109, 111
You Can't Take It With You (movie),
  121